ROAR
of the SEA

TREACHERY, OBSESSION, AND
ALASKA'S MOST VALUABLE WILDLIFE

DEB VANASSE

ALASKA
NORTHWEST
BOOKS®

Edited and indexed by Emily Bowles

Cover: Seal rookery, by Henry Wood Elliott. Courtesy of the Phoebe A. Hearst Museum of Anthropology and the Regents of the University of California (Catalog Number: 17-234)

Library of Congress Cataloging-in-Publication Data

Names: Vanasse, Deb, author.
Title: Roar of the sea : treachery, obsession, and Alaska's most valuable wildlife / Deb Vanasse.
Description: Berkeley : Alaska Northwest Books, an imprint of West Margin Press, 2022. | Includes bibliographical references and index. | Summary: "A history following Captain Alex MacLean and Henry Wood Elliott's fight over the highly prized Pribilof Island fur seals in the late 1800s and early 1900s"-- Provided by publisher.
Identifiers: LCCN 2021040751 (print) | LCCN 2021040752 (ebook) | ISBN 9781513209579 (paperback) | ISBN 9781513209562 (hardback) | ISBN 9781513209555 (ebook)
Subjects: LCSH: Northern fur seal--Alaska--Pribilof Islands--History--19th century. | Northern fur seal--Alaska--Pribilof Islands--History--20th century. | Sealing--Alaska--Pribilof Islands--History--19th century. | Sealing--Alaska--Pribilof Islands--History--20th century. | Pribilof Islands (Alaska)--Environmental conditions--19th century. | Pribilof Islands (Alaska)--Environmental conditions--20th century.
Classification: LCC SH361 .V36 2022 (print) | LCC SH361 (ebook) | DDC 639.2/9097984--dc23
LC record available at https://lccn.loc.gov/2021040751
LC ebook record available at https://lccn.loc.gov/2021040752

2022LSI

Published by Alaska Northwest Books®
an imprint of

WEST MARGIN PRESS
WestMarginPress.com

Proudly distributed by Ingram Publisher Services

WEST MARGIN PRESS
Publishing Director: Jennifer Newens
Marketing Manager: Alice Wertheimer
Project Specialist: Micaela Clark
Editor: Olivia Ngai
Design & Production: Rachel Lopez Metzger

CONTENTS

Shuffling past hordes of bachelors and beachmasters and other matkas, she locates her hungry pup. He bleats a welcome, then curls into her, latching onto a teat. For the moment, they are safe.

OTHERS WILL NOT BE SO LUCKY. A reign of terror is mounting. By summer's end, the pirates will have slain tens of thousands of seals. MacLean, it seems, is unstoppable.

Or he would be, if not for a self-appointed savior to the seals. More doer than thinker, artist and naturalist Henry Wood Elliott is every bit as contentious as his adversaries, of which he has many. In the halls of Congress, in the press, and in the White House, Elliott confronts pirates of all stripes, including corporate executives and corrupt government officials. Alex MacLean, at least, is forthright in his profiteering.

In America's burgeoning conservation movement, Elliott is an outlier, an accidental activist who is neither sportsman, seeker, nor wealthy elitist. Born in 1846, he grew up with his nation. During the turbulent Civil War years, he found refuge at the Smithsonian, an institution as nascent as the naturalists it trained. As the war ended and the nation pressed westward, it became clear how little the country's scientists, let alone its ordinary citizens, knew of the Western territories it claimed. Elliott joined a cohort of budding scientists who aimed to study and classify America's flora and fauna specimen by specimen.

On the Pribilofs, also called the Seal Islands, Elliott found himself far from his Ohio home. Trekking among throngs of seals, he learned by watching and sketching and making notes. Thirty-three years later, he now speaks with such authority on seals that people have taken to addressing him as "Professor Elliott," though he has not even a high school diploma, much less a university affiliation.

An artist, he paints in the tradition of the American romantics, capturing the essence of large, luminous landscapes that dwarf human figures. But his approach to wildlife is practical. Advocating for the seals, he confronts the excesses of an era ridden with greed. As with the emerging field of natural history, and as with America itself, the evolution toward his calling has been jagged and sometimes painful. Driven by an unwavering commitment to speaking truth, Elliott has become something of a force of nature himself, at turns diplomatic and brash. Though witty and self-deprecating, he lashes out at all who threaten his findings, his reputation, and the seals he feels called to protect.

In his quest to save the matka and her kind, Elliott suffers setback after setback. Wealthy, credentialed opponents attack him at every turn. Turned out from his government work, he is bleeding assets and can scarcely support his ten children. In the end, he will make history, but history will spurn him. Still, his tenacity will set a course for wildlife protections that will one day save species the world over.

Part One
1886–1896

*For a man to have an ideal in this world,
for a man to know what an ideal is,
this is also to have lived.*

—Gerald Stanley Lee

ONE

THE MAKING OF A PIRATE

*W*AFTING FROM THE HARBOR OF Victoria, British Columbia, the salt-scented breeze held the promise of spring, and with spring came cash. Thanks to the sealing fleet, the town was booming. In Bastion Square, workers were tearing down the gallows of a notorious hanging judge so they could construct a new concrete courthouse atop the plot of ground where the criminals were buried. Down the street, Alex MacLean's good friend Tommy Burnes was building a fancy red-brick, Italianate-style hotel, where he would rent rooms by the hour to prostitutes and their clientele.

Behind this new project stood the American Hotel, a simple wood-sided structure also owned by Burnes. Beyond the swinging doors of the American's saloon, a merry crowd belted out lines from a popular song:

He was a pal of mine, he shared my hopes and fears:
But, oh, for the scenes that fancy brings back from those golden years.

On this night, Alex MacLean and his brother Dan were buying five-cent beers all around. None would leave thirsty. In the morning, their crews would assemble at the docks, each MacLean brother at the helm of a separate vessel. Following the fur seals on their northward migration to the Pribilofs, they would battle the elements, the US Revenue Service, and one another for bragging rights to the biggest catch of the season. Belowdecks, each schooner would carry an ample stash of whiskey, an enticement to sailors who understood the brutal work ahead.

Originally of Cape Breton Island, Nova Scotia, the MacLeans were Gaels, a people descended from pirates. As far back as the third century CE, these "Scotti," as the Romans called them, raided Britannia by sea. Driven from their Highland homes after a series of uprisings, many from clan MacLean emigrated to Nova Scotia, or "New Scotland," in the late eighteenth and early nineteenth centuries. Among these was Alex and Dan MacLean's grandfather, who farmed a two-hundred-acre parcel in the East Bay region of Cape Breton Island.

If Nova Scotia is shaped like a torch held off Canada's eastern seaboard, Cape Breton forms its flame, separated from Nova Scotia's main island by the Strait of Canso. Burning blue near the center of Cape Breton is Bras d'Or, a large inland sea. Nearby, the MacLean family farm occupied land the Mi'kmaq had once used to portage between the East Bay of Bras d'Or and the Sydney River, which leads directly to the Atlantic Ocean. A green jewel of an island with some of the world's most dramatic coastline, Cape Breton evokes the Scottish Isles. In this new land, Gaelic culture thrived among the tight-knit MacLeans, who were renowned for fighting and seafaring. In story, song, and dance, they retained a strong sense of heritage.

But all was not paradise. Within decades of the MacLeans' arriving from Scotland, a potato blight and a wheat fly infestation struck Cape Breton. Some left the island, but Alex and Dan MacLean's parents stayed on, working the family farm. Then, only months after Alex was born in 1858, his father died, leaving the boys' mother with six children to raise.

At nineteen, Dan went to sea, shipping out from nearby Sydney harbor. Nine years his junior, Alex stayed behind, working the farm, but the sea called to him as well. At fifteen, he began crewing fishing boats, joining other Bluenoses, as Cape Breton islanders were called. Some say the moniker derived from a blue-ended potato grown on the island, others that it came from the stain local fishermen got from wiping their noses on knitted blue mitts. No matter the term's origins, locals took pride in what was intended as derision.

Bluenose captains had a reputation for manhandling their crews to get more work out of fewer men. They also earned a reputation as splendid seamen. Many crewed on American fishing boats, earning partial shares of the catch. In his younger days, Alex gained experience on both steamers and schooners, sailing out of Boston, Philadelphia, and Baltimore. But his passion was for the sail. Crossing the Atlantic, he favored the bustling port of Liverpool, England, the unofficial refuge of the American Confederate Navy during the Civil War. Closer to home, he fished for mackerel and laid telegraph cable out of Halifax on the main island of Nova Scotia.

In port, Cape Bretoners prodigiously spent their earnings. Men with names like Wild Archie and John the Weasel staggered from one saloon to the next, undeterred by the hefty fines intended to discourage their raucous behavior. One night in January 1879, twenty-one-year-old Alex MacLean left his boat without his captain's permission, intent on joining the fun. When he returned, a watchman confronted him, an affront that Alex answered with his fists. Arrested on charges of assault, he spent the next five days in jail.

A few months later, Alex signed on with the *Santa Clara*, a magnificent 1,535-ton, full-rigged clipper under the command of one of the most esteemed captains in the California trade. After six months' journey around Cape Horn, the ship reached San Francisco, a city that had grown quickly following the California gold rush. The fog-shrouded hills were much like the landscape Alex had left behind in Cape Breton, but on the streets he encountered a mélange of people and languages. As cosmopolitan as New York City, three-quarters of San Francisco's residents were either first- or second-generation immigrants from countries including France, Germany, Italy, Greece, Spain, Finland, Portugal, Norway, Japan, and China.

Alex quickly became familiar with the town's Barbary Coast district, where every other building was a saloon with a lusty name such as The Bull's Run and The Cock of the Walk. Under the glow of gaslights, the discordant sounds of cursing, drunken laughter, and pianos, banjoes, and bagpipes filled the alleys and streets. From the doorways of red-curtained dens of inequity, women beckoned to miners, farmhands, and sailors. Down passageways hidden from the law, cigar-smoking gamblers pressed their luck at cards. Lured by women and drink, greenhorns risked being shanghaied from the Barbary Coast. When drugged or passed out, the unlucky ones were sometimes taken aboard ships where crews were lacking. When they came to, the vessels would have already set sail. For his part, Alex was far too savvy for such a fate. Besides, he went willingly to sea, though he would return to San Francisco often, enjoying the excitements of the city's netherworld.

In 1880, Alex joined up with his brother Dan, who had also come west, and together they ventured north to Victoria, British Columbia, a major stopping point for London-bound ships. Founded on an ancient Indigenous trading site and, later, a Hudson Bay fort, Victoria rivaled San Francisco in both wealth and squalor. Like San Francisco, Victoria boasted a thriving uptown district that was worlds apart from its seamy waterfront of saloons, opium dens, and brothels. Again, the MacLean brothers preferred the more raucous districts where the men—and the women—were wild and free.

When the MacLeans arrived in Victoria, pelagic sealing—seal hunting in the open sea—was a small but growing industry, pursued mostly by independent traders of Scottish descent using Indigenous crews. Initially, these operations were locally financed, often by the traders themselves. Because they purchased dried sealskins from Indigenous hunters, traders in villages along the west coast of Vancouver Island were well aware of the fur seals' migrations and had already begun turning profits from them. Among the best known of these traders was James Warren, hailing from the Canadian province of Prince Edward Island, a Gaelic enclave north of Cape Breton. In the *Thornton*, a schooner that would figure prominently in the international conflict over the Pribilof seals, Warren sailed between Indigenous villages along Vancouver Island's west coast, trading booze for furs. At one point, he was apprehended for smuggling gin and rum and did time in jail. Upon release, he then led a gunfight in which fifteen Indigenous men were killed.

Dodging murder charges, Warren managed to entice a different Indigenous group of Vancouver Island people, the Nuu-chah-nulth, to hire out their experienced seal hunters to the *Thornton*. Hunting from canoes, the Nuu-chah-nulth were adept at killing fur seals migrating north to the Pribilofs. Traditionally, they killed seals for both the skins, which they fashioned into clothing, and the meat. When traders began clamoring for seal pelts, the hunters sold them the surplus.

Sealing ventures could be risky, especially when spring storms blew in. In 1875, one such storm swamped seventy canoes, killing a hundred Nuu-chah-nulth. Warren proposed an approach that had the potential to save lives while increasing his profits. He loaded Nuu-chah-nulth hunters and their cedar canoes onto the *Thornton* and set sail. Each morning, he lowered the canoes and the hunters over the side of his ship. While migrating, fur seals feed mostly at night and sleep by day, afloat on the water. For the experienced Nuu-chah-nulth hunters and their harpoons, the sleeping seals were easy targets.

The fact that Warren and other traders were already well established in pelagic sealing weakens Dan MacLean's claim that he and Alex took up sealing rather by accident. By Dan's account, he spent eighteen months sailing the coasts of British Columbia and Alaska in a seven-ton sloop called the *Flyaway*. Along the way, he claimed to have discovered both gold and coal. In addition, he said he came up with the idea of going after seals simply because he used to see them bobbing in the water.

Back home in Cape Breton, folks loved a good story. Many might have believed that a sailor could cruise along the Alaska coast and happen upon gold and coal. But those familiar with prospecting in the West knew such discoveries required a good deal of overland trekking—and even then, the odds of success were slim. Successful prospectors also filed claims, and Dan MacLean never had any to show. There was also the question of how Dan had financed what amounted to a pleasure cruise. A seven-ton sloop is a small craft, unsuited to the commercial transport of passengers or cargo. However, such boats were perfect for smuggling whiskey into Indigenous villages. Smuggling was exactly the sort of venture that would have aligned Dan with men like Warren, who was making a tidy sum off migrating seals.

Compared to Dan, Alex had a rather dull time in his early days on the West Coast. He crewed aboard a Fraser River sternwheeler, then helped lay telegraph cable from aboard a Canadian revenue cutter. These were only temporary gigs. Whether by smuggling or prearrangement with a San Francisco investor eager to cash in on the fur seal trade, Dan and Alex acquired sufficient funds to travel from

Victoria back to the East Coast in the fall of 1882. Alex later said he had simply wanted to take a trip, but the brothers seemed to have had some plan in mind, because they stopped in Boston on their way to Nova Scotia and gave up their British citizenship to become Americans. Neither ever explained why they made the switch, but it did position them nicely for encroaching on the Pribilofs, where foreigners were decidedly unwelcome.

The following spring, the MacLean brothers were back on the West Coast. From San Francisco, they set sail on what would be their first sealing venture aboard a nearly new forty-eight-ton schooner, the *City of San Diego*. American investors who financed ventures deemed piracy by their own government were understandably more secretive than their Canadian counterparts. In all likelihood, the 1883 voyage of the *City of San Diego* was financed at least in part by San Francisco furrier Herman Liebes, who would become a key figure in international wrangling over the seals.

On this voyage, Dan MacLean advanced several paygrades, from sloop runner to co-captain of the vessel. Alex was the ship's navigator. The other co-captain, James Cathcart, had run a similar operation in the region the previous year, one apparently funded by Liebes. Instead of harpoons and cedar canoes, Cathcart's hunters used guns and rowboats, following the seals not just along Vancouver Island but all the way north to the Pribilofs. Most pelagic sealing was done farther south, as the United States objected to seals being hunted in the Bering Sea, waters they claimed as their own. As a result, the *City of San Diego* had the northern sea mostly to itself that summer.

At dawn, the crew would lower armed hunters in butcher boats into the waves. Doing double-duty as a puller, or oarsman, Alex manned one of these boats. Spreading out in different directions, the hunters would approach sleeping seals from the leeward side. At a distance of thirty to forty feet, they would begin to shoot. Many of the seals would sink before the hunters could retrieve them. Others would swim away, wounded. In the end, whatever seals the hunters salvaged, they skinned immediately, the pelts being lighter than the whole animal for transport.

Toward summer's end, the *City of San Diego* tracked the seals as they migrated south. When they reached Victoria, Dan and his co-captain brought the ship into port. The MacLeans were tight-lipped to officials about where they had traveled and what they had been up to. When pressed for details, the more experienced Cathcart said they had gone looking for whales and seals were only the bycatch. Rumors continued to swirl about the extended voyage. Some said the MacLeans had made land raids on the Pribilofs. Whatever the truth, the rewards were hefty—a whopping $200,000 in profits, if one believed the scuttlebutt.

After a typical spending spree in Victoria's waterfront saloons, Alex had enough cash left over that year to purchase a 25-percent interest in the *Favorite*, a Canadian vessel from the Victoria sealing fleet. Built in 1858 of stout Douglas fir, the *Favorite* was a grand schooner that carried an incredible 1,300 square feet of sail between its two masts. At the helm in 1884, Alex MacLean transported Indigenous hunters and their canoes from Vancouver Island all the way to the Bering Sea. Compared to white men armed with rifles, Alex found the Indigenous people more adept with their harpoons and less expensive to feed, since they would eat seal meat.

Dan, too, bought into his own schooner. Unlike Alex, he preferred a crew of white men with rifles. Ever competitive, the MacLean brothers wagered over which method would generate the most profit. The result was a draw. Alex's Indigenous crews eventually grew unhappy with being away from home from spring until fall. Missing important months of subsistence activities that kept their families fed and clothed, they demanded a larger share of the profits. Alex refused, and soon both MacLeans were using mostly white men armed with guns to hunt seals.

At sea, Alex MacLean insisted his crews scrub every bit of blood and blubber from the decks after the killing was over, but there was no wiping clean the impact his enterprise had on the seals as a species. No matter the men or method, sealing was an ugly business. Pursued on the high seas, yearlings made easy targets. So did matkas, migrating north in their final months of pregnancy. The MacLeans knew full well that their men killed mostly young seals and pregnant cows. They knew that most seals sank after being shot, ending up at the bottom of the sea. Such practices foretold doom for the seals. But a pelt was a pelt, and the market was booming. Extinction was inevitable, Alex admitted. In the meantime, there were profits to be made. Like most pelagic sealers, Alex refused the label of pirate, though his accusers begged to differ.

For millennia, pirates have terrorized the seas, taking what was not theirs. Well before the dawn of the Common Era, pirates from Crete raided Mediterranean coastal towns, capturing women and children to sell as enslaved people. The Greek biographer Plutarch wrote of how pirates captured Julius Caesar, then demanded as ransom a sum that Caesar complained was only half his true worth. When confronted with the label, Alex MacLean rankled at being called a pirate, saying he was too wise for piracy, though throughout history the term "pirate" has been broadly applied. Renegade warriors who ransacked coastal towns, as the Vikings did during the ninth century, were called pirates. So were privateers who attacked cargo ships. So were those who attacked vessels at the behest of their sovereigns, as did Sir Francis Drake when Queen Elizabeth I sent him out on the seas to harass Spanish sailors.

Between roughly 1690 and 1720, an era that became known as the Golden Age of Piracy, men including Blackbeard and Black Bart and women including Anne Bonny and Mary Reid gained notoriety in the Atlantic and the Caribbean, where the slave trade proffered ample goods for plunder. Many of these Golden Age pirates began their careers the way that Sir Francis Drake had, as privateers engaged by monarchs to attack ships belonging to enemies of the realm. When their sponsoring monarchs settled their differences, these freewheeling mercenaries found themselves operating beyond the law. Previously sanctioned, their theft, murder, and sinking of ships became offenses punishable by death.

While most pirates of the Golden Age met their end at the gallows, their notoriety endured, in large part thanks to an author whose identity remains unknown. In 1724, "Captain Charles Johnson," as he called himself, published the swashbuckling collection *A General History of the Robberies and Murders of the most notorious Pyrates*. The book sold handsomely, inspiring the author to pen a companion volume, *A Complete History of the lives & robberies of the most Notorious Highwaymen*, which included even more sensational tales. Well over a century later, Johnson's success inspired Robert Louis Stevenson to imagine the pirate Long John Silver in his novel *Treasure Island*, released in 1883, the same year the MacLean brothers began sealing. In the straitlaced Victorian era, such outlaws fascinated readers as they roamed the sea, defiant and free, flaunting the rules of proper society.

Alex MacLean fits the romantic ideal of a pirate. Like pirates of the collective imagination, he was a handsome man of rosy complexion, standing tall for his day—nearly six feet—with steely gray eyes. While the infamous Blackbeard was said to have twisted ribbons and even burning matches into his thick black beard, MacLean was known for his eighteen-inch moustache, long enough for him to tie around the back of his neck. Like pirates of legend, MacLean had escaped the troubles of his youth by going to sea. He could be brutal, but he also had a keen sense of fair play. A natty dresser, he was also rumored to be a fine dancer. He was said to drink and curse and read philosophy. The latter may have been a stretch, an attribute granted to him by association with Jack London's fictional character Sea-Wolf. But when the real-life Sea-Wolf was called to testify before various authorities, he did impress them as a thoughtful and well-spoken man.

As is the way with the stories of many pirates, the facts of Alex MacLean's life tangle with the embellishments. Once, when his crew was readying a ship for sail, Alex reportedly came aboard in a fury. Without explanation, he ordered everyone except the first mate belowdecks. After locking the men in their quarters, Alex lit into the first mate. Was it true that the sailor had allowed Dan MacLean to steal Alex's best sailors? The mate admitted he had. At that, Alex reportedly removed his own starched shirt, hung it neatly over the ship's rail, and began pummeling the man with his fists. After thirty minutes of fighting, the mate said he had had enough. Having not the slightest injury himself, Alex supposedly took the man below and gently tended to his wounds. The mate vowed to get Alex's men back, and the combatants celebrated their truce with a round of drinks.

Like any pirate worthy of the name, MacLean supposedly loved to ride his ship hard through storm and gale. His code of conduct was straightforward. To punish transgressions, he would either leave a sailor to fend for himself on a nearby island or would cast him out to sea. If the man failed to survive, he had no one to blame but himself, MacLean reasoned. He also had few qualms about defying maritime law. Like the Golden Age pirates who raised the Jolly Roger, MacLean sometimes sailed under a flag of his own design. When authorities came after him, he did his best to outrun them. When they closed in, he offloaded illicit cargo onto other ships and feigned innocence. He also bribed guards and changed names and nationalities to suit his purposes.

In the end, the question of whether Alex MacLean deserved to be called a pirate hinged on a key question: whether the plunder he took—the Pribilof fur seals—were in fact government property of the United States. And at the heart of that dilemma is the question of whether wildlife, being wild, can be owned at all.

TWO

BACHELORS TO THE SLAUGHTER

*A*S STEWARDS OF ALL THE land and sea offered up for their use, the Unangax̂ of the Aleutian and Pribilof Islands, like other Indigenous Peoples of the Bering Sea, claim responsibility for, but not ownership of, wildlife. During the time the MacLeans were plundering seals, outsiders of the colonial mindset were far more rigid in their thinking. To these outsiders, wildlife was a resource for humans to exploit, regardless of who was first on the lands in question. From this perspective, maritime wildlife was a literal free-for-all.

On land, colonists might push aside Indigenous Peoples, claiming territory for themselves. But beyond a nation's coastal waters, no one owned the open seas—not even by Western ways of reckoning—nor did they own the creatures that swam in them. Regardless of a ship's origin, its crew might fish wherever they chose. They might also chase whales, an industry that thrived in the nineteenth century. To satisfy a seemingly insatiable demand for oil and baleen, seamen in both the Atlantic and Pacific slaughtered whales wherever they could find them, and no one accused them of piracy.

Like whales, fur seals migrate in the open ocean, well beyond national boundaries which, under maritime law, extend only three miles from shore—the so-called "cannon-ball limit" of distance that could be defended from land. When the seals are most vulnerable—that is, while breeding, giving birth, and raising their pups—they crowd onto small, remote islands like the Pribilofs. In this way, the species thrived for two million years. But no creature with the profit potential of a fur seal can hide forever. Whalers were the first to exploit them, taking seals when whales were scarce, beginning with the species native to the southern hemisphere. As a commodity, fur seals were worth far less than whales to humans, but there was a market for their pelts among the Chinese. The Chinese employed a trade secret for extracting coarse guard hairs from seal fur, making it soft and desirable as trim for the garments of the wealthy. And compared to running down and harpooning a whale, killing seals was easy. Crowded onto breeding grounds off the coasts of South America and the islands of Oceania, where they had always been safe, southern fur seals were akin to the proverbial fish in a barrel.

From the coast of South America to Australia and New Zealand and into the waters of Antarctica, whaling ships went from island to island between 1783 and 1812, destroying whole herds of fur seals. An experienced man could skin sixty seals in an hour, leaving the carcasses to rot. No one gave any thought to either seal ownership or extinction, the prevailing notion being that if one's own crew failed to take every last seal from an island, the next crew would finish the job. From the Galápagos, Guadeloupe, the South Shetlands, South Georgia, Alejandro Selkirk Island, the Falklands, New Zealand, and islands in the Indian Ocean, an estimated five million seals were killed during this thirty-year period.

As southern fur seal populations plummeted, merchants sought undiscovered breeding grounds. As with points farther north, the remote islands where the fur seals bred were often shrouded in fog, meaning that large populations of seals might go unnoticed. Although occasionally recorded on early maps, "phantom islands"— islands which seemed to shimmer into view only during storms— would elude seafarers in clear weather. Still, hunters clung to the hope that if a phantom island were to finally reveal itself, it would be crawling with fur seals.

North of the equator, far from the well-trafficked whaling and trade routes of the central and southern Pacific, northern fur seals escaped whalers' attention. Unwittingly, sea otters provided a diversion for profiteers, at least for a time. At six hundred thousand hairs per square inch, a sea otter pelt is twice as dense as a fur seal pelt, and there are no guard hairs to extract. For these reasons, the Chinese traders preferred otter furs when they could get them, exchanging tea and porcelain in return. With their proximity to China, Russian traders were well positioned to exploit sea otters, which live only in the northern hemisphere. In pursuit of these valuable furs, Russian fur hunters and traders, known as promyshlenniki, trekked across Siberia and then traveled eastward by boat to the Aleutian chain.

When Russian explorer Alexei Chirikov first spotted the Aleutians through a bank of fog in 1741, he thought he had reached the North American mainland. Arriving by boat four years after Chirikov, the promyshlenniki knew better. They also knew there was good money to be made from the sea otters that frequented Aleutian waters. But the promyshlenniki had a problem—unlike fur seals, sea otters rarely came ashore, not even to breed or give birth. And while well versed in trapping land mammals, the Russian traders lacked the patience and skill to pluck these nimble creatures from the sea.

Their solution was to coerce the Unangax̂ into providing them with otter pelts. Called Aleuts by the Russians, the Unangax̂ were known to be experienced maritime people, reading winds and currents from an early age, paddling kayaks through rough ocean waters, and throwing harpoons with precision. They took virtually everything they needed to survive from the sea. Out of driftwood, bone, and ivory, they fashioned tools and weapons. From the skins of sea otters, seals, walrus, birds, and fish, they made clothing, containers, and bedding. From the largest skins, they fashioned kayaks light enough to be carried by a child and fast enough to keep pace with large sailing ships traveling ten miles per hour.

Under Unangax̂ stewardship, the rich and productive Bering Sea ecosystem had remained stable for thousands of years. That changed in 1745, when the Russians infused the region with their profit motive, pilfering pelts from the Unangax̂ and ravaging their villages. The Russians took women and children hostage, releasing them only when Unangax̂ hunters paid a tribute in sea otter pelts. When the Unangax̂ attempted revolt, they quickly discovered that weapons crafted of wood and bone were no match for Russian firearms. A rough lot, the promyshlenniki killed Unangax̂ men for access to their women and burned entire Aleutian settlements when the Unangax̂ people tried to defend themselves. In one especially cruel incident,

Russians tied twelve Unangax̂ together and shot a musket ball into them to see how far it would go. With that, Unangax̂ resistance ended. Within fifty years, the promyshlenniki killed off two-thirds of the Unangax̂ population through homicide, disease, and deprivation. Simultaneously, they killed off most of the Aleutian sea otters.

The Russians then turned to northern fur seals. Fur seal pelts fetched a lower price than sea otter, so they needed a large supply. Not satisfied with the pelt numbers the Unangax̂ had procured for them as the seals passed by on their spring and fall migrations, the Russians sought to locate the northern islands they'd heard the Unangax̂ mention, teeming with seals.

Because they had traditionally taken only enough seals for their subsistence use, the Unangax̂ had no reason to seek out these "seal islands," but the promyshlenniki were keenly interested in finding them. In 1786, Russian navigator Gavriil Pribylov sailed north from the Aleutians in search of these breeding grounds. After three weeks, he spotted through the fog the smaller of the two sought-after islands. Naming the discovery after his ship, the *St. George*, Pribylov left some of his crew to spend the winter there, effectively claiming the uninhabited island for Russia. On a rare fogless day, these men then spotted the second, larger island.

To their great relief, Pribylov returned the following year as promised. On the feast day of St. Paul, he landed on the larger island, and so he named it St. Paul Island. Together with three tinier islands, also uninhabited, St. Paul and St. George collectively became known as the Pribilofs. This was the hoped-for bonanza—as it turned out, three-quarters of the world's vast population of northern fur seals bred and raised their young on these unlikely Pacific outcroppings. But to amass their furs, the Russians needed a labor force. Once again, they exploited the Unangax̂. From the Aleutian chain nearly three hundred miles across the sea, they relocated Unangax̂ men to do the bloody work of harvesting seals from their breeding grounds.

Isolated from the resources and vibrant culture they had developed on the Aleutians, the transplanted Unanga^x had little choice but to do the Russians' bidding. But as Russia expanded its hold on the lands that the Unanga^x called "Alaska," management of the remote islands proved a challenge. As evidenced by the freewheeling promyshlenniki, the further one got from St. Petersburg, the greater the challenge of maintaining control of the colonists. Taking stock of the situation, Russian empress Catherine the Great assigned her nation's fur trading interests in the New World to what eventually became a single private entity, the Russian American Company (RAC).

Even with this consolidation, management of the Pribilof seal operation was slipshod. One year the RAC had to destroy seven hundred thousand sealskins that they had failed to salt properly, a necessary action to preserve the quality. There were more skins where those came from, they reasoned. Though no one attempted a count, there appeared to be millions of Pribilof seals. Harvesting what seemed an endless bounty, the Russians killed all ages of seals indiscriminately—pregnant and nursing matkas, pups and yearlings, "beachmasters" (breeding males), and "bachelors" (nonbreeding males). Before long, it became obvious that the seal population was plummeting. Realizing their error of their ways, the Russians quit killing pups, then beachmasters, and then matkas. Eventually, they slaughtered only the bachelor seals. Every five years, they also declared a moratorium on all killing, giving the seal numbers a chance to rebound.

To further protect their profits, Russia made a bold declaration in 1834: because they owned the entire Bering Sea, the fur seals that bred there belonged exclusively to them. Claims of ownership over oceans or seas, by virtue of a concept dubbed *mare clausum*, were not altogether new. In Rome's heyday, its emperors had claimed jurisdiction over the entire Mediterranean. During the Renaissance, Venice collected tribute from trading ships in the Adriatic. By the seventeenth century, Great Britain had claimed much of the North Atlantic, calling it the English Sea. But whatever traction these claims gained in their day, the prevailing principle became *mare liberum*, meaning "free seas." On this principle, the United States and other world powers rebuffed Russia's 1834 declaration. American whalers continued to ply Bering Sea waters, though they paid little attention to the seals.

Within decades, the United States would do an about-face, making its own *mare clausum* claim to the Bering Sea and using it to brand pelagic sealers, including Alex MacLean, as pirates. The 1867 Alaska Purchase precipitated this reversal. Despite the RAC's improved sealing practices, Russia's profits from their North American holdings had steadily declined during the nineteenth century. Supplying the far-flung territory also proved problematic. By the 1850s, the entire Alaska colony had become a liability, and Russia began looking to offload it.

With an empire that spanned the globe, Britain would have happily annexed Russian America to its Canadian territory, but after the Crimean War, the Russians had little interest in making a deal with a nation that had defeated them. This put the United States in a prime negotiating position, especially since American merchants were already shipping food, clothing, and other supplies to Russian America, the area encompassed by modern-day Alaska. The American Civil War had interrupted diplomatic discussions over this territory, but with the war's end in 1865, US Secretary of State William Seward renewed his efforts to purchase the territory. He took some ribbing in the press for his efforts to annex "Walrussia," as reporters called it, but whalers understood the region's value. So did fishermen, who were impressed by the abundance of salmon and cod in northern waters, and so did the few who knew of the lucrative Pribilof fur seals.

In 1867, Seward inked his deal, agreeing on behalf of the US to purchase Russia's American holdings for $7.2 million, or roughly two cents an acre. Going forward, the Unangax̂ word Alaska, meaning "great land," would be used to identify the territory that became, for all intents and purposes, an American colony. Now that the United States owned the Pribilofs, the idea of also owning the seals had much greater appeal, and the question became how to assert that ownership.

In the aftermath of the Alaska Purchase, there was no need for piracy on the high seas, as sealing on the Pribilof breeding grounds became a free-for-all. Profiteers streamed north, eager for a piece of the action. Distance and geographic isolation precluded government intervention— the Alaska territory was vast and the question of how it should be governed was as yet unsettled. In the interim, the War Department was in charge. But there were few rules to enforce, certainly none dealing specifically with the profits to be made from the seals. Besides, the 150 troops stationed in faraway Sitka were themselves a lawless bunch.

It was a treacherous time for the seals and also for the Unangax̂, an unintended test of Adam Smith's notion that the free market would self-regulate. On the Pribilofs it did not, at least not in any sustainable way. At the end of the 1868 sealing season, Captain J. W. White of the United States Army finally made it to the Pribilofs to assess how the unregulated free market had fared. The picture was far from pretty. Not even under the most reckless Russian rule had there been such bloody slaughter. On St. Paul Island alone, some 250,000 seals had been killed in a competitive frenzy among profiteers. White feared that if there were another season like this one, the species would be wiped out. The Unangax̂ had not fared much better—what little payment they had received for their work had been mostly in whiskey and fancy clothes. On the spot, White issued an edict: all killing of the seals on the islands was to cease immediately, and all whiskey was to be rounded up and destroyed.

The moratorium would last less than a year. An East Coast entrepreneur named Hayward Hutchison, who managed to place himself in the right place at the right time by mixing it up with the right people, saw to that. Hutchison had made his first fortune selling stoves to the Union Army during the Civil War. Securing the financial backing of some of San Francisco's most well-heeled businessmen, he outmaneuvered competitors to purchase the RAC's trading posts, merchant vessels, and warehouses almost as soon as the Alaska Purchase was signed. On the Pribilofs, he ingratiated himself with the Unangax̂ by aligning with a trusted Russian Orthodox priest and installing a well-liked Unangax̂ foreman to oversee the Unangax̂ workers.

Organizing as the Alaska Commercial Company (ACC), Hutchison and his investors set out to convince Congress they should be granted a ninety-nine-year lease on the Pribilof seal operation, an arrangement that would give them sole rights to the seals. Aided by well-connected shareholders, Hutchison greased a fair number of palms in Washington, DC. Failing to procure a ninety-nine-year agreement, he settled for a twenty-year, government-sanctioned monopoly on the Pribilof seals. In exchange, the ACC agreed to turn over a portion of their profits to the US Treasury. To the ACC, there was no question that the US government owned the seals that they were leasing. Accordingly, company officials reasoned, anyone who plucked seals from the water anywhere along their migration route was stealing from them and from the government, plain and simple. From the perspective of officials who likewise perceived a potential decline in tariffs from the sale of fur seal pelts, that made men like Alex MacLean pirates.

In 1885, MacLean's second year of commanding his own ship, US customs officials in San Francisco responded to ACC complaints of piracy by assigning the crew of a revenue cutter, the *Corwin*, with protecting the Pribilof seals. Considering how tough it was to locate pirates in the 772,000–square mile Bering Sea, let alone catch them, this was a lot to ask. The *Corwin* already had a large and diverse set of assignments in the vast Arctic waters, from conducting rescues and searching for lost ships to transporting explorers, delivering mail, intercepting whiskey smugglers, and hauling criminals off to stand trial at Sitka.

At the helm of the *Corwin*, "Hell Roaring Mike" Healy was accustomed to doing the impossible. The son of an enslaved African woman and her white slave master, Healy had achieved his rank by concealing his race. Hot-tempered by nature, he had run away to sea in his youth, gradually working his way up to the position of captain with the US Revenue Service. Cruising at up to fourteen knots an hour under power of both steam and sail, the *Corwin* approached St. Paul Island at the end of June 1885. Matkas were by then heavy with pups and hauling out of the sea by the tens of thousands, contributing to the ruckus of beachmasters and bachelor seals that had arrived weeks earlier. With a lookout stationed at the mast to search for pirates, Healy anchored the *Corwin* offshore.

By this time, MacLean and other interlopers were well aware that the ACC and the US government were after them. Still, they kept taking seals. Sheltered by fog, they pressed close to the islands, passing word from ship to ship about the *Corwin*'s location. Healy waited as long as he could for the fog to lift, but eventually he had to pull anchor and steam north to attend to other pressing government business. In early September, he returned. Boarding the *Corwin*, the US Treasury agent assigned to the Pribilofs informed Healy that pirates from several vessels, including MacLean's, had killed thousands of seals that summer. The slaughter had stopped only when the pirates had gotten word of Healy's imminent return and sailed south to Victoria and points beyond.

Frustrated, Healy pointed out to his superiors how much revenue the pirates were diverting from the US Treasury. He also complained that Canadian officials in Victoria were encouraging the pilfering with claims that pelagic sealing was perfectly legal. And Healy provided a reality check—one revenue cutter simply could not handle all that needed doing in the Arctic. In a nod to the gravity of the seal situation, he proposed that the US Revenue Service assign one cutter exclusively to apprehending seal pirates and another to all the other duties.

Treasury officials agreed to the plan. Given Healy's experience in Arctic waters, he would captain the *Bear*, attending to basically everything except the seals. At the helm of the *Corwin* would be Charles Abbey, who had naval experience making blockades during the Civil War. In the Bering Sea, his sole mission would be to find and catch seal pirates. In 1886, Abbey reached St. Paul Island at about the same time Healy had the previous season, when the matkas were hauling out and birthing their pups. But the fog was especially thick that summer, and Abbey had trouble even finding the islands. For fifty-four of the next fifty-eight days, either fog or rain hampered his pursuit of the pirates. He heard gunfire, so he knew the pirates were there, but in the fog he became disoriented, and his attempts to navigate by dead reckoning proved futile.

After much frustration, Abbey finally tracked down the *San Diego*, a schooner owned in part by James Cathcart, the captain who had first taken the MacLean brothers sealing in the similarly named *City of San Diego*. Seizing the vessel, Abbey found more than five hundred sealskins in its hold. He attached a tow rope, then hauled the *San Diego* 270 miles southeast to Unalaska, on the Aleutian chain. By the time he returned to the Pribilofs, it was late July. The rookeries were disbanding, and the matkas, beachmasters, and bachelors were all taking to the water, as was their habit, making them prime pickings for the pirates.

Among the pelagic fleet, word spread that the *Corwin* was again in the vicinity. But with so many seals in the water, the pirates were disinclined to disperse. Perhaps more for Alex MacLean than the rest, there was sport in eluding capture. He did, however, take the precaution of transferring five hundred sealskins from the ship he was commanding, the *Favorite*, to the *Onward*, another vessel in which he was part-owner. In the meantime, Abbey nabbed two butcher boats belonging to the *Thornton*. He seized the mother ship and attached a tow rope. With the *Thornton* in tow, Abbey apprehended four more butcher boats within a half-hour. A short time later, he seized the ship that had launched them, the *Carolena*.

Towing both the *Thornton* and the *Carolena*, Abbey searched in the long summer twilight for additional offenders. A third vessel eluded him, as did a fourth. The *Onward*, owned in part by Alex MacLean, had no such luck. Shortly before 5 a.m., Abbey boarded the vessel. As before, MacLean was one step ahead, having transferred pelts this time from the *Onward* back to the *Favorite* so that only four hundred pelts remained in the hold. But by Abbey's orders, four hundred pelts were four hundred too many, so he tied up the *Onward* behind the *Carolena* and the *Thornton*.

Engines churning out steam, the *Corwin* chugged toward Sitka, some 1,200 miles to the southeast, where Abbey intended to turn the three pirate ships over to US authorities. He may not have realized that he and the officials who had dispatched him were on a collision course with history. The ships he was towing had sailed from Victoria. Outside Canadian waters, Great Britain had jurisdiction over them. Tensions between the United States and Britain were already simmering, and Abbey's success with the pirates was about to aggravate the situation.

THREE

PORTRAIT OF THE ARTIST
AS A MEGATHERIUM

*F*OR SIX-YEAR-OLD FRANK ELLIOTT III, a train trip with his father was a grand adventure. Traveling from Cleveland to Pittsburgh in 1886, they rode in the train's parlor car. In Pittsburgh, Frank swung a lunch basket at his side as he trotted beside his father, crossing the station to board the train that would carry them to Washington overnight. In the sleeping car, he watched in fascination as a porter made up the beds. After climbing into the lower berth, he promptly fell asleep to the clacking of the wheels.

Even more exciting than all of this was going with his father to the Smithsonian Institution when they reached Washington. His father spoke of the place often, but for Frank to see its wonders with his own eyes brought pure amazement. The Smithsonian really did have a castle, just as his father had said. When his father showed Frank the tiny room where he had slept when he was younger, Frank declared his desire to sleep in that very same place, all by himself, the way his father had. But his father said no, it was only the Megatheria—whatever that meant—who got to sleep there, and they were no more. Instead, Frank and his father returned to the big brick house where they had rented a room to sleep. They had to be well rested, his father said, because Sunday was going to bring about more tromping around the city as they called on people his father knew. Important people—Professor Baird from the Smithsonian, Mrs. Hutchison from the ACC, and some senators too—so Frank would have to be on his best behavior.

When they got back to the big brick house, Frank had to admit it felt good to stretch his tired legs on the bed. Before drifting off to sleep, he asked his father again how long three weeks were. Grand adventure or not, he missed his mother, and maybe even his five sisters. He knew they must be jealous of him getting to go on their father's winter campaign. One time, before Frank was born, two of his sisters, Grace and Flora, had traveled with their mother and father to Alaska, which Frank supposed was even farther from Ohio than Washington, DC. There, they had visited their mother's family and seen the seals their father was forever talking about.

But that was years ago, and he doubted his sisters had seen anything half as exciting as he had today. For one thing, he was pretty sure there was no Smithsonian in Alaska. The Smithsonian did have in its collection some of Alaska's people, maybe even some of Frank's own ancestors on his mother's side. Not living people but—even better—Alaskan mummies. Wrapped in furs and grass blankets, they had been found in a cave warmed by active fumaroles, which Frank's father said were steamy openings in the earth that might one day explode into volcanoes. Frank could have looked at the mummies all day, especially knowing it was his own father who had arranged for them to be brought to Washington.

Frank found volcanoes and mummies a lot more exciting than the important people he would meet. Equally exciting were the pirates his father spoke of in grave tones. These pirates were not searching for buried treasure the way Long John Silver had. They were after seals, which his father said were a sort of treasure too, because people paid lots of money for sealskin coats. And his father should know, because no matter where they went in Washington, the talk always came around to seals, seals, seals.

IN 1886, FRANK'S FATHER, HENRY WOOD ELLIOTT, was the world's foremost expert on the fur seals of Alaska's Pribilof Islands. Timed for when Congress was in session, Elliott's "winter campaigns," such as the one young Frank joined him for, dated back to 1873, the year following Henry's first foray to the Pribilofs. Of average height and build, Henry Elliott's physical presence was unassuming. More notable than his long face and sturdy chin was his blue-eyed gaze, conveying earnest intent. Talented, good natured, and passionate in his every pursuit, he was described by friends as irrepressible.

Born on November 13, 1846, near the Lake Erie shoreline in what would become Lakewood, a western suburb of Cleveland, Ohio, Henry was the firstborn of Franklin Elliott, a horticulturalist who had moved to the state two years earlier, and Sophia Hopkins, Franklin's wife of ten months. Henry's middle name, Wood, was a nod to the Ohio Supreme Court Justice whose home his parents were caretaking at the time, a dwelling far statelier than their circumstances would have otherwise allowed. This incongruence would prove a pattern in Henry Elliott's life, his circumstances often stretching him beyond his means.

Elliott entered the world at a time when Americans' ideas about nature and wildlife were still young and evolving. For the colonists, nature had been primarily a set of obstacles to be conquered as they carved out spaces for themselves in the lands they occupied. As settlers expanded westward from the colonies, the notion of frontierism took hold, exalting the rugged individuals who tamed the wilderness. New England's transcendentalist thinkers in the 1830s embraced the frontier notion of individual autonomy, but they also took an exalted view of nature, perceiving it as a means for discovering spiritual truths. Transcendentalist Ralph Waldo Emerson urged people out of the cities and into the countryside to experience the healing qualities of nature as an antidote to the effects of industrialization. But when Emerson wrote in the 1830s of "wild" places, he was referring to pastoral landscapes and rural towns, not the wilderness at the continent's farthest reaches. Emerson and others in the Transcendental Club, as they called their group, lived mostly in and around Boston and rarely left the area. Neither Emerson nor fellow transcendentalist author Henry David Thoreau ever traveled farther west than Missouri, and neither depended on the land to survive.

Henry Wood Elliott's early experiences were of a practical bent. His father had settled the family in Ohio, which at the time was considered part of the West, and ran a nursery and seed business. When nature delivered ice storms and early frosts, the family suffered. Seen in his cultivation of several new varieties of fruit trees, Franklin's interests leaned less toward transcendentalism and more toward Charles Darwin's controversial work on natural selection. As

Darwin's seminal 1859 book *On the Origin of Species* permeated American thought, the influence of transcendentalism faded, though not without having set a foundation for future work in conservation and preservation. In Henry Elliott's life and work, both wonderment with nature and the difficult questions arising from Darwin's theories would play a part.

Through his nursery business, Franklin Elliott became good friends with neighbor and gentleman farmer Dr. Jared Kirtland, an esteemed physician with a large country practice who also taught medicine and served in the Ohio legislature. Dr. Kirtland pursued his agricultural interests by commissioning the building of an estate he called Whippoorwill. There, he developed expansive gardens in which he cultivated six new varieties of pears and twenty-six varieties of cherries. A staunch abolitionist, Kirtland also made Whippoorwill a stop on the Underground Railroad. But his most enduring legacy is arguably his mentoring of up-and-coming naturalists, including Henry Wood Elliott.

In addition to the Elliotts, visitors to Kirtland's Whippoorwill estate included esteemed naturalists Alexander von Humboldt and Louis Agassiz. Going forward, Elliott would cross paths with many of Louis Agassiz's disciples, often to his detriment. To the extent that Agassiz's temperament rubbed off on his protégés, they tended toward self-confidence and, in the extreme, arrogant ambition. Kirtland, in contrast, was a genial soul who seemed more content with tending his orchards than with attempts at notoriety. His tutelage contributed to Henry Elliott's mostly idyllic childhood despite his brother's death, his own bouts of illness, and the near disaster of the family's finances.

In 1856, when Henry was ten years old, a hard frost destroyed his father's $30,000 peach orchard. On top of that, a bank panic led to the collapse of Franklin's seed business. Facing financial ruin, Franklin Elliott turned to Dr. Kirtland, who enabled his purchase of twenty-two acres in Rockport, near Kirtland's Whippoorwill estate. There, Franklin reestablished his orchards. In addition, he grew grapes that garnered statewide acclaim and he tested out rare varieties of shrubs and flowers. He also built a rambling home overlooking a pond that he stocked with goldfish which, as they multiplied, ended up in fishbowls all over town. In winter, there were skating parties on the pond, where many a local romance got its start. In summer, there were tennis and croquet games on the grounds.

It was in this home that Henry fell ill and evaded war. In 1862, the War Between the States was pulling young men of all stripes into action. At age sixteen, Henry might have had thoughts of going off to fight for the Union. Instead, he spent his time recuperating in bed and painting fruits and flowers for a manual his father was preparing for the government regarding crops that would feed Union soldiers. With Kirtland's encouragement, Henry accompanied his father to Washington to deliver the manuscript with the drawings. There, he met with Kirtland's friend Spencer Baird, a naturalist who was fervently building collections at the Smithsonian Institution even as the war raged on.

At the time, the Smithsonian was but a faint shadow of what it would later become—the largest research, education, and museum complex in the world. After British chemist and meteorologist James Smithson bequeathed his substantial fortune to the United States for the purpose of increasing and diffusing knowledge in 1829, Congress had deliberated for more than a decade before agreeing, for the most part, on what the Smithsonian should be. Some thought the funds should go to a university. Others wanted an observatory, a museum, a publishing house, a national library, or an institute of scientific research. Eventually, the Smithsonian Institution would come to encompass all of these except the university.

In 1850, Spencer Baird became the first curator of the Smithsonian's museum. Starting with two boxcars filled with his own personal collections, he set out to build the museum's holdings of natural history artifacts unique to North America. Like Kirtland, Baird had become one of the nation's leading naturalists primarily through self-study, with John James Audubon serving as his mentor. Baird also had the perfect combination of attributes for recruiting young naturalists to build the Smithsonian's collections. Bearing a passing resemblance to Abe Lincoln, though his face was fuller, his features not as coarse, and his beard redder, Baird commanded respect but was always up for a good laugh.

Baird's team of budding naturalists inducted newcomers into

what they called the Megatherium Club. Named after a genus of a long-extinct, elephant-sized, South American ground sloth, they were an all-volunteer force of aspiring naturalists working under Baird's somewhat loose supervision. As one of their own put it, when five o'clock came and the Megatheria took their prey, their most interesting traits were revealed, the beasts roaring with delight at their own revelry, offsetting the ardors of their work.

At sixteen, Henry Elliott was young for the Megatheria's most raucous adventures. For a time, they denned up in a cottage occupied by one of their founding members. To feed themselves, they kept hens. Hens led to eggs, and eggs led to eggnog, which led to playing music all night and other general rowdiness that infuriated the neighbors, who complained of the wild beasts. Informed that their shenanigans were besmirching the Smithsonian's reputation, the Megatheria handed over the hens to Baird's daughter Lucy, the assumption being that without eggs there could be no nog, and without nog, the mischief would cease.

It did not, though the neighbors must have breathed a collective sigh of relief when the Megatheria moved from the cottage into sleeping rooms in the Smithsonian Castle's main tower. In these drafty cuddies, the great beasts consumed yet more ale and organized sack races down the halls. Smithsonian Secretary Joseph Henry, the handsome, broad-featured director of the Institution, also lived in the Castle with his family, but that did little to squelch the revelry. When sufficient alcohol was consumed, the Megatheria would assemble beneath the windows of Secretary Henry's quarters and serenade his daughters.

Several of these fun-loving naturalists would become Henry Elliott's lifelong friends. But first, he had to prove himself to Spencer Baird by collecting specimens back in Ohio that summer. With Kirtland's training, this was easily accomplished. Having satisfied Baird, Elliott quit high school before his senior year and attached to the Smithsonian's Megatheria as a "cub," as they called the youngest among them. In addition to the tedious work of sorting and classifying specimens, Elliott handwrote correspondence for Joseph Henry. The smallest of the bunch, Elliott was also tasked with dashing to the peak of the Smithsonian Castle's main tower on certain clear nights, where he would pop the door to the roof so President Lincoln could ascend and observe Secretary Henry's tests of signaling devices for the Union Army. Conveying coded messages, the blinking lights and flashing rockets made quite the spectacle in the Washington night sky.

The capital city was along the most active front in what would become the nation's bloodiest war. Confederate strategists were convinced that if they could only take Washington, the North would surrender. As forty thousand formerly enslaved people and fifty thousand wounded soldiers sought refuge there, the town's population tripled. Among the largest of its makeshift hospitals was a one-thousand-bed facility headquartered in what was then the National Armory, on the grounds of the Smithsonian. In a complex that included twelve pavilions plus officers' quarters and a chapel, Clara Barton and Walt Whitman were among those who tended the wounded.

At work in the tower, the Megatheria kept mostly out of the fray. As the war dragged on, smallpox and typhoid spread through the city. Against the latter, the Megatheria's consumption of ale had something of a prophylactic effect, alcohol being safer to drink than the city's fetid water supply. Some, like Kirtland's former student Ferdinand Hayden, enlisted and went off to battle. Others, including another Kirtland protégé, Robert Kennicott, paid a $300 commutation to avoid military service.

Having looked up to Kennicott during his stay at Kirtland's Whippoorwill, Elliott's admiration for him must have soared when the dashing scientist strode into the Smithsonian Castle in 1862, fresh off a three-year expedition to the hinterlands of what would become the Yukon Territory and Alaska. Traveling by canoe and dog sled in the company of Hudson Bay voyageurs, Kennicott had hunted and trapped and collected specimens, returning from the Arctic with 282 birds, 230 mammals, 151 fish, and scads of plants and insects for the Megatheria to sort and label.

Since his time at Whippoorwill, the lanky Kennicott had grown even more handsome, his hair dark and flowing and his eyes soulful. At age twenty-seven, he enjoyed a reputation as a brilliant up-and-coming naturalist who handled poisonous snakes as if they were mere eels, boasting that no venom could harm him. There were, of course, no snakes in the Arctic, but he had enjoyed ample hair-raising adventures there too. Kennicott's achievements validated Baird's notion that in a nation as bright and new as America, a young man could accomplish as much or more than an old one.

Among the Megatheria, Kennicott established himself as a bright and shining light. From their ranks, he recruited what became a Scientific Corps that would accompany the Western Union Telegraph Expedition as it laid lines from British Columbia to Alaska, then beneath the Bering Sea to Russia. The Corps was Baird's idea, arranged by his "warm friend" who also happened to be Western Union's treasurer. Traveling alongside the company's surveyors, loggers, pole setters, road builders, and line stringers, the Corps' members would forge into the North American wilderness gathering specimens for the Smithsonian's collection. As Elliott would later write, Kennicott "was the very ideal man to go into the wilderness with other men and show them the way."

As the youngest of Kennicott's recruits, nineteen-year-old Elliott would get his first taste of real wilderness and real hardship on the telegraph expedition. On March 9, 1865, he and five other members of the Smithsonian's Scientific Corps left New York aboard the SS *Golden Rule* bound for the West Coast via the Isthmus of Panama. Almost immediately, they ran into stormy seas, and by the time they reached Panama, they were exhausted.

The group's troubles compounded when, upon arriving at the Isthmus, they discovered that waters in the San Juan River had dropped considerably. What should have been a two-day journey to the Pacific ended up taking sixteen days as they ferried supplies back and forth over the ninety-two-mile route. But the treks also opened an entirely new world of wildlife species to the Corps. Emerald-scaled Jesus Lizards, *Basiliscus plumifrons*, as long as a man's arm, dropped from trees along the river, then skittered across the water for up to fifteen feet before sinking. At dusk, multitudes of insects buzzed in thick clouds over waters where large-toothed sawfish, freshwater sharks, and crocodiles lurked. Making the most of the opportunity, Kennicott urged his team to collect specimens "day in and day out."

Amid this frenzied activity, Kennicott contracted yellow fever. It was not known at the time that mosquitoes transmitted this viral, hemorrhagic disease that causes fever, chills, nausea, vomiting, headache, and muscle pain. Even today, there is no cure for yellow fever—the only treatment is to make patients comfortable. In the nineteenth century, this meant a day of "laying in" followed by a day of normal activity until the disease ran its course. After a period of remission, 15 percent of yellow fever patients relapse into jaundice caused by deteriorating kidney function, which results in bleeding from the eyes, nose, and mouth. Fortunately, Kennicott avoided this fate. But instead of lying in as recommended, he became "fairly self-possessed with the idea he could fight off this fever" by self-medicating with whiskey and brandy. By early May, when the group finally reached San Francisco, Kennicott was reportedly consuming several glasses of spirits a day, beginning early in the morning.

In San Francisco, Kennicott, Elliott, and the rest of the Corps officially joined the Western Union Telegraph Expedition. The project's chief of operations, a former military officer, handed out dress uniforms and designations of rank. He likely also advised the young men to steer clear of the vile goings-on in the city's Barbary Coast district. The Corps was divided into three contingents. "Major" Kennicott set out with one group for the mouth of the Yukon River. Another group set sail for the Bering Sea to survey the area where underwater cable would be laid. The third group headed for British Columbia to begin an overland slog north, intending to meet Kennicott's team at the headwaters of the Yukon River.

Assigned to the British Columbia contingent, Elliott traveled from San Francisco through the tiny town of Seattle, population eighty-one, to a settlement on the outskirts of Vancouver. There, he joined a crew who followed wagon roads north, laying telegraph lines as they went. Where there were no roads, the men hacked through swaths of giant Douglas fir in what Elliott described as hard country full of swamps, heavy timber, and nearly impenetrable undergrowth. The Western Union superintendent in British Columbia, another former military man, complained that the province was nothing but rum mills, broken miners, loafers, and swindlers. By comparison, he said, banishment to Siberia would be paradise. Buoyant and tenacious by nature, Elliott kept his spirits up. Yet as he labored alongside the telegraph crew, he fretted at his failure to collect specimens. Assuring him that collections would be far easier to make once they had hacked a route through the wilderness, the project superintendent urged Elliott to continue his physical work with the crew.

News traveled slowly in the more remote parts of the continent at this time—hence the need for a telegraph line—and thus, many months passed before Elliott learned of Robert Kennicott's untimely and mysterious death. Short on rations, Kennicott's group had been forced to winter along the frozen Yukon River at a village nearly one thousand miles from their destination. Enduring months of bitter cold and scant daylight, Kennicott suffered sluggishness and frequent headaches. When spring finally came, he rose early one morning and scribbled a note that began, "in case of any accident." Then he set off toward the Yukon River, humming a cheery tune. His men found him hours later lying face-up on the riverbank, his arms folded across his chest, his broad-brimmed black hat knocked from his head, his eyes half-closed, his face calm and peaceful. Some suspected suicide, some murder, and others the general ill health that had plagued him from childhood, accelerated by his bout with yellow fever and attempts at self-treatment. Without him, the Megatheria would never be the same.

On top of this bad news, Elliott and his fellow Corps members learned that following a previous failed attempt, a transatlantic telegraph cable had been successfully lain beneath the Atlantic Ocean, negating the need for a Pacific route. In 1867, the Western Union Telegraph Expedition was called off and the Scientific Corps returned to the Smithsonian. Restless, Elliott did not remain in Washington for long. Ashamed of how few specimens he had collected, he returned to British Columbia, becoming a telegraph operator along a stretch of line that the crew had completed before the project fizzled out. He confessed to Baird that while he had written several letters to friends at the Smithsonian about losing all interest in wildlife, he had burned the letters rather than sent them.

But Baird refused to give up on his young protégé and arranged for Elliott to join a twenty-man expedition to Wyoming led by

Ferdinand Hayden. Like Kennicott, Hayden had studied with Jared Kirtland at Whippoorwill before joining the Megatheria. Quick and exuberant, he went about his fieldwork with such abandon that the Sioux called him the "man who picks up stones running." Possessed of a long face, deep-set eyes, and a prominent chin, Hayden was not the handsomest man in the Megatherian lair, but he was nonetheless known for his vanity and the meticulous attention he paid to his hair.

Writing to Baird of the collection of fossils and bones he had amassed with Hayden's crew in Wyoming, Elliott joked of the tremendous set of whiskers he was growing. As he did in British Columbia, he helped out with whatever needed doing. The physical labor caused his hands to stiffen, making him wonder whether they might ever again do the "elegant work" he had done at the Smithsonian. Lest he seem to be praising his own artistic efforts, he added a question mark after "elegant."

That Elliott questioned the quality of his own art is unsurprising. Though the drawings he had made for his father's horticulture book had helped secure his spot at the Smithsonian, Elliott still had no formal artistic training—until a second expedition with Hayden the following year, when he found the opportunity to study with artist Thomas Moran. An acclaimed painter of resplendent landscapes, Moran joined Hayden's 1871 expedition at the urging of the Northern Pacific Railroad. Like Baird, who valued top-notch illustrations as a means of prodding Congress to fund the Smithsonian, the railroad's director knew that artwork depicting the natural beauty of the American West would entice otherwise skeptical homesteaders to settle there, ensuring a supply of rail passengers.

At the end of this second expedition, Hayden wrote up his findings. Presented to Congress with Moran and Elliott's illustrations, Hayden's report spurred lawmakers to set aside a portion of the explored lands as America's first national park, Yellowstone. With this success in hand, Elliott was eager to learn where Baird might send him next. For a time, he was slated to travel to China. When those plans failed to materialize, he jumped at an assignment in the Pribilof Islands, where Baird had arranged a post as an assistant US Treasury agent. This time, Baird assured him, the job would not interfere with his efforts for science. Rather, Elliott would investigate on the Smithsonian's behalf the natural history of the northern fur seals, which despite their proven value to the United States had yet to be studied in any meaningful way.

After riding west on the newly completed transcontinental railroad and then sailing north from San Francisco, twenty-six-year-old Henry Elliott arrived on St. Paul Island in April 1872, having traveled on the first supply boat to reach the Pribilofs after the winter ice receded. From the start, he was spellbound. After sketching and painting cards to send home, he set out to explore the island, hiking over rocky uplands, mossy flats, and shimmering dunes. Taking a scientist's perspective, he made notes on everything—flora, fauna, and even the beach sands, which had shells of *Foraminifera* and skeletons of *Diatomacea*, both planktonic animals, mixed with finely ground lava and friable gray slate. With an artist's eye, he noted how these sands changed color as they dried, from steely black to dusty purple and gray. From the island's ponds, he netted and then preserved new species of fish to send back to the Smithsonian. At low tide, he gathered seaweed, whelks, and sea urchins that the Unangax̂ ate raw. He marveled at the flocks of birds returning from their winter migrations, especially the bright, fearless, chattering choochkies, which he likened to "plump little auks."

Trekking through moors and up hillsides, Elliott delighted in the spreading grasses and "gaily-colored lichens and crinkled mosses" of the treeless landscape. Happily, he noted a dearth of bothersome insects—even the dreaded mosquitoes that plagued mainland Alaska were absent here. Innocuous green-and-gold carabus beetles muddled over the ground, and only a single species of dragonfly flitted over lakes and ponds. He discovered fox dens tucked into the island's basaltic formations occupied by a type of fox unique to the Pribilofs, its fur color ranging from white to a deep gray tinged with blue, depending on the season. Wary of the foxes, voles darted among the grasses. Mice plagued St. Paul village, where the Unangax̂ kept cats as deterrents. No one kept dogs anymore. Assuming that dogs would harass seals, American government officials had rounded up and shot all the dogs on the island a few years before.

But what most fascinated Elliott were the seals. In May, the beachmasters—the big, breeding males—arrived from their winter feeding grounds in the Gulf of Alaska. At first, these beasts seemed shy and not quite ready to leave the water, perhaps sensing that after coming ashore they would neither eat nor drink for several weeks. In June, "seal weather" consisting of gray banks of fog and off-and-on drizzling rain set in. Having migrated north, hordes of bachelor seals—males who had yet to breed—hauled up on the island. Crowding close, these young upstarts attempted to depose the beachmasters from the turf they had already claimed. With heads averted, mouths open, and teeth glistening, the seals lunged at each other, a rapid *choo-choo-choo* sound rising from their throats. If an intruder failed to back down, the scene could turn violent. "Their fat bodies writhe and swell with exertion and rage," Elliott wrote of these battles. "Furious lights gleam in their eyes; their hair flies in the air, and their blood streams down."

As seals filled the rookeries, Elliott sketched and measured and made notes. He also performed experiments, spraying beachmasters with fine mustard-seed shot to see if he could drive them from their posts. Stretching up to full height and looking their challenger squarely in the face, the beachmasters would roar and chug and lunge before finally retreating. As soon as Elliott quit harassing them, they reclaimed their turf. He marveled at their sheer numbers—millions upon millions, it seemed—and the cacophony of growling and whistling and roaring that he likened to Niagara Falls' churning boom. Day and night, the din never ceased.

Heady with excitement, Elliott anticipated the matkas' arrival. The matkas were the last of the seals to make land. Heavy with pups, they hauled out of the sea in late June just as the wild violets, gentians, and creeping pea vines blossomed over the islands. Describing the matkas, Elliott wrote:

> The head and eye of the female are exceedingly beautiful; the expression is really attractive, gentle, and intelligent; the large, lustrous, blue-black eyes are humid and soft with the tenderest expression, while the small, well-formed head is poised as gracefully on her neck as can be well imagined; she is the very

picture of benignity and satisfaction, when she is
perched up on some convenient rock, and has an
opportunity to quietly fan herself, the eyes half-closed
and the head thrown back on her gently-swelling
shoulders.

Upon arriving at the islands—and after having been pregnant for
nearly a year—the matkas pulled themselves over the rocks to the
rookeries. As they passed, frustrated bachelor seals grabbed at them
with their teeth. Such attacks would sometimes continue even after
a matka reached her destination. If a bachelor seized her by the neck,
the beachmaster who reigned over that patch of ground might
respond by sinking his teeth into her back, making the matka the
object of a cruel tug-of-war. Despite these challenges, the matkas
managed to give birth within two days of hauling out. Then they
would mate, becoming pregnant again.

Smitten though he was by the seals, Elliott's attentions were not
entirely given over to them. The fur seals were an incredible sight—
but so was a pretty sixteen-year-old woman named Alexandra
Milovidov. Of course, this love would not be so simple either.

FOUR

A Matter of Race

STANDING A HEAD SHORTER THAN Elliott, Alexandra
Milovidov was beautiful, with dark eyes and black hair that fell
nearly to her waist. Her ancestors included Indigenous women and
fur traders from Russian outposts on America's western shores. Both
of her grandmothers—one likely Tlingit and the other Unangax̂—
had been transported to Fort Ross, California, as part of a Russian-
forced relocation. In the common parlance of the times, this mixed
racial heritage made Alexandra a member of the Creole class. In
stratified nineteenth-century society, Creoles received opportunities
withheld from other Indigenous Peoples. Before requiring the labors
of Creole boys in the Pribilof killing fields, the Russian American
Company (RAC) shipped them to Sitka for schooling. Upon
matriculation, these young men owed the company a period of
indentured servitude after which they were granted the status of
"free Creoles."

Alexandra's father was a free Creole who worked as an RAC agent,
first on Kodiak Island in the Gulf of Alaska and then on the Pribilofs.
At St. Paul, he replaced a manager who was despised for his brutal
treatment of the Unangax̂. His employer gave Milovidov strict
instructions—he was to set an example that would prompt the
Unangax̂ to obey him out of love and respect. Should trouble arise,
officers from the annual supply ship would judge the offenders. Under
no circumstances should Milovidov resort to corporal punishment. If
Unangax̂ workers wanted to return home to the Aleutians, he should
remind them that life was hard everywhere. Unlike many Alaska
Natives at the time, the men had jobs on the Pribilofs and could

purchase supplies from the RAC company store—what more could they want? Never mind that their wages were a pittance compared to the RAC's profits and the debts they were encouraged to rack up at the store left them ever indentured.

Judging from his tenure on St. Paul Island, Alexandra's father got along well with the Unangax̂. During the difficult period of transition from Russian to American rule, he made a strategic voyage to Sitka, where he became an American citizen. But eighteen months before Elliott's arrival, when Alexandra was only fourteen, her father died suddenly. At age thirty-seven, her mother became a widow with four children.

From her mother, known for her hospitality, Alexandra had acquired an easy grace. Her ready smile and lively eyes charmed Elliott, as did her intelligence. In Washington, Elliott had played croquet and attended church with those he fancied. On the island, the lusty seals formed the backdrop for his romance with Alexandra.

Theirs was a whirlwind courtship. In July, three months after Elliott's arrival on St. Paul Island, an itinerate Russian Orthodox priest married the young couple in the little onion-domed church on the hill. By virtue of her marriage, Alexandra was counted among the eight "American citizens" in St. Paul that summer, as photographed by an ACC agent. Indigenous residents, including Alexandra's Creole siblings, were not considered American citizens because they were not white. But as the new Mrs. Elliott, Alexandra no longer suffered this particular discrimination, at least not among the white people on the island.

As the brief Arctic summer began its retreat, Henry Elliott settled into married life with Sasha, as he affectionately called Alexandra. Already, the rookeries were beginning to break up. The beachmasters were plunging into the ocean to eat and drink at last, the skin on their necks and shoulders loose and sagging from their weeks of fasting. Back on shore, matkas and pups roamed freely. On the dunes, wild wheat, *Elymus arenarius*, turned brown, and Unangax̂ women gathered dark, watery crowberries, *Empetrum nigrum*. The seal fog dispersed and mighty cumulus clouds often towered overhead. The handsome red-legged turnstones, shorebirds that summered on the island, began their journey south. Also bound for warmer climes, flocks of jacksnipe and plover touched down on the island, then departed as suddenly as they had arrived. Save a few stragglers, the seals, too, headed south, in reverse order of their arrival—first the pups, then the matkas followed by the bachelors, and finally the beachmasters. Elliott could hardly wait for their return next spring.

For several weeks, he was forced to abandon his fieldwork so he could help build the new Government House where he and Alexandra would spend the winter. The project, which replaced substandard RAC quarters, was finished only days before the season's first sleet storm arrived. Isolated even during the best of weather, the Pribilof Islands became a tiny universe unto themselves with the onset of winter. Even by local standards, the winter of 1872–3 was especially severe. "It is the wind that tortures and cripples outdoor exercise," Elliott wrote. "It is blowing, blowing, from every point of the compass at all times; it is an everlasting succession of furious gales."

During this dark, lonely season, the Pribilof Islanders drank copious amounts of tea from samovars, highly decorated Russian tea urns. Holes were drilled through the ice so the women could haul water in buckets from freshwater lakes a mile from the village. Some of the men passed the time with gambling games learned from the promyshlenniki. Some drank kvass, a fermented homebrew made from flour and sugar. A local orchestra, including two of Alexandra's brothers, entertained villagers at community dances. On Sundays, lay priests led services in the Russian Orthodox church, the male parishioners standing on one side of the chapel and the women on the other. At the end of December, the entire village celebrated Slaviq, also called Russian Christmas. For three days and nights, villagers paraded from house to house, following lay leaders who led the procession while spinning a big wooden Slaviq star. Reminiscent of traditional potlatches, the celebration included religious exhortations, feasting, and gift giving at every house along the route.

As storms rolled in one after the other, Elliott felt chained to his room. The north wind pushed great fields of ice toward the island, intensifying the sense of isolation. Though not especially heavy or thick, the ice hushed the surf's roar, adding to the uncanny silence that had replaced the seals' din. On the rare days between storms, Elliott trudged through the snow on paths he had followed with far greater ease in the summer. During one especially brutal March blizzard, the mercury hovered near four degrees Fahrenheit, and the wind blew for six days straight, topping out at eighty-eight miles per hour. Unable to stand upright in the gale, villagers resorted to crawling from house to house on all fours.

Wind whistling at their door, Alexandra taught her husband Russian and shared folktales and legends she had learned growing up. Henry Elliott used these months of seclusion to compile his notes and sketches into the book he intended to publish, one he expected would establish him as an expert on fur seals. Waxing poetic about the seals' sensibilities and intelligence, he wrote in great detail of how they fought and played and bred and bore their young. He mapped their rookeries and haulouts. From these maps, he attempted the seemingly impossible feat of estimating the Pribilof fur seal population.

Elliott's sketches and paintings made that winter evoke his sense of wonder at his surroundings. The landscape looms large, skies billowing with clouds. Rendered in watercolors, the rookeries seem almost surreal, the seals appearing in unimaginable numbers. In one detail, they appear almost jovial, a big beachmaster lording over his "harem," as Elliott called the matkas who occupied a beachmaster's turf. In a few scenes, he painted himself among the seals, a small and insignificant observer.

As winter progressed, Elliott grew ever more confident he would find his destiny at the intersection of science and art. His Pribilof assignment would end the next summer, and after returning to the mainland, he planned to tour the nation in Chautauqua style, giving lectures on the seals and displaying his artwork by limelight as a sort of traveling show. The most recent improvement to the magic lantern slide projector, limelight was an intense form of illumination created when a flame heated cylinders of quicklime. For ten cents, a person could take in a limelight show, which often included nature scenes.

By the time the long winter nights finally ceded to long sunlit days, Elliott had completed his manuscript plus more than one hundred sketches. As spring took hold of the islands and the ice floes drifted off to sea, snowbanks slowly shrank and meltwater trickled into the earth. Returning northward, long-tailed ducks, *Harelda glacialis*, glided into the open reaches, their sonorous *dh-naah-nadh-yahs* bringing welcome cheer after the winter's silence. In May, as the first beachmasters straggled toward shore, Alexandra gave birth to Grace, the first of what would eventually be ten Elliott children.

At the end of July 1873, the young family left the Pribilofs, making the long journey by boat and then by train to Rockport, Ohio, on the outskirts of Cleveland, where Elliott's parents lived. During an era when even some prominent abolitionists espoused the notion of racial purity, some among Elliott's family and friends no doubt looked askance at his bride. Among Indigenous people, those with white bloodlines might get preferential treatment, but overall, society discouraged intermarriage between Native Americans and whites. The perceived threat of race mixing had also been used by some Democrats as recently as 1864 in their attempt to unseat President Lincoln. Toward this end, two journalists had coined the incendiary term "miscegenation," which they promoted anonymously in a pamphlet that hyped fear of race mixing in order to turn voters away from Republican candidates. Many scientists also deemed mixed-race unions harmful. Knowing this, Elliott delivered the news of his marriage to one of his Smithsonian colleagues without mentioning Alexandra's race. Instead, he pointed out that although she had been raised in Alaska, she could play the piano.

As with all the Pribilof Unangax̂, outward displays of assimilation were survival skills of sorts. As a people, they had traditionally hunted seals only for subsistence, eating their meat, rendering their blubber for oil, and fashioning clothes from their skins. So that the seals would continue to give themselves up to them, Unangax̂ custom called for the hunters to return the seals' bladders to the sea. But to survive their forced servitude under the Russians, the Pribilof Islanders had been forced to adapt. Even as their Elders continued extolling the right ways to behave within nature, the Unangax̂ had little choice but to engage with an economy that insisted the best use of a seal was for its pelt to be salted, stretched, and shipped to some faraway market. Indeed, Alexandra and her people were doing well to hang onto any of their traditions at all. Schools, the Russian Orthodox church, and the Alaska Commercial Company, which took over for the RAC after the Alaska Purchase, supplanted the way of life that had sustained their people for millennia.

Though remote and unique in a multitude of ways, the Pribilofs mirrored conditions in the mainland United States, where Charles Darwin's theory of natural selection was liberally misapplied to explain away social stratifications and justify racial oppression. Those who failed to adapt were simply destined not to survive, or so went the rationale of outsiders who forced one group of Indigenous People after another from their ancestral lands. Justifying their colonial enterprises, these so-called "civilized" people ranked Indigenous Peoples along a continuum of how "savage" they were. While Elliott was adamant that Alaska Natives not be pushed onto reservations as Indigenous Peoples on the mainland had been, he still judged them as others of his race and class did, asserting that some were by nature more praiseworthy than others, meaning that they showed more evidence of assimilation. Unsurprisingly, he placed his wife's people at the top of this false hierarchy.

Alexandra's charm and beauty may have helped tamp down questions about her culture and race. As she settled into life in Ohio, people took note of her clear skin, ready smile, and dark hair, which she often wore coiled neatly atop her head. Rumors circulated that her father, a Russian American Company agent, had held the prestigious title of "governor." Though undoubtedly homesick for family and friends in the Pribilofs, Alexandra enjoyed tending the flowers that surrounded the Elliotts' Rockport cottage. The family even had their own pond, plus a big lawn where Elliott's sisters played croquet. On one occasion, the Episcopal church staged a theatrical there, complete with magic lanterns that changed the yard into a fairyland.

Sadly, such magic was not to last.

FIVE

ROTTEN ROW

*A*FTER HENRY ELLIOTT RETURNED FROM Washington to Ohio with six-year-old Frank in the summer of 1886, he learned of Lieutenant Abbey's mixed success hunting seal pirates in the *Corwin*. The lieutenant had seized four ships—earlier, the *San Diego*; and now the *Thornton*, the *Carolena*, and the *Onward*, which was owned in part by Alex MacLean. At the helm of the *Favorite*, MacLean had escaped capture, but only barely.

Abbey was already towing the *Thornton*, the *Carolena*, and the *Onward* when he spotted the *Favorite* running to the southeast at full sail, a classic MacLean maneuver. Powered by steam as well as sail, the revenue officer had the advantage. When he caught up with the *Favorite*, Abbey demanded that MacLean leave the Bering Sea immediately, though Abbey was in no position to enforce this mandate. He already had the crews of three seized vessels aboard the *Corwin*, which was straining to tow three captured ships, all heavy with furs. He could not take on another ship. His order to leave did not faze MacLean in the least. For the next seventeen days, MacLean remained in the Bering Sea, dropping butcher boats, American *mare clausum* claims be damned. When he finally left, he had three thousand seal pelts stashed belowdecks.

Lieutenant Abbey kept the offending officers aboard the *Corwin* but offloaded the crews of the seized ships at Unalaska, leaving them to find their own passage back to Victoria and San Francisco. Abbey then towed the pirate ships to Sitka, headquarters of what then passed for government in the Alaska territory. There, authorities took the officers into custody and ordered their ships hauled out on a stretch of beach in Sitka that soon became known as Rotten Row.

The former capital of Russian America, Sitka boasted a modest mansion, Baranov Castle, and a stately Russian Orthodox church, but otherwise, it was a rough-hewn settlement. Following the 1867 Alaska Purchase, Sitka became the de facto capital of the new United States territory. For the first decade of American rule, this distinction as capital meant little, as there was no territorial government. Instead, Congress used the 1868 Customs Act to entrust oversight of the sprawling territory to a single customs collector who, in addition to managing commerce, was charged with enforcing the region's only two laws, one that banned the sale and importation of liquor, and another that banned firearms. Enforcement of these laws was sporadic at best. To assist the lone customs collector, the War Department initially stationed troops at Sitka, but these soldiers engaged in much of the same drunkenness and criminal behavior as the citizens. The Army pulled out in 1877, replaced by a naval gunboat to help keep the peace.

The 1884 Organic Act had made Alaska an official judicial district, providing for a bare-bones government that was based in Sitka. Under the provisions of the act, Alaska's governors were appointed nearly three thousand miles away in Washington, DC. The first of these governors was forced to resign after less than a year, having purportedly shipped to himself a personal supply of scotch whiskey that he had disguised as canned tomatoes. By 1886, the first judge appointed to the Alaska district had also left in disgrace. The second judge, Lafayette Dawson, was accused by critics of being a "drunken judge."

It was Judge Dawson who ruled on Abbey's seized pirate ships. Arguably, a matter of such importance and with the potential for international repercussions was beyond his pay grade. Regardless of a judge's expertise, disputes over maritime law were notoriously difficult to arbitrate. The Treasury edict granting Abbey the authority to seize any and all seal-hunting vessels within the Bering Sea was in effect a bold claim of *mare clausum* or, from the US perspective, *mare nostrum*, meaning "our sea."

A ruling based on *mare nostrum* was sure to ruffle some feathers in nations opposing limits to their maritime ventures. By the nineteenth century, the concept of free seas prevailed, but as with most rules, there were exceptions. A country could station ships as needed to defend its ports. A hostile vessel first spotted within a nation's territorial waters, defined as three miles from shore, could be chased and challenged on the open seas. Some countries also claimed the right to enforce customs and revenue laws beyond the three-mile limit. And, apropos to the verbiage US officials used to describe men like MacLean, nations could pursue and punish pirates wherever they found them.

Ruling on the seized ships and their officers, Judge Dawson reiterated the broad claim of *mare nostrum*. Citing the boundaries of the territory Russia had conveyed to the United States in 1867, he affirmed that the Bering Sea now belonged to the United States, and Abbey's orders to seize the ships had been within the nation's rights. He levied fines of $300 and $500 on the officers and mates Abbey had taken into custody. Their vessels, forfeited under Dawson's ruling, remained on Sitka's Rotten Row.

These punishments enraged officials in Victoria who claimed that the Bering Sea was no different from any other international waters, which allow free passage for international commerce. The fines and the schooners left to rot were bad enough, but outrage grew further when officials in Victoria learned that the elderly captain of the *Onward* had died in Sitka. He was reported to have been so distressed at his arrest that he had become a raving madman and run off into the dense forest surrounding Sitka, where he had died of exposure.

None of this sat well with Great Britain. Between disputes over fishing rights in the North Atlantic and over the exact location of the northern boundary between Alaska and Canada, tensions between the United States and Britain were already high. When British officials learned of Dawson's ruling, they filed a protest with the US government. To avoid escalating the crisis, President Grover Cleveland instructed his attorney general to release the seized ships from Rotten Row.

But the matter was far from over. The pirates, including MacLean, wanted compensation for their lost revenues and the damage to their ships, which had not held up well on Sitka's soggy, wind-battered shores. With this in mind, the MacLean brothers positioned themselves to benefit from any cash settlements Britain might pursue on behalf of the Canadian sealers. A British shipowner making such claims would be in better standing than an American shipowner, so Dan MacLean renounced his American citizenship and Alex transferred ownership of the *Onward* to him. Why it was Dan who changed citizenship and not Alex remains unclear. Unless pressed, neither brother was much inclined to share his motives.

Back home in Cape Breton, the newspapers reported proudly on the MacLean brothers' accomplishments. Already the two were becoming legendary. According to some reports, Dan MacLean had shanghaied some of his fellow Cape Bretoners into crewing for him. Back east, he had invited seven unsuspecting young men to dine aboard a boat he was preparing for a run from Halifax to Victoria. While the men were enjoying the free food and ale, Dan lifted anchor. As the wind carried the boat from shore, he promised his new crew double the wages they could earn back home. As the story has it, he kept his word.

In 1887, the MacLeans and their fellow pirates were back on the Bering Sea, encouraged by the Canadian minister of marine and fisheries who publicly applauded their pluck and daring. Following the release of the Rotten Row vessels, President Cleveland's Treasury Department again dispatched two revenue cutters to patrol the Bering Sea. As one pirate put it, dodging gunboats became half the fascination of the enterprise. The revenue cutters captured fifteen sealing ships that season—six Canadian and nine American. Protesting the taking of his vessel, one Canadian ship captain complained that he had not personally harmed a single seal, that all he had done was drop butcher boats into the sea. By his reasoning, he could not be held responsible for what his crew did after he cut them loose.

Seizing on Judge Dawson's ruling, an attorney for the ACC wrote a forty-eight-page pamphlet defending the US right to control sealing not only on the Pribilof Islands but throughout the Bering Sea. To President Cleveland's secretary of state, Henry Elliott addressed a separate appeal, expounding on the dangers of pirates who, more often than not, killed pregnant matkas while they were sleeping. He also warned of pirates spreading gill nets to catch seals, a practice that could quickly decimate an entire herd. The government must protect the fur seals, Elliott admonished, not simply for their monetary value but because they were fascinating subjects of biological study.

None of these arguments swayed the British. In January 1888, Rear Admiral Algernon Heneage, captain of the Royal Navy's Pacific division, ordered a twelve-gun warship from Hawaii to the Bering Sea, where it was assigned to protect the British Sealing Fleet, as he called the pirate vessels. Typifying the excesses of the British Royal Navy, Heneage had made a name for himself with his immaculate wardrobe that included 240 shirts that had been shipped to the Pacific in an airtight container and which were returned to London periodically for laundering. Before prayers, he removed his uniform, lest any naval captain be seen bowing to a higher power.

Concerning the American seizure of British vessels, Heneage agreed with an official from British Columbia—who was also an investor in the Victoria sealing fleet—that the real pirates were the American cutter captains who captured Canadian vessels. Heneage ordered the captain of the twelve-gun British warship to start seizing US revenue cutters if the capture of Canadian ships continued. What had begun as a remote enterprise generating rich rewards for both corporate shareholders and the US Treasury was becoming a huge diplomatic headache.

The threat of a British warship capturing a US government vessel got President Cleveland's attention. He was running for reelection in 1888, and tensions with Britain remained high. Both Democrats and Republicans added anti-British planks to their party platforms. Hoping to avoid all-out war, Cleveland ordered his Treasury Department to stand down in the Bering Sea while his secretary of state opened talks with the British. For this, he was deemed a British sympathizer. Matters took a turn for the worse in September, when a letter from a British ambassador surfaced. In it, the ambassador responded to a man named Murchison who sought advice on which American presidential candidate would be more favorable to the British. The ambassador assured him that while Cleveland might tough on the Brits, he genuinely wanted good relations with the mother country. Later, it was discovered that Murchison was a persona feigned by a political hack to get a rise out of the ambassador. By then, the damage was done—Cleveland lost the election.

Lest he be forever remembered as a British sympathizer, one of Cleveland's last lame-duck measures was to sign legislation requiring all future presidents to issue what amounted to annual preemptive arrest warrants for seal pirates. Two days later, his successor, President Benjamin Harrison, put some teeth in these warrants by ordering revenue cutters back to the Bering Sea. But while the cutter captains had the new president's outward backing, their reticence in the summer of 1889 suggested an administration squeamish about the prospect of a seal war. The cutter *Rush* stopped Dan MacLean's *Triumph*, but as was the usual practice, the crew had already hidden their cargo of sealskins belowdecks. Rather than search the vessel, the cutter's captain let Dan off with a warning.

In a separate incident, the *Rush* ran out two of its guns while in pursuit of another pirate ship. Closing in on it, the cutter captain yelled out a command to stop, and the sealing captain complied. But instead of seizing the ship, the *Rush* captain ordered one of his men aboard to command the pirates to sail directly to Sitka and turn themselves in. Unsurprisingly, the pirates failed to comply. Instead, they headed for Victoria, warning the US official that should he force the issue, the pirates' seal hunters would kill him. And it wasn't just the *Rush*—stops made that summer by a second US revenue cutter, the *Bear*, yielded similar non-results. Canadian officials took note of how pirates were gaining the upper hand in the region. This might be the perfect time to send backup, one official advised, in the form of another British warship.

The combination of reticent revenue officials and emboldened pirates spelled trouble for the seals. The pelagic catch that year yielded nearly forty thousand skins, a death toll that did not account for seals that sank upon being shot (which was by some estimates 90 percent) nor the orphaned pups that starved. Based on Elliott's calculations, the Pribilof seal population was in freefall. Without decisive action, there would soon be no seals left.

SIX

By the Numbers

*T*O STAND OUT IN A crowd of millions is not easy, and yet Old John managed it. His age alone distinguished him, evidenced by the battle scars etched in his thick skin. One of his flippers was missing a digit, though whether he had lost it in a fight or been without it since birth was unknown. Like all northern fur seals, Old John compared favorably to cats and higher primates in cognitive ability. Demonstrating higher-order thinking skills, he could have learned to understand words had anyone tried to train him. He also had a superb memory. But it was not memory, as humans know it, that drew him to the Pribilofs every spring. Pure instinct, ingrained in his species over a span of two million years, compelled Old John's annual return to the islands.

In the waters adjacent to their northern breeding grounds, Old John and his fellow seals enjoyed plentiful food. The complex Bering Sea food web is like no other on the planet. If the Bering Sea were a clock, the Aleutian chain of islands would define its lower rim, running from the four o'clock to seven o'clock positions. Along the upper rim, spanning from the ten o'clock to four o'clock positions, runs a shelf zone dense with nutrients. Currents create an upwelling effect that stirs these nutrients toward the surface, a phenomenon called a cyclonic gyre. Because of this gyre, the Bering Sea is home to some of the largest populations of marine invertebrates, fish, birds, and mammals in the world. Those who migrate south to avoid the harsh winters return in the spring when the gyre's algae and plankton bloom, providing ample food for spawning fish which in turn provide food for the seals.

In the middle of these rich feeding grounds sits St. Paul Island, where Old John hauled out from the water each spring. The island and its closest neighbor, St. George, are part of the Ring of Fire, a zone where tectonic plates beneath the Pacific Ocean chafe against continental land masses. Long ago, magma rose from beneath the sea floor to form basaltic islands like the Pribilofs. For the fur seals, breeding on such remote outcroppings became an evolutionary necessity. Fur seals are descended from the same ancient common ancestor as bears, otters, wolves, and dogs. As some of these prototype land mammals began spending more and more time in the water, they developed webbed feet, making them adept at swimming. Over millennia, these land-sea creatures evolved into several separate species of mammals, including the northern fur seal, that were better suited for locomotion in water than on land. The seals' webbed feet became flippers, yet they still bred and birthed their pups on offshore islands where fierce winds, pounding surf, and dense fog kept them safe from humans, at least until the Russians intruded.

No one knew for certain how many years Old John had been migrating to and from the Pribilof Islands. He spent three-quarters of each year in the water and the other quarter on land, where he fulfilled his duty to the species by breeding. Like other beachmasters, he was so devoted to guarding the turf he claimed for his "harem" that he neither ate nor drank until the breeding season was over, a period of sixty days or longer. When bachelor seals challenged him, he fought them off, roaring and biting at his foes. Most beachmasters reign for less than two years before ceding their tiny fiefdoms. Old John had lasted longer than most.

Captivated by this seal who distinguished himself in a crowd of millions, Henry Elliott had sketched Old John back in 1872. His front flippers were like bluish-black hands, Elliott wrote, complete with knuckles and vestigial nails. Lighter and slenderer than the forefeet, the hind flippers resembled a pair of flattened, shriveled black leather gloves. Above a glistening mane, Old John's head was small in proportion to his massive form. In shape, it resembled the head of a Newfoundland dog, especially about the muzzle and jaw. Elliott described the beachmaster's large, expressive eyes as both burning with vengeful light and shining with tenderness.

Because Elliott considered himself a man of science, he took measurements, formulated theories, and conducted experiments. But when it came to the seals, he was never entirely objective, effusing over them the way Alexander von Humboldt had effused over nature in general. Like a man in love, Elliott penned poetic descriptions of the matkas, the bachelors, and the beachmasters. In paintings, he would often depict one seal set apart from the rest. In *Life Study*, for instance, a single beachmaster towers above his companions. In *The Last One of a Million*, a single seal is seen alone on the January snow, the rest of herd having journeyed south months ago. In *White Hunters. Pelagic Sealers at Work*, a single seal stares down the barrel of a pirate's gun. These renderings seem eerily prescient of how isolated Elliott himself would become in his quest to save the seals. In ways he did not yet realize, he would also come to fit his own description of Old John, alternately shining with tenderness and burning with vengeance.

In 1872, during his first year on St. Paul Island, Elliott had resolved to make a census of the seals, a project no one before him had attempted. Even today, with all our advanced technology and instruments, counting wildlife remains a challenge, with different methods often yielding different results. Before Elliott's attempt, the only Pribilof seals deemed worthy of counting were the dead ones. Skinned and dried and salted into pelts that were taxed and then sold in the London fur market, sealskins were meticulously accounted for.

To estimate how many living, breathing seals gathered on the Pribilofs, Elliott first calculated the average space a seal occupied. This was no small task. Up to seven feet long and tipping the scales at six hundred pounds, a beachmaster like Old John occupied a four-by-four-foot patch of ground, by Elliott's estimate. For every beachmaster, he assumed twelve to fifteen matkas. At five feet in length and 140 pounds, each matka was a good deal smaller than a beachmaster, occupying a space Elliott estimated at two feet square. Because the matkas made forays into the water to eat and drink, Elliott assumed that at any given time, one-quarter of them were in the water. Their pups took up little space, weighing in at only ten to twelve pounds at birth.

Then there were the nonbreeding females, yearlings who were too young to have pups; Elliott accounted for them by adjusting their space downwards by 10 percent. Complicating matters further were the bachelor seals, which by July had given up trying to depose the beachmasters from their turf. The bachelors were the most carefree of the seals, shuttling to and from the water in a way that confounded attempts to determine how much space should be allotted them. Adjusting for size differentials, Elliott determined that each seal, no matter the gender, age, and breeding status, occupied on average a two-by-two-foot patch of ground. The seals' fate, not to mention the course of history and Elliott's own future, would largely hinge on this figure and its underlying assumptions.

Having arrived at a per-seal space estimate, Elliott then applied it to each rookery, which the seals conveniently occupied with the same degree of crowding no matter the overall size or location. Elliott mapped and measured the rookeries on St. Paul—Reef, Gorbotch, Lagoon, Nah Speel, Lukannon (or Lukanin), Keetavie (or Kitovi), Tolstoi, Zapadnie, Polavina (or Polovina), and Novastoshnah—and applied his per-seal space estimate to each one to arrive at a total count. He repeated the process on St. George Island, calculating the populations of Starry Arteel, North, Little Eastern, and Great Eastern rookeries. All told, Elliott determined the total population of Pribilof fur seals to be 4.7 million in 1872. He did not claim perfect accuracy, but when challenged he would stand by his figures. Barring pestilence or other unforeseen disaster, he believed that this population could, under proper management, be maintained indefinitely, though he cautioned that a count should be undertaken annually to ensure that the numbers remain steady.

As American capitalism hurtled toward the gross inequalities of the Gilded Age, Elliott's numbers mattered because they translated to dollars. As with so many of America's vast resources—forests, waterways, or wildlife—the thinking was that the seals were assets to be managed. From the ACC's annual quota of one hundred thousand seals, the company generated on average 50-percent returns for each of its lucky sixteen shareholders. Between the annual lease fee and the per-skin tariffs collected by the government, the US Treasury likewise benefited, swelling by $365,000 each year—

netting roughly $5.8 million during the ACC's twenty-year lease—at the seals' expense.

Maintaining that the Pribilof seal population had reached equilibrium, Elliott believed the profit potential for the ACC and the government could continue indefinitely. Americans could have their seal coats and their seals too, despite—or, as some would later claim, because of—the "culling" of the bachelor seals. In this assessment, Elliott epitomized the utilitarian spirit of his era. Even as he marveled over the seals' beauty and intelligence, even as he painted them in wondrous scenes, he initially expressed few qualms about their killing. It was as if his mind had two windows, much like the Government House where he and Alexandra spent their first winter as a couple. From one Government House window, Elliott could look out over the rookeries where beachmasters bellowed and matkas nursed their pups, and from the other window, he could gaze over the killing grounds. At dawn, under the watchful eyes of ACC boss men, Unangax̂ sealers would run along the beaches, waving sticks and driving the bachelor seals inland. There, close to the salting houses, they would deliver a swift blow to each bachelor seal's head, crushing its skull. They finished the job by stabbing the seal in the chest. This was the bloody method the Russians had introduced, forcing generations of Unangax̂ to kill seals in unfathomable numbers. The ACC continued using this method of slaughter.

Modern wildlife advocates would rail against such brutality. Yet for all the good Elliott would one day do for the seals, the split-screen of wonder and horror gave him little pause. Back home in Ohio, farmers raised cattle and hogs to be slaughtered. As agriculture became industrialized, the brutal treatment of livestock at Chicago's Union Stockyards and adjacent packinghouses caused no public uproar until Upton Sinclair's *The Jungle* was published nearly four decades later. In fact, people flocked to the facilities to witness how the killing was done, a process that by Elliott's reckoning was far less humane than what took place on the Pribilofs—a method, he wrote, that could not be improved on.

For the ACC and the Pribilof Unangax̂, killing became a way of life. In *The Killing Gang at Work*, Elliott painted a mother and small child into the foreground of a melancholy scene in which Unangax̂ workers raise their clubs against a dark, indistinct mass of seals. Alongside the living are the blanched carcasses of the dead, though Elliott's representation is so indirect that they might be mistaken for chunks of bleached driftwood.

As a beachmaster, Old John would not end up a blanched carcass on the hunters' killing field because the scars on his hide made his fur undesirable as a coat. How he eventually died was a mystery. At the end of one summer, he simply went off into the ocean and never returned.

OVER A SPAN OF FIFTEEN YEARS, 1872–1887, Elliott went back and forth to the Pribilofs several times, sometimes on official government business and sometimes in conjunction with the ACC. He was not on the company books as an employee, nor was he an official lobbyist. Rather, in a looser affiliation, he served as an expert on contract. Though he had never finished high school, company officials called him Professor Elliott, a title he did not bother to correct. On his winter campaigns in Washington, he spoke with the right people at the right times about matters relating to Alaska, especially the seals. In reports, articles, and interviews, he opined on the mutual benefits of the Pribilof lease arrangement to the ACC, the government, and the Unangax̂ people. Even the seals were thriving under ACC management, or so he thought.

Elliott was not fulfilling his dream of touring the nation and giving limelight lectures on the seals, nor had he sold his collected paintings for $15,000 as he had hoped to do. He did publish books and articles, and his winter campaigns kept him front and center as an expert on the Pribilof seals. That he knew the islands, their people, and the seals as few outsiders did was indisputable. Unlike others who came and went from the islands, Elliott had married into a prominent Pribilof family, and whenever he returned, he was welcomed by friends and relatives. Thanks to Alexandra, he spoke passable Russian and a bit of Unangam, the language of the Unangax̂. When he had questions about the seals, he often consulted village Elders, relying on their observations over those of scientists, some of whom had spent only a day or two on the islands and others who opined about the seals without ever having observed one. During this time, the ACC kept a close watch on the pirates. At one point, they even deployed a Gatling gun, a rapid-fire weapon developed during the Civil War, to the Pribilofs. As part of his work, Elliott kept close watch on the pirates too. But after 1876, he did this mostly from afar. Busy with his family, his Ohio orchards, and his winter campaigns, he relied on US Treasury agents' reports for assurance that the seals were holding their own. In 1886, the year he took young Frank to Washington for his winter campaign, he felt confident this was the case. The Pribilof agent at the time, a former dry-goods merchant named George Tingle, reported that there were 4.7 million Pribilof seals in 1886, the same number Elliott himself had estimated in 1872. In his 1887 report, Tingle painted an even rosier picture, reporting a count of over six million seals.

However, when reviewing the 1889 report submitted by the new Treasury agent Charles Goff, Elliott knew something was amiss. After years of reading that the rookeries were in splendid condition and the entire operation up to standards, he was now getting a different sense of things. Noting a precipitous drop in the seal population, Goff had urged the government to adjust the ACC's harvest quota from one hundred thousand to sixty thousand seals.

Never in the nineteen years of the company's monopoly had any agent proposed the seal harvest quota be cut, much less by 40 percent. The problem had to be the pirates. As word had spread of the successes enjoyed by Alex MacLean, his brother Dan, and other seal pirates, the Victoria fleet had grown by leaps and bounds. In 1883, the year the MacLeans began sealing, hunters from eighteen ships were taking seals from the water, and nearly all were operating off Canadian shores. By 1889, the fleet had more than tripled, with the greatest activity in the Bering Sea, where matkas could be shot going to and from their feeding grounds.

Then again, Goff was new to his post in 1889. Perhaps in his inexperience he had misapplied Elliott's method of estimating the seal numbers. The duties of a US Treasury agent were minimal and consisted primarily of overseeing the work of the ACC, with whom the agents were chummy, and filing an annual report. As such, the positions tended to be doled out as political favors, and not always to the most capable personnel. Charles Goff had likely landed the post through his influential brother. He was only thirty-three years old and fresh off a silver-mining venture.

To determine whether Goff's alarm was warranted, Elliott needed to travel to the Pribilofs and assess the situation for himself. During his 1890 winter campaign, he pressed Congress to fund his visit. Concerned at the potential revenue loss from Goff's recommended quota cut, legislators approved the allocation. Elliott eagerly packed his trunks for the journey. Alexandra and their two oldest children would travel with him. The other five would stay behind in Rockport, where Elliott's sisters could look after them. Alexandra's last visit home had been in 1875, when Grace was still young; now she was nearly a grown woman. With a burgeoning network of rail lines and steamship routes, travel had become easier, but the trip still took weeks. The Elliotts would have to leave Ohio in May, just as fruit was forming in the orchards, if they were to arrive in time for Henry to make a thorough study of the seals' situation.

THEY REACHED ST. PAUL ISLAND IN JUNE 1890, not long after the ice had gone out. The hillsides were greening and the air was fresh with the smell of spring. For Alexandra, there was a joyous reunion with her mother and brothers and sisters, now grown. She and her two daughters settled into village life in St. Paul. Meanwhile, Henry Elliott met with Charles Goff, the agent who had sounded the alarm on the seals. It was time to get down to the matter and see where the numbers actually were.

As it turned out, Goff was far from inept. His estimates were accurate, but he had gotten crossways with his supervisor, George Tingle, who had inflated the seal count by millions. Another agent, William Gavitt, also questioned Tingle's integrity, accusing him of threatening Unangax̂ workers with physical harm if they failed to share their wives with ACC employees. In one specific instance, Gavitt claimed Tingle had refused a young Unangax̂ woman the right to marry an Unangax̂ man because Tingle wanted her sexual favors to go to white men. Tingle denied these improprieties.

Elliott empathized with Goff's troubles. Years earlier, during his own stint as an assistant Treasury agent, he, too, had run afoul of his supervisor, Charles Bryant, a cantankerous former whaler who claimed without evidence that he was responsible for Congress funding the Alaska Purchase. Because the Elliotts had shared the Government House with Bryant and his wife, Henry had been careful to maintain good relations with his boss, but like others on the island, he had privately chafed at taking orders from a man known in the village as "a conceited old goose." Though Bryant claimed to be an expert on the seals, he rarely bothered to make the trek to the rookeries. In Elliott's view, the problem went beyond mere puffery—an agent who took no interest in the seals was not the sort of person who should be recommending harvest quotas. Upon leaving the islands in 1873, Elliott had discreetly suggested to an ACC director that a younger, more engaged agent would be better for the post.

As Elliott went over the numbers with Goff, the younger man shared a troubling revelation—unable to meet its 1889 quota, the ACC had ordered its workers to kill fifty thousand one- and two-year-old seals, and Tingle had done nothing to stop them. To make matters worse, Tingle was back on the island in 1890 with a new position. Confronted with Goff's accusations, Tingle had declared his assistant a weak-minded liar, then quit his Treasury post. Almost immediately, the North American Commercial Company, which, to the ACC's dismay, had procured the next twenty-year lease, hired Tingle to oversee their Pribilof operations.

At the time, Elliott cared little about which company held the lease, but Tingle's role as company supervisor certainly complicated Elliott's investigations. And with Goff assuming the role of lead Treasury agent, tensions ran high, to say the least. Nonetheless, Elliott set about taking measurements of the rookeries to use in a new population estimate. Though the beachmasters were only now beginning to make an appearance, the rookery boundaries should have been easy to determine, as the areas would be worn clean of vegetation by so much activity year after year.

Right away, Elliott noticed a problem. Mosses and lichens and grasses were growing within the previous boundaries of the rookeries. Areas that should have been worn bare by seal activity looked like bluegrass meadows. Elliott trekked from rookery to rookery, documenting his alarm in his field notes. At Reef Rookery, he visited Old John Rock, named for the legendary beachmaster with the missing digit. In 1872, Elliott had needed a stick to nudge seals aside in order to clear his path. Now there was not a beachmaster in sight.

Scattered across Lukannon, another rookery, Elliott found a few beachmasters, but rather than the feisty beasts he remembered as being of "wonderous strength and desperate courage," these seals appeared sluggish and indifferent. After the matkas arrived, he visited a rookery on St. George. Stunned, he shut his notebooks and gazed over a scene of utter desolation. From this spot in 1873, he had heard nothing but the beachmasters' booming roars. Now he heard only the mewling of pups and the cries of their matkas. Without beachmasters to mate with, the matkas seemed restless. Away from the rookery, they gathered on grassy patches, their bewildered pups huddled in pods of their own.

Everywhere, Elliott saw devastation. In places where platoons of bachelor seals had once waddled back and forth to the sea, there was not a single seal. At the bold, sweeping hill of Tolstoi, which Elliott called the most picturesque rookery, he made a sketch, one with grasses filling the foreground and seals nowhere to be seen. In his 1872 rendering of the same location, Elliott had recorded great masses of beachmasters and matkas congregating above the water's edge, separated by the usual corridors from the bachelors. Beneath his new sketch, Elliott penned a caption: "sickening contrast."

Assembling his findings, Elliott was dumbfounded. Certainly, the pirates were part of the problem, especially because they indiscriminately killed matkas. Recently, a revenue cutter captain had determined that matkas accounted for all but six of the skins aboard one vessel he had stopped. In the ship's hold, he also found the tiny black skins of their pups, cut from their mothers' wombs. The seal hunters themselves calculated that for every seal they had shot and recovered, at least four others had sunk to the depths.

The beachmaster population was in bad shape too, and the pirates could not be blamed for that. Since Elliott's 1875 Pribilof visit, the ratio of beachmasters to matkas had shifted. Then he had observed the ratio of about fifteen matkas to each beachmaster. Now he was observing up to fifty matkas in each harem. For the most part, the breeding males appeared old and tired, and yet the bachelors poised to take over breeding were also dwindling in number.

Before this visit, Elliott had naively assumed that the government and the ACC were acting together in good faith to protect the seals, if for no other reason than the profits they enjoyed from the pelts. He also assumed that Treasury agents were following his instructions, making annual counts of the seals and adjusting the quotas as needed. But as he pored over record books, he discovered that several years earlier, the ACC had begun taking bachelor seals from areas set aside as reserves. Though the seals were ill equipped for land travel, workers had forced them into long death marches from the reserves to the killing grounds so they could be dispatched closer to the salting houses. Elliott decried these death marches as inhumane. He also pointed out that matkas and yearlings were getting swept up in these expansive drives. Workers attempted to cull them out before slaughter, but mistakes were made. And any seals that were spared were, by that point, weak and vulnerable from their overland trek.

Elliott tried to ask Unangax̂ workers about the marches. In the past, they had been forthcoming with him about their practices, but now they remained silent. He suspected that George Tingle had threatened the Unangax̂ with reprisal if they told what they knew. Openly, the former Treasury agent turned company manager was warning workers that if they failed to make the company's quota— never mind the declining seal population—they risked starving that winter. Since Tingle oversaw the company store, which was the only place within three hundred miles that the Unangax̂ could buy food, this was no idle threat.

In the report Elliott prepared for Congress in 1890, he estimated the Pribilof fur seal population had dropped by 80 percent since 1875, when he last visited the islands. Declaring this no time for half-measures, he proposed a two-step solution. First, the American government needed to enlist the help of the British as well as the Russians, whose lesser seal islands were also targeted by pirates. Together, these nations needed to issue and enforce a total ban on pelagic sealing in the Bering Sea that would remain in effect until a joint commission could assess the situation and propose a permanent solution. In addition, Elliott said, the Americans must institute an immediate seven-year moratorium on the commercial harvest of Pribilof seals. He believed this was the only way to save the breeding males. In 1834, the Russians had declared a similar moratorium, and the depleted seal population had rebounded.

Elliott knew his proposal would meet with resistance. Americans could agree on stopping the pirates, but the land harvest was another matter. Men of wealth and influence were turning handsome profits on the seals, and their focus was on their balance sheets. Indeed, American greed and carelessness were already causing the sharp decline of previously abundant species like the whooping crane, the passenger pigeon, and the American bison, and little was being done to save these creatures. Even preservationist John Muir assumed a grimly utilitarian stance, positing that grazing cattle were more important in the long run than bison. "We are a selfish people and look only to the present," Elliott wrote in his report.

Until the end of the eighteenth century, the general thinking, even among scientists, was that God had uniquely and perfectly created each species on earth to forever occupy its niche in nature. The notion that a species might vanish implied that God's plan was less than perfect. Only in 1796 did French naturalist Georges Cuvier dare to suggest that a species could indeed be obliterated. Like Elliott, Cuvier had learned natural history by doing it. Relocating from a small French town on the Swiss border to Paris, he worked at the newly founded Paris Museum of Natural History. When he was only twenty-six, he shocked his fellow naturalists with his theory of extinction. Using skeletal remains, Cuvier identified three species that had gone extinct. One was the woolly mammoth, whose bones were initially presumed to be elephant remains carried to Siberia by apocryphal floods. Another was the American mastodon, whose elephant-like bones had previously been thought to belong to a living mammal dubbed the "incognito." The third was the Megatherium, the giant sloth after which the club of naturalists at the Smithsonian had been named. Using bones discovered in Argentina and shipped to Spain, Cuvier reconstructed the giant sloth's skeleton.

After Cuvier went public with his bold theory of species extinction, he discovered that people all around the world had been gathering curious fossilized remains that did not match the skeletons of living creatures. Using these as evidence, he extrapolated another forty-one extinct species. In doing so, he founded the field of paleontology. In his manuscript *Essay on the Theory of the Earth*, published in 1813, Cuvier proposed that multiple catastrophes had befallen the planet in years past, wiping out species now known only by the fossils they left behind. Soon, fossil hunting became a global pursuit. Wealthy individuals hired explorers to search on their behalf for evidence of extinct species not yet identified. So many were found that people began to question whether catastrophic events were the cause, as Cuvier had proposed. Even before Darwin published *On the Origin of Species* in 1859, some scientists were suggesting that species went extinct because they failed to thrive.

As the notion of survival of the fittest went mainstream, it was applied far more widely than Darwin had intended. Robber barons of the Gilded Age used it to justify ruthless behavior in the marketplace. Those who resented the emancipation of enslaved African Americans used it to claim racial superiority. And although Darwin's theory was at odds with literal interpretations of biblical creation, it was also used to affirm the Old Testament idea of man's dominion over the earth. As the thinking went, man was the fittest of all creations, and any species that could not withstand human exploitation was clearly destined to fail.

Some species went extinct more quickly than others. Steller's sea cows, hunted for their meat and oil, vanished only seventeen years after German naturalist Georg Steller first documented their existence on a Bering Sea island west of the Pribilofs. Resembling manatees, the sea cows were holdovers from the Pleistocene Era. When they went extinct, naturalists blamed it on the species being slow moving and having a small range compared to other marine mammals. Later, scientists would discover that Russian and American fur traders had hastened the demise of the Steller's sea cow not only by hunting them but also by decimating the sea otter population. Without sea otters to eat them, sea urchin populations had skyrocketed, and the urchins had decimated the Bering Sea's kelp beds—the primary food source for sea cows.

By the end of his 1890 Pribilof assignment, Henry Elliott feared the northern fur seal was going the way of the Steller's sea cow. Something had to be done. His beloved seals were at the foundation of everything that mattered to him—his art, his livelihood, even his marriage. He could scarcely abandon them now.

SEVEN

UNDER WRAPS

*R*EPORTING ON HIS 1890 PRIBILOF visit, Elliott wrote that the seals faced speedy extinction unless the United States took decisive action to restore and preserve them on land and at sea. But for the measures he proposed to succeed, he would have to get past the public's general indifference to extinction. He would also have to contend with tense international relations, underhanded political dealings, and the wiliness of men like MacLean and his wealthy patrons, including San Francisco furrier Herman Liebes, who would figure prominently in the fur seal controversy. In short, the road to change would be an arduous one.

From the outside, it looked like the US government was taking some measures to address the issue. Assuming office in 1889, President Benjamin Harrison had dispatched revenue cutters to patrol the Bering Sea for seal pirates, but their efforts were half-hearted, perhaps because the new president had no wish to start a war with Britain. He assigned his secretary of state, a powerful statesman named James G. Blaine, to open seal talks with the British, who defended the interests of the Victoria sealers. But demands for monetary damages for the ships that had spent time on Rotten Row, including MacLean's *Onward*, complicated the issue. So did some serious conflicts of interest involving the Harrison administration and the North American Commercial Company (NACC).

The British told Secretary Blaine they wanted a moratorium on the land harvest of seals before they would do anything to stop the pirates at sea. That prospect did not sit well with President Harrison's friends and associates who had organized the NACC so they could bid on exclusive twenty-year rights to the land harvest. These were powerful people, including Darius Ogden Mills—one of the nation's wealthiest men, whose son-in-law, owner of the *New York Tribune*, was Harrison's close friend and political ally—and Blaine's business associate Stephen B. Elkins. Also contributing to the $3,000,000 in capital needed for the NACC venture were the wealthy Rothschilds of London and Jay Cooke, owner of the Northern Pacific Railroad.

Lesser known but hugely significant to the NACC was Herman Liebes, a primary stakeholder in the corporation. Astute and energetic, Liebes had emigrated from Germany and established himself in San Francisco as a manufacturer and importer of furs in 1864. At first, he specialized in carriage robes, manufactured in the single room where he also lived. As he shifted to trading in Pribilof sealskins, his enterprise quickly outgrew its small quarters.

When the government granted the ACC a twenty-year seal monopoly beginning in 1870, many San Francisco merchants, including Liebes, were outraged. They formed an Anti-Monopoly Association and hired Charles Leege to be their front man. In 1875, Leege published a widely circulated pamphlet on the merchants' behalf. In it, he laid out reasons why the monopoly was working to the detriment of Alaska and the nation. He decried the bribery and political favors that had led to Congress awarding the ACC lease. He cited poor treatment of the Unangax̂ as proof that the ACC was mismanaging the project. He also singled out Henry Elliott for special criticism, contending that he was nothing but a company hack.

The Anti-Monopoly Association pamphlet prompted a congressional investigation, but no wrongdoing was found. Leege later admitted to having fabricated much of his material. Meanwhile, Liebes, realizing there were other ways to chip away at the ACC's profits, sent eight seal-hunting vessels into the Bering Sea. In 1881, two of these ships anchored north of St. Paul Island for most of the summer, with no apparent purpose besides raiding unguarded beaches for seals. On foggy days and moonlit nights, hunters would steal off the ships and row to shore. Infiltrating the rookeries, they killed and skinned as many seals they could, leaving the carcasses to rot.

Eventually, Liebes was handling 75 percent of the pirated seal pelts. Though never as openly as some Victoria traders, he had longstanding ties to the MacLeans, beginning with their first sealing trip in 1883. He always gave the pirates leeway to do as they pleased, including slaughtering matkas. As long as the MacLeans went where the seals were, Liebes was happy. As he traded in pelagic seal pelts, Liebes also kept his eye on the twenty-year Pribilof lease, scheduled to go up for bid again in 1890. Stirring up trouble in the northern Pacific, his seal pirates were the bane of the US government, so Liebes had been careful to keep his involvement under wraps. When the NACC organized ahead of the 1890 lease bidding, Herman Liebes and his cousin and business partner, Isaac Liebes, both became shareholders.

With wealthy backers and ties to the Harrison administration, it was perhaps no surprise that the NACC secured the lease to the Pribilofs. ACC shareholders were outraged. Theirs had been the higher bid, and they owned all the infrastructure needed for the remote operation. They grumbled over the backroom deal, even though it was similar to one their own company's founders had arranged when they secured the 1870 lease. Before the new lease was awarded, a US Treasury agent stationed in the Pribilofs warned his superiors that Liebes was backing seal pirates. Only weeks later, the agent withdrew his complaint. He also quit his job with the Treasury, having procured a better one with the NACC. This informant-turned-employee was none other than George Tingle, the man who had inflated the seal count and disparaged Charles Goff for raising the alarm about the health of the herd.

With Tingle no longer making noise about Liebes's association with the pirates, the US Treasury secretary merely required the furrier to take an oath swearing that his company would have no further dealings with pelagic sealers. Liebes complied, and the NACC lease went forward. Liebes then reorganized his company, putting his cousin Isaac in charge. Isaac was not bound by Herman's oath, so the new Liebes corporation kept right on working with pirates, including MacLean, who was spending more and more time in San Francisco.

At the end of the 1889 sealing season, rumors circulated that MacLean's ship—that season it was the *Mary Ellen*—had gone down in a storm. In truth, MacLean had sailed straight past Victoria to

San Francisco, where he delivered all his seal pelts to Liebes. His motley crew cavorted around the city in the month that followed, no doubt dropping a good portion of their earnings into Barbary Coast saloons and brothels. Then in the spring of 1890, as the NACC was jockeying for the Pribilof lease, MacLean put his wife and young daughter on a steamship back to Victoria, gathered up his crew, and set out for more adventures aboard the *Mary Ellen*.

MacLean dropped anchor at Drake Bay, thirty miles north of San Francisco. Matkas were starting north from California's warm waters, and several pirate ships were already in the bay, hoping to apprehend them. Ahead of whatever difficulties they might encounter on their way north, the pirates were in a festive mood. MacLean opened his ample stores of rum and they all set to drinking. When night fell, he and the captain of another ship began to argue and soon came to blows. The other man landed a punch close to MacLean's moustache—a great affront, as he took much pride in his facial hair. Adding insult to injury, the other captain then tossed MacLean into Drake Bay's chilly waters.

Not to be outdone, MacLean swam back to his ship. Eyeing the signal gun, a small bronze apparatus used to launch flares, he ordered bags of potatoes to be brought up from below. He loaded the potatoes into the signal gun, then began firing them at the other captain's ship. Before long, potatoes were flying from vessels all around the bay. After a few spud-related casualties, none of them serious, MacLean called a truce and invited everyone onto the *Mary Ellen* for a jamboree.

Such stories of MacLean and his escapades stand in contrast to the very real dangers of seal pirating. Seafaring annals recount the grim tolls of ships that wrecked on the northwest coast, capsized, foundered or burned at sea, or vanished without a trace. An additional notation appears within many of these logs: "All hands lost." Captains whose ships prevailed despite these hazards still had to worry about their butcher-boat crews. Shrouded in fog, these rowboats would drift from the mother ship, sometimes pulled along by strong currents, and the hunters sometimes could not find their way back. If they survived on the open seas, it was thanks to the creatures they were bent on killing—they sustained themselves by eating seal meat.

When gales struck, the hunters also made drags from seal carcasses to steady their small boats. Sometimes, they were rescued. Sometimes, they disappeared without a trace.

Over time, Alex MacLean lost fifty-nine men to various hazards. In addition to those who floated away in butcher boats, never to be seen again, three of MacLean's men died in a thresher shark attack. One died of smallpox, and another was shot—though not on purpose, MacLean hastened to explain. Despite his habit of marooning sailors who gave him trouble, he claimed he had never intentionally killed any of his crew.

None of these dangers gave Herman Liebes pause. He was in the business to turn a profit. In many ways, Alex MacLean was the ideal partner, one who kept his mouth shut when it mattered and who had few qualms about bending the rules—or ignoring them altogether. A prime example was the scam the pirate pulled off at the end of the 1890 sealing season. Pulling into a remote port on one of the easternmost Aleutian Islands, MacLean ordered his crew ashore. He unloaded and sold all his supplies to a storekeeper, then took his ship back out and purposely ran it into the rocks. Afterwards, he collected a sizable insurance payout that totaled a good deal more than what the vessel was worth.

In matters involving fur seals, subterfuge went well beyond MacLean and his benefactors—it ran through the highest levels of government, as Henry Elliott would soon discover. Elliott must have known that the conclusions and recommendations of his 1890 Pribilof report would generate controversy. In the 336-page document, Elliott detailed, rookery by rookery, the seals' dire situation. He admitted his folly in having trusted the ACC to act in the species' best interest. He reported how company agents, determined to meet their annual quotas, had authorized death marches, decimated reserves, and killed yearling seals. Elliott had little reason to think the NACC would do any differently, especially with George Tingle as their Pribilof superintendent.

Referencing the near elimination of southern fur seals during the previous century, Elliott warned the US government to act swiftly to save the northern fur seals. To restore the population of breeding males, he urged a seven-year moratorium on all commercial killing of Pribilof seals. In fairness to the new leaseholders, he proposed that the government pay a cash settlement to the NACC for the lost years of the lease. At the time, Elliott knew little of Liebes's involvement with the pirates. If he had known more, he might have recommended canceling the lease altogether. On the issue of seal pirates, Elliott proposed that diplomats from both the United States and Great Britain appoint members to a joint commission charged with conducting an extensive investigation of pelagic sealing.

On November 27, 1890, Elliott submitted his report to Treasury Secretary William Windom. Aware that the report's findings and recommendations would surely have diplomatic repercussions, Windom summoned Elliott to a meeting with Secretary of State James G. Blaine. The three men met at Blaine's home. Once likened to a plumed knight poised to throw his shining lance at every brazen traitor to US interests, Blaine was now in ill health and mourning the deaths of two of his children.

The situation in the Bering Sea remained tense. After seal talks between the United States and Great Britain broke down, the British Navy stationed four warships—two in Yokohama and two in British Columbia—with orders to advance if Canadian and British interests needed protection in the North. Six British naval cruisers were also poised for action. Outwardly, the Harrison administration stood its ground—US revenue cutters would continue seizing and even dismantling any vessel with sealskins aboard, no matter the flag it flew. But behind the scenes, the administration was rattled. To avoid escalating tensions, Windom asked that only one revenue cutter, the *Rush*, be sent to the Bering Sea that summer. Coming upon pirates, the *Rush*'s captain was to issue only warnings—no seizures, no arrests.

In short order, the pirates discovered they could send out butcher boats within plain sight of the *Rush*. The revenue cutter would respond by simply running a wide circle around the offenders and then slowly steaming away. In 1890, MacLean and his colleagues brought in over forty thousand sealskins, a new record. While winter offered a brief respite from the strife, in a matter of months, tensions over seal hunting would escalate all over again, and the British naval fleet remained ever at the ready. On the American side, there was even talk of deploying twenty-three armed naval cruisers to patrol the Bering Sea. As a writer for the *New York Herald* warned, it would take no more than a hot-headed naval commander to set off a seal war.

Amid these tensions, Secretary Blaine was concerned about Elliott's suggestion of a seven-year moratorium on the Pribilof land harvest. The British had been clamoring for a moratorium, too, arguing that if the United States were genuinely concerned about extinction, a temporary halt to the land harvest only made sense. In addition, a moratorium would be a good faith concession, something the British could use to placate Canadian interests while they brokered a solution to the pirate problem. But Blaine was not yet willing to concede to British demands on this point. He knew his friends at the NACC—and the president's friends—would come undone at any alteration in the terms of their new lease. They were after profits at the same levels the ACC had enjoyed, and government compensation for a moratorium would not have offset what they might otherwise have earned.

With these considerations in mind, Blaine said Elliott's Pribilof report was too volatile to release while negotiations with the British were ongoing. Any suggestion that land slaughter by the United States was contributing to the seals' demise would concede a point to the British, and Blaine wanted every bargaining chip to remain on his side. Elliott understood these diplomatic concerns, but since 1886 when the first pirate ships reached Rotten Row, the seal talks had been starting and stalling, starting and stalling. At the rate the seals were declining, there was little time to waste. Elliott agreed to withhold his report, but only if Blaine promised to prioritize negotiations with the British, dangling the prospect of a land-harvest moratorium as incentive to get them to agree to a temporary prohibition on pelagic sealing—a modus vivendi, it was called—so a joint commission could get to work on a long-term solution.

Having reached what he thought was an understanding with Blaine, Elliott sat on his report. A skilled diplomat, Blaine was thought to have even more political clout than President Harrison. Surely Elliott could trust him to uphold his end of the deal, working behind the scenes for terms that would save the seals.

But the NACC was also working behind the scenes. Alarmed at

the declining seal numbers, Treasury Agent Goff had cut short the 1890 land harvest. In response, NACC principals had convinced Windom to fire Goff. When Blaine privately shared Elliott's findings and recommendations with the NACC, they also discouraged Windom from ever again contracting services from Elliott, accusing him of "secret" dealings with the ACC. At the same time, NACC lobbyists pressed for an unlimited land-harvest quota for 1891 to make up for the previous shortened season.

Meanwhile, Blaine's behind-the-scenes work with the British continued. At first, he pushed for a ban on the pirates with no change at all to the land harvest. But President Harrison preferred the terms Elliott had suggested—a temporary halt to all killing, on both land and sea—and so Blaine was compelled to present that option too.

The British seized on this new offer. Presenting a dispatch from his higher-ups, the chief British negotiator told Blaine they would accept a full land-and-sea moratorium. Disgusted, Blaine threw the dispatch to the floor. The British negotiator coolly pointed out that any further endangerment of the seals could scarcely be blamed on Her Majesty's Government.

For Elliott, initial revelations of these concealed dealings came in April 1891, when a Washington socialite brought him distressing news. At a party, she had overheard a NACC attorney brag that despite the grim population tallies, the government had secretly granted the NACC a land-harvest quota of sixty thousand seals for 1891. Elliott was furious. In agreeing to suppress his report, he'd been clear that the land harvest should be suspended as a bargaining chip with the British. Why was it now being authorized, and in secret?

All bets were off. Had Windom still been in his post, Elliott could have pressed him about the secret quota, but Windom had died three months before of a heart attack. Unsure where Windom's replacement stood regarding the seals and the NACC, Elliott asked his Ohio congressman, William McKinley, to ask the new Treasury Secretary, Charles Foster, about the secret seal quota. Foster repeated the false claim that Great Britain had refused any sort of halt on pelagic sealing, stating that, with negotiations at a standstill, he had seen no reason to deny the NACC its profits.

At the time, Elliott knew nothing of the British dispatch authorizing a land-and-sea moratorium. Still, Foster's response didn't ring true—if negotiations were truly stalled, why keep the quota a secret? Elliott knew politicians could be duplicitous, but there were real consequences here. And it was not as if the seals could save themselves. Someone had to intervene, and if not him, then who?

Elliott decided to make a bold move. Still under contract with the US Treasury, he arranged a meeting with the British ambassador. The question he posed was direct: was it true that Britain had refused any sort of moratorium on pelagic sealing? Absolutely not, the ambassador said. The British had offered a temporary ban on pelagic sealing, and Blaine had refused it.

For Elliott, this was a moment of truth. In his yet-unpublished report, he had warned there could be no half-measures or the seals might never recover. Now the question was whether he intended to heed his own advice. He could no longer trust Blaine to uphold his end of their arrangement, nor could he trust Foster, who, in his new position as secretary of the US Treasury, had falsely said that the British had refused a moratorium. Elliott's only recourse, it seemed, was to let the truth speak for itself. Because Blaine had reneged on their agreement, Elliott no longer felt bound to withhold his report.

Bypassing official channels, Elliott released his findings independently, becoming one of the nation's earliest whistleblowers for an environmental cause. He published a summary of his recommendations in a Cleveland newspaper, urging that all seal butchers on both land and sea be stopped. He also published a letter in a New York paper exposing the secret quota and Blaine's duplicitous dealings with the British. The next day, Treasury Secretary Foster informed Elliott that his services as a Pribilof seal expert were no longer required, stripping him of the job he needed to support his family, which now included seven children.

In 1891, there were no laws protecting whistleblowers. At some level, Elliott must have known that his decision to go public would endanger his government position. He must have known it would strain alliances he had forged during his many years of winter campaigns. He must have understood that his reputation would be on the line. But perhaps, like most whistleblowers, he felt his first allegiance was to his conscience. And he also felt a strong sense of duty to the seals, which would not survive without action.

After Elliott went public, President Harrison had little choice but to rescind the secret quota. Over NACC objections, his administration also authorized British observers on the Pribilofs as a preliminary step toward further negotiations. In exchange, Great Britain agreed to enforce a one-year ban on pelagic sealing. These terms fell far short of Elliott's call for a seven-year moratorium and a full-fledged joint commission, but at least they were a step in the right direction.

DEFIANCE

CANADIAN SEAL PIRATES WERE FURIOUS with the British for agreeing to shut down their 1891 season. What about compensation for damages, including lost revenues, owed by the United States for seizing Canadian ships in open waters? What about the US arrests of Canadians engaged in what the pirates claimed was a lawful pursuit? What about procuring a promise that the United States would never again seize a foreign vessel in the Bering Sea? As of 1867, Britain was no longer supposed to be treating Canada like a colony. Financially, Canadians were officially on their own. They had a mandate to defend themselves against foreign aggressors. But to those in Victoria, the British governor-general was only looking out for the mother country, not the best interests of Canadians who should have been able to do as they pleased at sea.

Betrayed by Britain, the pirates refused to give up a season of sealing. Ban or no ban, they were out in force in 1891. In what was becoming a revolving door operation for the pirates, vessels seized by the United States were returned, resold, renamed, and sent back out to take more seals. Such was the case with the ship MacLean commanded that season. In 1887, the United States had seized a vessel called the *Aida*. On MacLean's recommendation, Herman Liebes had purchased the ship after US authorities released it. Liebes renamed it the *J. Hamilton Lewis*, an unvarnished attempt to garner favor with the up-and-coming Washington state politician of the same name who was helping to arbitrate yet another dispute between the United States and Britain, this one over the border between Canada and Alaska.

At the helm of the *J. Hamilton Lewis*, Alex MacLean sailed north in the spring of 1891, plying the waters off the west coast of the United States and Canada, killing seals as they migrated north. Early on, he lost three men when a butcher boat failed to return. When he stopped in Sitka to replenish the vessel's fresh water supplies and smoke out the rats infesting the hold, one of his men took a boat and a gun and deserted. Near Kodiak Island, another man did the same. MacLean picked up two replacements, but one of these was soon stabbed in the chest by a fellow sailor.

For all the adventure a life at sea might portend, dependable sailors had long been hard to come by. Sailing demanded grit, strength, and endurance. Ocean voyages meant months of isolation at sea, staring at the same companions day after day, with only a bunk and a sea chest to call one's own. A ship's forecastle, the belowdecks area that served as living quarters for the crew, was generally dark and cold. Food was often tainted and water sour. Hygiene was poor. Sleep was catch-as-catch-can between four-hour shifts. During storms, rest was near impossible. No matter how much a man prayed, he might get tossed overboard in the waves or go down with a ship that sank in a gale. Small wonder the men who went willingly to sea were essentially drifters. Rarely did they stick with their calling beyond their mid-forties. Few old sailors' homes were needed because there were few old sailors.

A popular sailors' ditty captured the essence of what it meant to crew on a schooner:

> *I'll sing about a sailor man that sails upon the sea*
> *In coasters and deep-water ships, wherever they may be,*
> *Incurring needless hardships in earning others' wealth.*
> *Now this is true what I tell you, for I've seen it all myself.*

Aboard a sealing ship, the most dangerous place was the tiny deckhouse cabin where the hunters—these days, a mix of white and Indigenous men—loaded shells. Heedless of the open kegs of gunpowder, the hunters often lit pipes and cigarettes, smoking into the night as they worked. Adding to the potential for disaster, a stove used for melting lead to cast bullets burned hot in the cabin. As one

Liebes employee admitted, these conditions were ripe for accidents.

Amid so many hazards and hardships, schooner captains often relied on men called "crimpers" to provide sailors. These unscrupulous men would come aboard ships as soon as they docked, promoting "boarding houses" to the seamen as places where they could enjoy prostitutes and whiskey. In these dens of inequity, the sailors would blow through their meager earnings and rack up debt. Then the crimpers would step in again, this time securing an advance on wages from a future voyage. Caught in a cycle of debt and deception, sailors had little choice but to keep going to sea. Crimpers did not limit their marks to seafaring men either. Roaming the waterfront, they shanghaied landlubbers too, getting them too drunk to stand, then wheeling them off to schooners that were short on crewmen. By the time the shanghaied men came to their senses, the ships would be out to sea and they would have become sailors, like it or not.

HEADING NORTH FROM SAN FRANCISCO IN 1891, Alex MacLean saw the warnings posted at every port where he stopped for water and other provisions: by order of the British government, sealers were barred from hunting in the Bering Sea. He would end up heeding the warning, but not by choice. Since the early days of MacLean's career, the pelagic sealing season had grown longer and the pirates had expanded their reach into Asiatic fur seal enclaves. In January, seal hunters would intercept seals that wintered off the Oregon and California coasts. In March, they would head north, killing seals along the shores of Canada's Queen Charlotte Islands and Alaska's Inside Passage. In June, they would put in at Unalaska or another Aleutian port, load up on fresh water, and then strike out for the Kuril Islands, a volcanic archipelago stretching from the Japanese island of Hokkaido to Kamchatka, Russia. There, they would spend a few weeks hunting seals from a small Asiatic herd before heading to the Pribilofs, where they would arrive at about the same time as the matkas.

Alex MacLean and his brother Dan followed this route in 1891, skirting along the Aleutians to a group of four islands called the Commander Islands in the northern Kurils. Like the Pribilofs, the

Commander Islands were originally uninhabited except for the seals. In 1741, Danish cartographer Vitus Bering had wrecked his ship there, an inglorious end to the mission that would give Russia control of Alaska. Bering died while awaiting rescue, but the ship's resident naturalist, Georg Steller, survived, as did his observations of the sea lions, sea cows, and fur seals he encountered. Far fewer seals bred on the Commanders than on the Pribilofs, but there were enough for the Russians to exploit. As they had on the Pribilofs, they forced Unangax̂ from the Aleutians to relocate to the Commanders as a labor force for killing fur seals.

Russia had no part in the one-year modus vivendi on pelagic sealing. Instead, they claimed a thirty-mile no-kill zone in the waters surrounding the Commander Islands. Unlike the on-and-off pursuits attempted by US revenue cutters, the Russians meant business. Apprehended pirates could be sentenced to a life of hard labor in Siberian mines. In his poem "Rhyme of the Three Sealers," Rudyard Kipling warned of this fate:

> For life it is that is worse than death, by force of Russian law
> To work in the mines of mercury that loose the teeth in your jaw.

None of this deterred the MacLean brothers, but it did give some of their men pause. As their schooners approached the Commanders, eight of Dan MacLean's crew mutinied, refusing to board the butcher boats. Confining them to the hold without food, Dan forced a change of heart. Between the two MacLean ships, twelve butcher boats were eventually lowered, bound for shore in the Arctic summer's midnight dusk. Making land, the crews raided the rookeries and killed seals. Russian guards spotted the pirates and started shooting. In the scramble to get back to the boats, one of Dan's men drowned and Dan himself took a bullet, though the wound seems to have been superficial. Dan MacLean sailed fast for the open sea, headed for the Pribilofs, where he would have attempted another land raid had his crew not staged another mutiny.

Not willing to concede so easily to the Russians, Alex MacLean remained near the Commander Islands, though well out of gun range. Near daybreak, he spotted a Russian man-of-war, a combat ship, steaming toward him. He ordered his crew to hide all evidence of the raid, then turned the *J. Hamilton Lewis* toward the southeast, driving it hard under full sail, a dangerous and difficult maneuver. The Russian man-of-war followed suit, increasing its speed. As dawn lightened the eastern skies, the man-of-war drew close to MacLean's schooner. The Russians hoisted their colors and fired a blank shot. MacLean dropped anchor and heaved to, allowing two Russians from the man-of-war to board the *J. Hamilton Lewis*. MacLean assured them that his crew had been hunting sea birds and catching fish, nothing more. But his crew's clean-up had failed to entirely conceal the truth. Belowdecks, the Russians found a tub of bloody water, a number of firearms, and a large amount of gunpowder.

Receiving this report, the Russian captain dispatched his lieutenant and six more men to seize the *Lewis*. MacLean would have none of it. He was in neutral waters, he declared, and no one had any right to tell him what to do. Up came the anchor, and the *Lewis* set off at full sail. With a shot from his revolver, the Russian lieutenant alerted his commander. The man-of-war fired a cannon ahead of the *Lewis*. Unfazed, MacLean kept driving the schooner hard away. Again, the man-of-war fired its cannon, this time landing a ball in the *Lewis*'s rigging. When this failed to stop MacLean, the Russian ship went full steam ahead. Catching up, the man-of-war turned sideways, blocking MacLean's course as the Russians fired shots into the *Lewis*'s starboard side.

Armed men from the man-of-war stormed aboard. MacLean called out the American flag as the reason his ship should be left alone, and he ordered his mate to cut the lines that the Russians had set to secure the *Lewis* for towing. A mate's knife and MacLean's insolence notwithstanding, the Russians took command of the vessel in the end. The man-of-war towed the *Lewis* to shore, where the captors lowered the American flag, shredded it, and raised a Russian flag in its place. They confiscated virtually everything aboard MacLean's schooner—butcher boats, guns, provisions, boots, clothes, and the hidden sealskins. MacLean and his crew were forced aboard the man-of-war, which then steamed south to the Russian port city of Vladivostok, near the Chinese border. Given neither berths nor rations, they had to scrounge food from the Russian crew.

In Vladivostok, MacLean and his men were marched through the city, then officially placed under arrest. By day, they hauled timbers and scrubbed boots to earn enough rubles to cover their meager meals. By night, they slept in a vermin-infested jail. Ever present was the threat of being sent to a virtual death sentence in a Siberian mine. Years later, MacLean would gloss over the circumstances of his capture, claiming he had enjoyed the finest time of his life while in Russia, when in fact his men had suffered emaciation, depression, and disease while in captivity.

Perhaps looking to avoid an all-out international incident, the Russians released MacLean and his men after ten weeks. A Russian vessel transported them to Yokohama, where they boarded a mail steamer and traveled in steerage to San Francisco. Disembarking on friendly soil shortly before Christmas, MacLean reportedly had a new swagger in his step along with a fierce new curl in his famous moustache. Others in his crew were less fortunate. Exposed to smallpox, they had to be quarantined, and one man died of the disease.

Not surprisingly, MacLean and his San Francisco financiers set out to milk the incident for all it was worth. For ten years, they pursued damages against the Russians for the seizure, claiming over $100,000 in losses. Deftly, Herman Liebes kept himself from the fray, as was his habit. Documents conveniently dated days before the Russian seizure showed that he had signed over the *J. Hamilton Lewis* to another investor. It would not do for someone so closely tied to the NACC to be affiliated directly with a notorious seal pirate like Alex MacLean.

IN 1892, AS THE YEARLONG AGREEMENT BETWEEN the United States and Great Britain was nearing its end, President Harrison began to consider that a seal war might be inevitable. Many in the United States, including politically ambitious Theodore Roosevelt, were obsessed with expanding the nation's naval power. With the 1823 Monroe Doctrine as justification, American imperialism was on the rise in the western hemisphere. By the end of the century, America would annex Hawaii and fight a war that would end in a takeover of the Philippines. Meanwhile, a Chilean crisis gave the US an excuse to move its naval fleet into the Pacific, where it was also better positioned for a seal war if tensions with Britain could not be otherwise resolved.

Days before the modus vivendi was set to expire, American and British diplomats averted crisis by extending its terms, the end goal being the formation of a joint tribunal that would rule on America's claim to sovereignty in the Bering Sea. The next task was to give teeth to the measure so the pirates would know both nations meant business. Gone were the days when one or two revenue cutters patrolled the Bering Sea. In 1892, a total of sixteen US warships and revenue cutters would enforce the agreement against pelagic sealing.

In command of this expansive fleet was Rear Admiral Robley D. "Fighting Bob" Evans. From the new steel warship *Yorktown*, Evans took his orders to heart, mustering the full zeal and energy of his commanding officers toward the aim of stopping seal pirates. In many ways, he embodied America's imperialistic tendencies. Assuming command of the entire North Pacific, Evans noted that even British naval officers were "practically under my command," owing to the agreement that had established the tribunal. Though he would not go so far as the Russians who torched some of the pirate vessels they seized, Evans did have a battle plan. He would begin combat by stopping the pirates' supply ship, never mind that its activities were not subject to the terms of the diplomatic agreement.

While military detectives combed waterfronts for evidence that would identify the supply ship, Evans headed north to the Bering Sea. It was the worst patch of water he had ever encountered, he later wrote, with fog so thick it seemed you could poke a finger and pop out a piece of it, as if releasing a cork from a bottle. And then there were the storms. During one especially bad gale, the *Yorktown* was forced into harbor. There, Evans sheltered alongside half a dozen ships that he suspected of piracy, though he lacked proof. Like a meeting of opposing generals before battle, he invited the captains of these ships to come aboard the *Yorktown*. Over cigars and drinks, he reminded them that he could easily put a hole through the sides of their vessels should they engage in any seal hunting.

Evans also succeeded in nabbing the ship that brought supplies to seal hunters in the Bering Sea. This forced MacLean and his fellow pirates to cut the season short. On the way back to San Francisco, some of MacLean's disgruntled crew defied orders. MacLean responded by shackling the offenders and keeping them belowdecks. By the time the vessel reached port, he had only one mate and four seal hunters manning the sails. In the ship's hold were pelts that a merchant identified as having come from a Pribilof rookery. Somehow, despite Evans's fleet of warships and revenue cutters, MacLean had managed a land raid. But the catch had been small and he was in a foul mood.

At a favorite Oakland watering hole, Heinhold's First and Last Chance Saloon, MacLean downed several drinks. When he went outside, two of his crew ambushed him, accompanied by a prize fighter they had hired. As the story goes, MacLean drew his gun, warning off the men. Then he lit into the prizefighter with his fists. Settling the matter in his favor, MacLean returned for another round at the saloon before rowing himself back to his schooner. He was determined to let no one—not disgruntled crew nor patrolling fleets with men like Evans—stop him for long.

NINE

STANDOFF

*B*ROAD-SHOULDERED AND STANDING OVER SIX feet tall, naturalist David Starr Jordan struck an imposing figure, but he was no match for a Pribilof fur seal. On a grassy clifftop on St. Paul Island, an enormous beachmaster, a breeding male weighing upwards of five hundred pounds, eyed the naturalist. Jordan eyed him back. All at once, the beachmaster lunged, breaking the standoff and throwing the naturalist off his feet. In tandem, seal and scientist rolled down the cliff to the graveled Bering Sea shoreline.

Jordan limped back to the Government House where the island physician pronounced his ankle sprained and advised a period of rest. But the energetic naturalist could not stand to be idle. Confined to quarters, he set about writing the story of Kotik, a fur seal pup, and his mother, aptly if unimaginatively called Matka and anthropomorphized by Jordan to have human physical features, thoughts, and emotions. In the story, Matka is one of the silken-haired seals on the Mist Islands. Upon wakening each morning, she brushes her throat nervously with her hands. One day, when Matka sets out for the water so she can wash her face, Kotik's father seizes her by the neck, flings her over his shoulder, and plunks her back where she belongs. But in Jordan's telling, Matka always gets her way in the end. She blows a kiss, then proceeds to the ocean to wash her face. This is the law of the Icy Sea, Jordan proclaims in the book—that a wife will do as she pleases.

Through the frigid waters, Matka swims many miles to feast on purple squid that taste like peaches and cream. Upon her return, she kisses her little Kotik, then averts her eyes because she does not want him to know she cares. On the Mist Islands, it is poor form to show either love or anger, Jordan writes. Groaning, Kotik's father sheds tears as he embarks on the Long Swim. Kotik and Matka soon follow.

The following year, when they return to the Mist Islands, Matka tells Kotik he must go away from her to another beach. Never again will she answer his call. An obedient yearling, Kotik does as his mother instructs so she can turn her attention to a new pup. But from across the sands, Kotik's face will remain ever toward her, even as he frolics with his companions at a new beach.

Then the humans' drive to the killing grounds begins. The drive is all good fun for Kotik until he sees his older companions being clubbed to death for their pelts. His little heart filled with anger, he charges at one of the club-wielding men. Jordan writes that he wishes he could have written a scene in which Kotik leads a revolt of his fellow seals, but this is a true story and he has vowed to tell only the truth. So, Kotik does not revolt. Instead, he sleeps, for on the Mist Islands, Jordan maintains, when one is unhappy, one sleeps very well indeed, and upon waking, all troubles are forgotten.

Kotik's fellow seals assure him that there have always been drives to kill seals, and there always will be. Otherwise, the Mist Islands would be too crowded and the beachmasters would trample the little pups. Play-fighting with a friend, Kotik acquires a scar. When he turns three years old, he eagerly awaits the drive because he is finally old enough to be clubbed. "He went into the drive again and thought himself the best of them," Jordan writes. But the men turn Kotik away. The trouble is the scar, which makes his skin only second-grade. Kotik slinks off, ashamed of his scar and of himself.

Jordan's story ends with the Pirate Kings sailing into the Icy Sea. Then comes the real tragedy, the blood of the silken-haired ones staining the waters and the cries of their little ones rising day and night as the pirates slay their mothers. One sad day, Matka's lifeless body, stuck through with a spear, washes up from the sea right in front of Kotik. As poor Kotik roars and groans, Jordan must turn his head from the green waters, finding no more brightness in the sands.

Penning *Matka and Kotik* in 1896, naturalist David Starr Jordan joined the ranks of the "nature fakers." While amping up the drama in their stories, nature fakers also sanitized violence. Works by such authors were popular in their day. When Jordan returned from the Pribilofs, he read the story of Matka and Kotik to an admiring crowd in Stanford University's chapel. As the university's first president, he could scarcely have expected a lesser reception. He commissioned a Stanford student to illustrate his story, then delivered the manuscript to a San Francisco publisher. Jordan's "true story" of Matka and Kotik enjoyed brisk sales, making celebrities of the seals. A half-century later, an up-and-coming producer named Walt Disney would turn a nice profit by releasing a film version of the Pribilof seals called *Seal Island*, for which he would win an Oscar.

David Starr Jordan would go on to write many more books. Having turned the attention of young readers to the nefarious doings of the Pirate Kings in the Icy Sea, he wrote more somber tomes to warn parents of the dangers of intermarriage among people of different races. In *The Blood of the Nation: A Study of the Decay of the Races Through the Survival of the Unfit*, Jordan wrote of race suicide, race degeneration, race improvement, and race progress, arguing that neither animals nor humans should be allowed to breed from inferior stock. By passing inheritances through eldest sons, Jordan wrote, the British had made themselves the fittest of all human races. He also warned readers that a republic would last only as long as the blood of its founders. Thus, he maintained, the United States was obliged to keep its bloodlines pure, turning back immigrants from southern and eastern Europe who were, according to Jordan, unsuited by temperament to mix with descendants of the British. Like *Matka and Kotik*, *The Blood of the Nation* was immensely popular in its day, going into several printings.

In scientific circles, Jordan was a bright, rising star. Raised in New York State, he enjoyed a privileged upbringing by Unitarian parents. Upon graduating from Cornell, he completed a one-year stint at a small Illinois college while applying for professorships at more prestigious institutions. When Cornell, Princeton, the University of Massachusetts, and Purdue all turned him down, he taught high school. His fortunes changed when he attended a summer program in natural history off the Massachusetts coast on Penikese Island, hosted by the venerable Louis Agassiz, director of

Harvard's Museum of Comparative Zoology and owner of the island. Everyone who was anyone in American science knew Agassiz. According to Henry Elliott's friend Robert Kennicott, de facto leader of the Smithsonian's Megatherium Club, Agassiz was selfish and egotistical, often stealing the thunder from others. Still, he was a man who made and broke scientific careers.

Agassiz had come to the United States by way of Switzerland, where he rubbed shoulders with Alexander von Humboldt, whose imperially funded adventures made him a powerful figure in the burgeoning field of natural history. Though premised on work done by others, Agassiz's studies of glacial ice in the Alps elevated his reputation. In America, he hit the lecture circuit and discovered an admiring audience for his ideas, which included the rejection of Darwin's theory of evolution and the conviction that racial mixing threatened the human race. Eventually, Agassiz quit doing actual scientific work and devoted himself wholly to his popular lectures as well as curating the Harvard museum and running his Penikese program of nature study.

Agassiz emphasized that in a place like America, where creation was ripe for collecting and cataloging, men should study nature, not books. Taking this advice to heart, David Starr Jordan spent several summers after his stint at Penikese Island collecting and cataloging fish for the US government, often at his own expense. At long last, he acquired a professorship at Indiana University, where he followed Agassiz's example of giving popular lectures. One of Jordan's favorite topics was a stirring rendition of how he had climbed the Matterhorn, presumably with more success than Agassiz, who had mistakenly summited the wrong peak.

By the time Leland and Jane Stanford went looking for someone to lead the university they were founding in Palo Alto, California, thirty-five-year-old David Starr Jordan's fortunes had shifted significantly. The Stanfords hired him to run their new school, making him the youngest university president in American history.

DAVID STARR JORDAN AND HENRY ELLIOTT WOULD come to despise one another. To those who knew them both, this came as no surprise. Jordan had much of what Elliott lacked—academic credentials, money to send his two children to boarding school, a crew to help with his field work, and the resources to travel widely. Unlike Elliott, who narrowed his work to the Pribilof seals, Jordan identified a thousand new species around the country, including a dragonfish he named for himself. And Jordan couldn't be accused of loving any animal with the sort of affection Elliott lavished on the seals—in the name of science, Jordan blew fish out of the water with dynamite and sprinkled poison in tide pools. Worse, Jordan championed the theory of polygenism, which held that the human races had descended from different ancestors and therefore could never be equal. From this theory, he derived his opposition to mixed marriages and "interbreeding," which meant he opposed Elliott's marriage and the very existence of his ten children.

In many ways, David Starr Jordan must have reminded Elliott of William Dall, a fellow Megatherium who had betrayed Elliott years earlier. Both Jordan and Dall were favorites of Louis Agassiz, and both had earned credentials and achieved recognition that had eluded Elliott. Both showed a preoccupation with self-image, and neither was averse to going behind a person's back if the purpose suited.

Dall and Elliott were the two youngest members of Kennicott's Scientific Corps. When the Corps began its work in 1865, Dall was with the contingent surveying the Bering Sea while Elliott was assigned to bushwhack through British Columbia under the command of construction superintendent Major Edward Conway. That winter, Dall asked that Elliott be reassigned so the two of them could work together in the Bering Sea. Elliott did not learn of the request until the spring. He wrote to Dall that much as he wanted to accept, he felt obliged at that point to keep his commitment to Conway. He also said he hoped he could join Dall in his scientific endeavors the following year.

In what would become a duplicitous pattern, Dall went behind Elliott's back, writing to Kennicott (who, unbeknownst to Dall, was already dead) that Elliott had refused his offer and given up completely on scientific work. Knowing nothing of this betrayal, Elliott roomed with Dall at the Smithsonian after the telegraph expedition ended in 1867, cheerfully illustrating a book on Alaska that would propel Dall to fame. When Elliott went to the Pribilofs in 1872, he discovered that Dall had published some incorrect assumptions about the seals. For instance, Dall claimed the seals reached the Pribilofs in mid-June, when in fact the beachmasters arrived in May. Dall also wrote that the seals wintered near the Aleutian Islands, when in fact the matkas wintered off the coasts of Oregon and California; that June was peak pupping season, when it was actually July; and that beachmasters kept pups from their mothers for the first three years of life, despite all evidence to the contrary. Dall said the seals mated in the water, when in fact they mated on land; and he said that the seals would tear a man to shreds if he dared venture among them, though Elliott had done this on countless occasions without incident.

In his 1873 book *The Seal Islands*, Elliott corrected these misconceptions, but he did not directly call out Dall for getting his facts wrong. They were friends, after all, or so he thought, and Dall could scarcely be expected to know the truth on these matters when he had made only superficial observations while passing to and from the Pribilofs. Assuming they remained friends, Elliott kept up amiable correspondence with William Dall. In turn, Dall wrote to the Smithsonian's Spencer Baird that Elliott was a fool. Ignorant of this affront, Elliott was thrilled to connect with Dall for three days during his 1874 return to the Pribilofs. During the visit, the naturalists engaged in what Elliott thought was a friendly disagreement over Dall's assertion that Alaska Natives should be forced onto reservations. Somewhere along the way, Elliott also made an offhand remark about the thousands of specimens Dall had collected in Alaska, saying they were gathering dust in the Smithsonian's basement. He seems to have intended this as a joke, perhaps underlain with some envy over Dall's impressive tally of specimens. Dall responded by firing off another letter to Baird, who promised Dall a dressing-down of Elliott.

The indiscreet remark and subsequent scolding had, in actuality, little effect on Elliott's long-term relationship with Baird and the Smithsonian. During his winter campaigns, Elliott continued using a desk in the Smithsonian's Castle. Each summer, as cherries and pears ripened in his Ohio orchards, he shipped baskets of fruit to the Baird family, with a friendly note tucked into each package. But there was no repairing his relationship with Dall. In 1875, the dubious Anti-Monopoly Association wrote a screed that excoriated Elliott and lauded Dall, who, unbeknownst to Elliott, had longtime ties to the association through one of its ringleaders. After that, the only correspondence between the former friends was in the *Nation* magazine, where Elliott and Dall argued in a series of letters over the extent to which the hunting of the Pribilof seals had influenced the decision to purchase Alaska. After much back-and-forth, the *Nation's* editor finally put an end to the sparring with a note saying the magazine would publish nothing more on the subject.

From his experience with Dall, Elliott knew to be cautious and not trust even the friendliest of fellow naturalists. Aside from the backstabbing, there was also the fact that David Starr Jordan had taken what was arguably Elliott's rightful place on the 1896 Pribilof Seal Commission, an assignment that originated in an 1893 Paris Tribunal decision arbitrating British and American tensions over the seals. The Paris Tribunal had met during an especially bad year for the seals. At the height of his glory, Alex MacLean was openly defying anyone who tried to stop his piracy. When a US revenue cutter chased after his 294-ton *Alexander*, a square-rigged sailing vessel that was also equipped with steam engines, MacLean fired the *Alexander's* two big guns straight across the cutter's deck and then proceeded about his business. According to a report in the Portland newspaper *The Oregonian*, MacLean reveled in the idea that he might soon surpass Captains Kidd and Morgan in the piratical hall of fame.

All told, MacLean and his fellow pirates took over 120,000 pelts in 1893, meaning they likely killed upwards of half a million seals, since so many sank after being shot at sea. Meanwhile, officials in Paris were sorting through arguments and proposals, among them Elliott's 1890 report, which had been previously suppressed by the US government. Published by the British, the report was part of sixteen volumes of evidence the tribunal considered. Despite open threats and accusations of treason, Elliott had shared his mothballed report with the British because he wanted the public to be able to study his findings in full.

After blowing the whistle over his suppressed report, a lesser man might have given up on the seals altogether. Elliott no longer had a Treasury assignment. No one was paying him for his expertise, nor did anyone share his zeal for protecting a single species of marine mammals on a pair of faraway islands. But Elliott had his passion, and he had his art. From his field notes and sketches, he painted a series of before and after images that gave form and color to the endangered seals' plight. In idyllic renditions from 1872, he showed a St. Paul hill with a small bidarrah, a traditional skin kayak, and its Unangax̂ crew in the foreground. He painted Lukannon Beach crowded with yearling seals. He painted seals as far as the eye could see at Polavina, a hauling ground that at the time was a reserve. He painted bachelor seals hauling out by the hundreds at English Bay as two Unangax̂ men stroll among the throngs on shore, causing not the slightest disruption.

Elliott's paintings from his 1890 visit show darker scenes. In one, seal pirates pursue their quarry on a choppy sea. Another depicts a pirate ship and three of its butcher boats. In one of the boats, a hunter tugs a rope attached to a harpoon embedded in a seal. Equally disturbing were Elliott's depictions of the hauling grounds, which by 1890 had turned lonely and desolate, with vegetation having crept in where seals had once crowded by the millions.

Armed with these paintings, Elliott renewed his winter campaigns to Washington, traveling from Ohio at his own expense. Hoping to spark conversations among lawmakers, he loaned his more sublime artwork to sympathetic congressmen who agreed to display them on their office walls. He also shared some of his paintings with the British ambassador, confident that the luminous images would move him to press harder for a solution to the seal crisis.

By the time the 1893 Paris Tribunal convened, a solution seemed within reach, and it could scarcely come soon enough. While Alex MacLean and his fellow pirates were decimating the seal population at sea, NACC superintendent George Tingle was overseeing aggressive land drives that included the killing of yearlings. But the tribunal's ruling fell short of what Elliott had wanted. While pelagic sealing was banned from May through July in a zone stretching sixty miles from the Pribilofs, seal pups depend on their mothers for milk well into the fall, so any pups whose mothers were killed by pirates after July were doomed to starve. The sixty-mile foraging zone was also inadequate, as the matkas traveled over a hundred miles to feed on pollock, anchovies, and squid.

The tribunal's decision also banned pelagic sealers from using firearms, and their ships were to be powered only by sail, not steam. But as Elliott well knew, those prohibitions would do little to stop a man like MacLean, a master at the sail with no qualms about sending out butcher boats loaded with spears instead of rifles. An even bigger flaw in the arbitration decision was that it only bound the United States and Britain. By hoisting another nation's flag, pirates could claim that none of the terms applied to them.

What was needed, Elliott knew, was an international treaty tailored to the unique habits of the seals. Because the species migrated, the treaty would need to include mutual concessions and joint control of the wildlife by the world's most powerful nations—the United States, Britain, Russia, and Japan. This was a revolutionary concept. Never before had nations with such diverse interests come together to protect migrating mammals. Elliott also felt the US needed to admit its own culpability in endangering the seals. That was not at all something industry titans and their government enablers wished to acknowledge.

In addition to the limits it placed on pelagic sealing practices, the tribunal's decision established a joint British-American commission to study the seals, a proposal Elliott himself had made. Recognized as the nation's premier expert on the Pribilof seals, he should have been an obvious choice for heading the commission. But after blowing the whistle on the government's suppression of his 1890 report, he had become a pariah. David Starr Jordan, however, was perfectly positioned for the assignment. As president of Stanford, Jordan courted wealthy donors, including politically influential California banker Darius Ogden Mills, one of the wealthiest men in America for a time. Mills had founded the NACC with the Liebes cousins and was a longtime associate of Leland Stanford, who had hired Jordan as his university's president. Mills also served on Stanford University's Board of Trustees, in effect making him Jordan's boss. Jordan spoke admiringly of NACC principal Stephen Elkins, describing him as a jolly fellow untroubled with idealism. Mills and Elkins may or may not have wielded their influence in getting Jordan appointed to the Seal Commission, but either way, Jordan's recommendations would align conveniently with NACC interests.

Having come around to the idea that the seals had intrinsic value as wildlife, Elliott despised Jordan's methods. Jordan once ordered the construction of an eight-foot wire fence around a group of young male seals, the idea being that it would keep them out of the water and away from the pirates. When the seals breached the barrier, he was forced to admit they were not as stupid as he had believed. Another time, Jordan ordered matkas to be branded like cattle, the idea being that the brands would decrease their value to the pirates. Eventually, Jordan admitted that the branding experiment had failed, and he discontinued the practice.

Unlike Elliott, Jordan was adamant about the Pribilof land harvest having nothing to do with the fur seals' imminent demise. As far as he was concerned, the pirates bore the brunt of the blame, along with the beachmasters, which according to Jordan indiscriminately trampled pups. Elliott had only rarely observed such trampling. Then there was *Uncinaria lucasi,* the thin, yellowish hookworm that Jordan said was killing seal pups. This claim puzzled Elliott. When dissecting seals, Elliott had often found tight balls of worms in their digestive tracts, but the seals had been healthy and robust, the worms seeming not to have affected them at all. How could these worms suddenly be causing a die-off of pups as Jordan claimed?

At the time, scientists knew little about parasites. Belonging to a phylum that has thrived for over four million years, hookworms are remarkably adaptive parasites of many species, including humans. Entering their human hosts through the soles of their feet, they infect millions of people around the planet, mostly in warm climates. Yet successful parasites do not typically kill their hosts, which is why many people with hookworms in their digestive tracks show no adverse effects. While their hosts are healthy, worms may even offer certain protections. But if a host is weak, the hookworm's sucking of blood from within can cause anemia in the host and eventually death.

Through the lens of modern science, it is possible to see how Elliott and Jordan reached different conclusions about hookworms in fur seals. Elliott made most of his observations when the herd was at peak health, while Jordan made his when the species was threatened. Recent studies show that hookworms have little effect on seal pups who get frequent feedings of rich milk from their mothers. Those lacking such nutrition, as they did when pirates killed their mothers, are more likely to die from hookworm infestations.

Disputes among scientists are nothing new, of course. Ideally, disagreements should serve as part of the scientific process, spurring those with conflicting theories to think more deeply about their data, examine controls and variables, make more observations, and adjust their conclusions if needed. But money, politics, and egos have ways of undercutting the scientific process. Isaac Newton sparred with Gottfried Wilhelm Liebniz over which of them had invented calculus, Charles Darwin had a similarly ugly fight with Richard Owen over which of them deserved credit for the theory of evolution, and Thomas Edison invested a good deal of time and money trying to discredit Nikola Tesla, whose alternating current would ultimately prove superior to Edison's direct current.

For all their differences, neither Elliott nor Jordan lacked for ego. To Jordan, Elliott was an uneducated hack undeserving of recognition. To Elliott, Jordan was at best a neophyte when it came to the seals, at worst a NACC shill installed to protect the company's profits. Early on, Elliott refrained from public criticism of Jordan. But not long after Jordan wrote his nature-faker story about Matka and Kotik, he also penned a letter to Samuel Langley, who had taken over at the Smithsonian following Baird's death in 1887. In this missive, Jordan raised doubts about Elliott's honesty and even his sanity, urging Langley to sever all ties with him on behalf of the Institution.

Elliott cared deeply about his affiliation with the Smithsonian, which had been a major part of his life since the age of sixteen. When he learned of Jordan's denigrating appeal to Langley, Elliott vowed to defend his turf against his adversary, not unlike a beachmaster. Jordan might be the darling of science and the NACC, but Elliott was determined to prove him wrong about the seals.

Part Two
1906–1914

It will be a question for your serious consideration...
whether it is not better to end the
practice by exterminating the herd ourselves
in the most humane way possible.
—Theodore Roosevelt

TEN

TWELVE GUNS

*H*AD THE DAY DAWNED CLEAR and blue, a Japanese assault on American soil would have been unthinkable. But on St. Paul Island, such weather is rare, especially in summer. And so it was that on July 18, 1906, Japanese frigates edged through the fog toward these US shores, manned by pirates who aimed to plunder America's most valuable wildlife.

A total of sixteen schooners, including one called the *Kensai Maru*, bobbed in a daisy ring around the island that day, the pirates threatening to escalate a global crisis that had pushed the world's most powerful nations to the brink of war more than once. The US revenue cutter whose crew might have held off a Japanese land raid was at that moment cruising southward through the Bering Sea toward Unalaska, on the Aleutian chain. There, the crew would happily disembark, toasting the bad luck of their remote assignment while their ship was restocked with the salted pork, hardtack, coffee, and coal that would sustain them—physically, at least—for the next godforsaken round of their duties. Left behind to defend the seals against the marauding Japanese were fifteen Unangax̂ men in servitude to the government and the NACC. Charged with protecting the island's rookeries, these guards were allotted twelve rifles to be shared between them.

The shape of St. Paul Island is roughly that of a diving seal. Southwest Point, the snout of the island, sniffs, as it were, toward Japan. Across thirteen miles of cinder heaps overgrown with wild parsnip, wormwood, sedges, and grasses, Northeast Point protrudes like a hind flipper, waving toward mainland Alaska. Stationed among the rocks on the western edge of Northeast Point were Mikhail Kozloff, called Michael by his boss, and John Fratis Jr. Entrusted to the pair was one rifle, a heady privilege for two young Unangax̂ men aged nineteen and twenty. Kozloff and Fratis could hardly have been more different, at least in appearance. Short and stocky, Kozloff was more inclined to frown than smile, while Fratis was lean, tall, and handsome. The eldest boy of nine children, Fratis had recently become head of the family, his father having died earlier in the year. He also had a fifteen-year-old wife and a new baby.

At eight o'clock that July morning, the sun shone only as a dim, backlit glow in the fog. Scanning the woolly haze, Fratis and Kozloff were pitched with adrenaline. Raised to hunt on land and sea, they were patient, alert, and adept. From a young age they had learned to identify subtle changes in wind, sea, and sky that might auger calamity. Their traditional training and the teachings of their Elders enabled their survival in a maritime environment that was challenging, to say the least. Whether that training had equipped them to prevail against the Japanese marauders remained to be seen.

By virtue of his age and status, Fratis would have been the leader of the pair, but it was Kozloff who handled the rifle, listening intently as guns fired back and forth in the fog. Though unable to discern where the shots were coming from or where they were aimed, he knew what they signified. Amid the frenzy of barking seals and sea lions, matkas splashed into the ocean. Despite the gunfire, they had to forage for food so they could feed their pups. Fratis and Kozloff knew as well as anyone that each pirate's bullet in essence killed three seals—the matka, her orphaned pup, and the next generation pup in her womb.

The rounds of gunfire also affirmed that Fratis, Kozloff, and the rest of the Unangax̂ guards stationed around the island were grossly outnumbered and outgunned. If the Japanese pirates were to descend en masse, it would be impossible for fifteen men to defend their homes and families, let alone the seals. The previous day, a shift in the fog had exposed one of the schooners racing toward Northeast Point. Taking cover behind a rampart of jagged rocks, Unangax̂ guards had watched as the pirates lowered a butcher boat into the waves, outfitted with a makeshift sail and jib. Greased cloth wrapped the oarlocks, silencing the oars and providing an added measure of stealth to the seal hunters.

Yesterday, luck had been with the guards. They had sent for reinforcements, who arrived from nearby posts to surround the pirates as they made land. In broken English, one Japanese pirate said they had only come ashore for fresh water, but the visible contents of the butcher boat—clubs and knives for killing and skinning seals—betrayed his story. Fratis and Kozloff knew the damage these objects could do. They had seen the evidence from previous raids conducted under cover of fog—broken clubs, bloodied rocks, and the carcasses of skinned seals left to rot.

Marched by Unangax̂ guards along the twelve-mile road to the village, the captured pirates from yesterday's raid were now awaiting their fate, but taking these prisoners had apparently done nothing to dissuade their comrades at sea. If anything, the gunfire had intensified. Sailors in the sixteen vessels seemed to be making a show of force, hoping to overwhelm the guards so the prisoners could break free. If that were the case, there was little that fifteen guards would be able to do to stop them.

Fratis and Kozloff watched, listened, and waited. The few words they exchanged were likely whispered in English, not in Unangam Tunuu, the native language of the Unangax̂. At a young age, Fratis and Kozloff had learned hard lessons from their government schoolteacher—for every word uttered in Unangam Tunuu, there had been a slap to the face, a tug of the ear, or verbal ridicule.

For more than a century the Unangax̂ had been forced to answer to the white men who came and went from their islands. The boss men—officials with the NACC and the US Treasury—who had assigned Fratis and Kozloff to this particular post on this particular day were no better equipped for armed battle than the Unangax̂ guards were. Charged with ensuring the welfare of the Unangax̂ as well as the seals, US Treasury agent Walter Lembkey was fighting a losing battle, and yet he returned year after year.

Stateside, some of America's wealthiest men continued to reap incredible returns on the work of men like Fratis and Kozloff. In contrast, no Unangax̂ worker earned a living wage. By government mandate, the Unangax̂ were trapped on the islands, what little pay they received coming in the form of stingy allotments of goods from the company store, such as one pair of shoes per year. They were given no milk, sugar, lard, candles, cooking utensils, tableware, or furniture.

And yet a life of deprivation was still a life worth defending. As Fratis and Kozloff watched from their hidden lookout, three butcher boats with a total of nine armed sailors materialized from the fog. In the lead boat, two Japanese pirates busied themselves with unfastening a sail. A third scanned the shoreline, rifle in hand.

Fratis and Kozloff leaped from hiding. "Hands up!" Fratis yelled.

Kozloff fired three warning shots, striking the waves that lapped alongside the lead butcher boat. Abandoning the sail, two of the pirates grabbed the boat's oars. Squinting, the third traced his rifle along the rocks, looking to return Kozloff's fire.

Fratis and Kozloff flattened themselves to the earth, pungent with the smell of wild parsnip and beach grass. Seconds passed. An eternity. Kozloff inched forward, peering out at the rocky shoreline below, teeming with bellowing, barking seals. Wisps of fog teased at the butcher boat as Kozloff held it in his sights. Adrenaline surging, he fired again. Once. Twice. Three times.

The two oarsmen slumped where they sat. The rifleman crouched, clutching his shoulder. Wind and waves buffeted the boat, sweeping it toward the island. Fratis and Kozloff scrambled over the rocks toward it. At the shoreline, they grabbed hold of the bow and dragged the boat onto the gravelly sands. They assessed the casualties—two pirates dead, one wounded. It was an incident sufficient in scope to trigger yet another international conflict over the seals.

The fog pressed in, swirling over and around the guards, who could no longer make out the rookery they defended. Beyond the bleating seals, the pounding surf, and the wind pummeling their ears, they heard volleys of gunfire, punctuated by cannon booms. All around the island, more butcher boats were advancing.

Again, the fog retreated. Fratis and Kozloff looked down the beach. What they saw horrified them. A Japanese schooner was anchored only three hundred feet from shore. Having already rowed to land, pirates were now spread all along the beach. They were clubbing seals, stabbing them. They were skinning some while the seals were still alive.

Without the fog for cover, the pirates scurried for their butcher boats, abandoning their gruesome work. Fratis and Kozloff walked among the wounded and dead seals, surveying the carnage. Beachmasters bellowed in pain and confusion. Their eyes smashed by the pirates' clubs into their skulls, they staggered over the sands on mutilated flippers. Though hardened by wind, weather, and servitude, the young Unangax̂ men wept as they moved among them, dispatching the mortally wounded, cursing the wanton waste. A world away from the endless congressional debates, presidential briefings, and diplomatic volleys over the fate of these seals, the guards had done the best they could to prevent this sort of carnage. Clearly, their efforts were insufficient.

When the sun finally set that July day, the tallies were grim. Five Japanese dead, two wounded, and ten prisoners awaiting transport to the mainland. For the seals, it had been a bloodbath that had brought them a step closer to extinction. By summer's end, the pirates would kill over twenty thousand more of their kind.

WHEN WORD OF THE RAIDS REACHED WASHINGTON, President Theodore Roosevelt deliberated over his response. Less than a year before, he had brokered peace talks between Japan and Russia, bringing an end to the Russo-Japanese War. But the truce was unpopular in Japan, where some viewed the terms as proof that their nation had failed to stand up to Western powers. Many Japanese were frustrated with America's meddling in Asian affairs. Though the Japanese ambassador admitted that the seal hunters should have stayed off American soil, he decried the shootings. Now Roosevelt had to smooth over Japanese casualties on the Pribilof Islands.

Having flexed its military muscle with Russia, Japan was a force to be reckoned with. In the aftermath of America's imperialistic acquisition of the Philippines, Roosevelt worried that Japan might try to seize the Pribilofs. As preemptive moves, he instructed his secretary of the navy to ready America's Asiatic fleet and dispatched a US warship to Alaskan waters. He knew anti-Japanese sentiments were running high across the United States. On the West Coast, labor groups had formed an Asian Exclusion League and were promoting an effort to force Asian students in San Francisco into a single school, away from white children. In California, politicians from both parties were calling for Japanese exclusion. News of the Pribilof raids was now adding fuel to the fire.

For Japan, pelagic sealing had become part of the global commerce forced upon them by Commodore Matthew Perry when his fleet of American warships opened Japan to the West in 1853. Then as now, the vast majority of the world's northern fur seals bred on the Pribilofs. However, a much smaller group, comprising about 25 percent of the world's total, frequented rookeries on the Kuril Islands, a chain of approximately fifty-six islands off the coasts of Russia and northern Japan. Japan's Indigenous People, the Ainu, had populated some of these islands since pre-modern times. In the center of the island chain, on several tiny, uninhabited islets, fur seals bred.

American and Canadian pirates first raided fur seal rookeries on the Kuril Islands in 1881. These raids mirrored the earlier devastation wrought on fur seals in the southern hemisphere. Within fifteen years, the Kuril herd of twenty-two thousand seals was virtually extinct, with only thirty seals remaining. The rest of the Asiatic fur seals, which bred on Russia's adjacent Commander Islands, migrated south along the Japanese coast each winter. By 1893, there were more than fifty North American pirate ships plying these waters. That same year, these pirates harvested over fifty thousand sealskins, with an untold additional number lost due to the wasteful methods of pelagic sealing. As in Victoria, the pirates overran the waterfront in Hakodate, the port city of Hokkaido, frequenting saloons and getting into fistfights. Unsurprisingly, NACC principal Herman Liebes kept a man in Hokkaido to look out for his pelagic sealing interests.

At first, the Japanese government banned its own citizens from killing seals at sea, but by 1894, in an about-face, they had begun paying Japanese pelagic sealers subsidies that covered nearly all expenses except the cost of their schooners. In Hakodate, the Japanese sealing fleet grew. Noting the profits foreigners were making, the Japanese government tried to use licensing as a means of restricting pelagic sealing to Japanese citizens only, but by then, foreign pirates like MacLean were well entrenched in the industry.

Further complicating the matter was the colonial practice of consular jurisdiction, which gave Great Britain judicial authority over the ports of countries that it deemed to have inadequate court systems. In effect, this left the British to enforce Japanese restrictions on the same Victoria-based pirates that the British were protecting in waters claimed by the United States.

North American pirates had long been hiring Japanese sailors to crew on their expeditions, but when Congress passed legislation in 1897 that prohibited Americans from pelagic sealing, pirates like MacLean also began registering their ships under Japanese flags. Even vessels that seemed to be Japanese operated were, upon closer inspection, often financed and owned by North Americans, with white men among their crews.

During the Russo-Japanese War, Japanese mercenaries had raided Russia's Robben Island, eliminating an entire population of migrating fur seals that might otherwise have been considered fair game for pirates. Interrupting what had become a substantial supply chain of sealskins obtained by pelagic hunters, the war had also driven sealskin prices to an all-time high. These factors prompted Japanese sealers to turn their attention to the Pribilofs in 1906.

In the aftermath of the July 1906 raids on St. Paul and St. George Islands, reports from around the globe suggested that the most notorious of seal pirates, Alex MacLean, had been behind the incident. MacLean had managed to escape extradition to San Francisco in 1905, but he was no longer at the helm of the ship known first as the *Carmencita* and later as the *Acapulco*. During the first half of 1906, he had been out of sight. He didn't resurface in Victoria until several weeks after the Japanese sealers were killed, fueling suspicions that he had masterminded the raids.

Like others in the Victoria and San Francisco fleets, MacLean had regularly chased seals from the Asiatic herd before heading to the Pribilofs. He had also hired Japanese seal hunters who fared no better under his command than their Western counterparts had. At one point, MacLean sailed into Yokohama with ten Japanese sailors in shackles, claiming that they were mutineers who had refused orders. The sailors countered that MacLean had abused them, chaining them to the deck and exposing them to the elements.

MacLean said that he had paid them in advance and would not abide their refusal to work. But everyone knew that sealers got paid at the end of a voyage, not the beginning. Perhaps MacLean's payments had been to crimpers. Perhaps he had simply lied. In any event, his ties to the Japanese sealing industry were yet another wrinkle in the tensions between the US and Japan.

In the years leading up to the 1906 raids, Henry Wood Elliott saw how correct he had been to question the effectiveness of the 1893 Paris Tribunal ruling on the seals. As he had predicted, the pirates had simply switched flags to nations that were not bound by the ruling and gone on about their nefarious work. Enforcement of the tribunal's judgment was also a problem. The Bering Sea was simply too vast an area to patrol effectively, and the pirates knew it. Though a signatory to the 1893 accord, the British were of little assistance to the United States in patrolling the waters. If America was serious about finding a lasting solution to the seal crisis, then the British wanted the United States to terminate the NACC lease, which would acknowledge that they shared responsibility for the seals' dwindling numbers. Britain had even tried using the Pribilof land harvest as a bargaining chip during the Klondike Gold Rush. The Klondike was in Canada, but primary access to it went through Skagway, Alaska. British negotiators proposed that the United States cede Skagway to Great Britain, and in exchange the British would quit insisting on termination of the Pribilof land lease as a condition to enforcement of pelagic sealing restrictions. The US declined the offer.

Meanwhile, seal coats were fetching ever higher prices around the globe. There seemed no end to what the market would bear. Elliott predicted that unless swift action was taken, the population of breeding male fur seals would be gone within a few years. His own prospects for financial and professional survival looked similarly dim. For more than a decade, David Starr Jordan and others with ties to the NACC had kept up their attacks on Elliott. Still, Elliott pressed on, showing his storytelling art around Congress and pleading with officials to do something to save the seals.

Meanwhile, his financial circumstances grew increasingly desperate. Without government work, Elliott had been forced to sell the twenty-two-acre estate he had inherited from his father. Gone were the Rockport cottage and the orchards he had so lovingly tended. Gone were the pond and the grassy lawn where his sisters had honed their skill at croquet and where the church had staged its theatricals. Gone were the roses and lilies that had given his wife Alexandra such pleasure in a place far from her Pribilof home. The Elliotts and their ten children now squeezed into a small house on Detroit Avenue in the Cleveland streetcar suburb of Lakewood, and Elliott had to figure out a way to feed them.

After sixteen years of fighting for the seals, Elliott's situation was much like that of the Unangax̂ guards Fratis and Kozloff—he was alone and ill equipped. Never before had any man given up so much to save a species. And the fight was far from over. When news of the 1906 raids reached him, he fell ill with anxiety. Still, he took comfort in the words of President Theodore Roosevelt, who as much as any public figure embodied the "man's man" of the era. If you must strike a blow, don't hit soft.

ELEVEN

SEA-WOLF

*T*HE FINAL YEARS OF THE nineteenth century had been unkind to Alex MacLean. In 1896, his brother Dan, who had sailed alongside him through storms of all kinds, died of consumption. In 1898, Alex's erstwhile benefactor Herman Liebes died in London, where he had been living for three years. The *San Francisco Chronicle* had at one point estimated Liebes's net worth—built in part on MacLean's piracy—at between four and six million dollars.

In the wake of these events, MacLean took a brief hiatus from sealing to pursue other money-making ventures. He joined a South Seas pearling venture that ended up being a scam, and he was also spotted in the Klondike during the height of the gold rush. Lured by rising seal fur prices, he was back in the Bering Sea in the early years of the twentieth century. As much as anyone, he knew the seals were going extinct—but until they were gone, there was money to be made.

Beginning in 1904, MacLean also had more reason than ever to prove up on his piratical reputation, thanks to Jack London's *The Sea-Wolf*. One of the nation's most popular writers, London was no stranger to piracy. At age fifteen, he had given up cannery work for a crack at adventure in Oakland's waterfront district, where oystering was in full swing. Like seal coats, oysters were all the rage among the wealthy, and an Oakland company had a monopoly on the industry. Eager for a piece of the action, oyster pirates sailed the bay under cover of night, raiding oyster beds owned by the company that had the monopoly. Guards protected the beds, but if an oyster pirate could slip past them, the profit potential was huge. In one night, a pirate might earn the equivalent of a month's salary from factory work.

Borrowing $300 from his childhood nanny, fifteen-year-old London bought an oyster pirate's boat and got into "the business." Along the waterfront, he soon became known as the Prince of the Oyster Pirates. When he decided he was done risking his life to steal oysters, he took up sealing and spent seven months on a schooner that plied the Bering Sea. Returning to San Francisco in 1893, the seventeen-year-old London wrote a story based on his adventures. In a fiction contest sponsored by the *San Francisco Call*, his story took first prize.

In 1898, London returned from a stint in the Klondike with a different sort of gold, one sluiced not from streams but from colorful characters confronting nature's most brutal challenges. Finding a receptive audience for the stories he wrote about these people, he published what would become one of his most acclaimed novels, *The Call of the Wild*, in 1903. For the better part of that year, he devoted himself to writing another novel, *The Sea-Wolf*, about a refined man and woman stranded at sea with a ruthless seal pirate.

London signed with *Century Magazine* to serialize *The Sea-Wolf* between January and November 1904, at which point his publisher would release the full text as a book. Brokering his literary success for a coveted assignment as a correspondent in the Russo-Japanese War, London headed for Japan at the end of 1903, leaving his lover to look after his publishing concerns. In Yokohama, he made the rounds at saloons he had frequented as a seal hunter. Moving to the war's frontlines, he managed to get himself arrested three times in a span of four months. As punishment for the third offense, punching a guard, London might have been sentenced to death if President Theodore Roosevelt, a fan of his stories, had not intervened.

London returned home to accolades for *The Sea-Wolf*, a narrative that gave context to the consequential drama playing out in real time over the Pribilof seals. In excruciating detail, the book depicts a ship's decks slippery with seal fat and blood, its masts and rails splattered red, with bare-chested butchers carving up the animals. When asked about his inspiration for the story, London revealed that the real-life model for his fiendish seal pirate Wolf Larsen was none other than Alex MacLean. London had never sailed with the notorious pirate, but he had heard plenty about him. MacLean claimed that, in fact, he and London did know one another. He said that one day the author had delivered him a copy of *The Sea-Wolf* in a cigar box to be read after MacLean set sail.

Whatever the connection between the two men, London's Wolf Larsen is a dead ringer for Alex MacLean. London describes the fictional Sea-Wolf with a handsome face, frank and open, square and full and altogether as beautiful as a man's face can be. He makes much of the Sea-Wolf's large gray eyes, at turns brooding and full of fire and softly warm. All Wolf Larsen lacks is MacLean's infamous moustache.

In London's telling, the Sea-Wolf is at times a model of culture and intelligence, while on other occasions he is brutish. This duality is central to the novel's theme. Accounts of MacLean's temperament likewise emphasize opposing traits: One minute he's in fisticuffs, the next he's tending the wounds of an opponent. One minute he's hot with anger, and the next he's shooting potatoes across his ship's bow in a piratical food fight. *The Sea-Wolf*'s narrator maintains that Wolf Larsen's rages are all for show, a way for a lonely man to position himself when set apart by his own virility and mental fortitude. Perhaps this was also true of MacLean, or perhaps he was simply mercurial by nature. Regardless, after the novel was published, MacLean's friends took to calling him "The Sea-Wolf."

For his part, Alex MacLean had been leaning into the role of outlaw even before the first installments of *The Sea-Wolf* began making the rounds in *Century Magazine*. In 1904, he sailed the double-masted wooden schooner *Carmencita* north from San Francisco under a Mexican flag, ignoring the papers that authorized him to sail the vessel only to Mexico. Along the way, the US revenue cutter *Bear* intercepted him. With typical aplomb, MacLean passed out cigars to the revenue officers, who took no action other than noting that the crew looked more Irish than Mexican. During a second patrol stop, officers asked MacLean his destination. In response, he gave a latitude and longitude that officials later realized would have put his ship in the middle of the Gulf of Guinea, off the African coast.

MacLean continued toward the Commander Islands, where he had been arrested thirteen years earlier, determined to show the

Russians he would not be intimidated. As it turned out, the Russian guards, better armed than their Pribilof counterparts, were of a similar mind. As MacLean's butcher boat crews rowed toward land, rifles sang like bees all around, according to one of the seal hunters. An oarsman cried out, then slumped to the floorboards, blood spurting from his mouth. Under heavy fire, his companions reversed course, heaving hard on the oars. Reaching MacLean's schooner, they hoisted aboard their wounded comrade, a twenty-two-year-old Missouri boy on his first sealing adventure.

As the wounded lad writhed in his bunk, MacLean's defiance broke. Heaving ho, the captain turned the *Carmencita* south, the wind-powered schooner a lonely dot in a desolate sea. At last, a steamship came into view. Steam was the enemy of sail. The clanging, dirty engines that produced it were anathema to men like MacLean. But this was no time for waxing nostalgic over the dying days of sail. The *Carmencita* tacked toward the steamship. Drawing near, MacLean convinced the steamship captain to transport his wounded crewman to the mainland for medical care.

The young man's bleeding had stopped, but he still had a bullet lodged in the roof of his mouth. Aboard the steamship beelining for Seattle, he must have felt no small amount of gratitude for the ship's grimy engines. Making land, he was rushed to a hospital. Feeling little allegiance to MacLean, whose illegal pursuit had caused his woes, the lad gave a full account of the attempted seal-hunting raid before going under the ether. It would be his final tale, his life snuffed out on the operating table.

If the incident gave MacLean pause, its effects were brief and minimal. He ended the season by sailing into Victoria's port with characteristic bravado, circling his schooner at full speed in a free-spirited flaunting of success during a season that had been a disaster. A pistol conspicuously at his side, he paid his surviving crew members one dollar each, the minimum required by law. The disgruntled men dispersed into saloons along Victoria's waterfront. Emboldened by liquor, two of the crew tracked down their captain. Using choice words, they expressed to him how they felt about risking their lives for a dollar apiece.

Having sailed a season with MacLean, they should have known

better. Even those acquainted with the sea pirate only by reputation knew better than to cross him. True to form, MacLean met the sailors' complaints that night with his fists. When all was said and done, he literally had blood on his hands. The crewmen survived, but their battered faces testified to lessons learned. Splayed out on a saloon floor, they pondered their poor judgment as MacLean announced to any who cared to listen that he was headed home to his wife and daughter.

In Washington, DC, authorities decided to get serious about apprehending MacLean. At the end of the 1904 season, they sent an undercover detective to prowl saloons along the waterfronts in San Francisco and Victoria, trying to track MacLean down. The detective claimed he was looking for a brother who had sailed with Alex MacLean, but the drunken sailors he encountered made poor sources and the detective learned little of substance.

Tipped off by US authorities, Mexico canceled its registration of the *Carmencita*. Determined to sail the vessel again, MacLean resorted to new layers of subterfuge in 1905. He tried to swap his Mexican flag for registration in Argentina, but embassy officials turned him down. He then returned to Mexico, this time working through an intermediary who, claiming Mexican citizenship, petitioned the Mexican consul in San Francisco to register a ship called the *Acapulco*. The intermediary claimed the ship had been recently built in Victoria for the purpose of transporting lumber to Mexico. The registration was approved, and in 1905 MacLean took the helm of the *Acapulco*, which looked nothing like a brand-new lumber-hauling ship because it was in fact the old *Carmencita*. On paper, the commander was not MacLean but one "Captain Alexander Woodside."

It was during the *Acapulco*'s 1905 voyage that MacLean offloaded his entire crew at Clayoquot, on Vancouver Island, and then later proceeded to round them all up from the saloon and put them back aboard ship. Some of these men were holdovers from the ill-fated 1904 voyage. Some were veterans of the Spanish-American War who knew nothing about sealing but were excellent marksmen. It was also during this voyage that MacLean obsessively clipped articles about himself from newspapers he gathered at each port of call.

With his financial backers in San Francisco set to stand trial for their involvement in pelagic sealing, he knew how much was at stake if he was caught.

Three times during the summer of 1905, patrol boats intercepted the *Acapulco* within three miles of the Pribilofs. Each time, MacLean identified himself as Captain Woodside. When asked if he and his crew were in fact Mexican, he answered, "Sí, señor." Looking over the rough men aboard, a revenue officer noted that, national origins aside, they were the worst-looking bunch of cutthroats he had ever encountered.

When the third patrol boat came steaming toward the *Acapulco*, MacLean switched tactics. Gathering his men on deck, he demoted himself from captain to navigator, then assigned a seasoned old sailor named Bill Thomas to the helm. As the authorities closed in, they called out for the *Acapulco* to drop sail. A patrol boat lieutenant set out in a rowboat for the *Acapulco*, intending to go aboard. In the choppy sea, he had trouble climbing the ship's ladder. Grinning, "Navigator" MacLean grabbed the officer by the collar and heaved him up the ladder and onto the deck. Affronted, the lieutenant demanded MacLean's nationality, to which MacLean of course replied, "Mexican." The day was cold, and MacLean offered the lieutenant a spot of rum to take the chill off. Demurring, the lieutenant demanded to see the ship's papers. Even without the rum, he somehow missed the fact that the *Acapulco* was 4,500 miles north of its declared destination.

After the lieutenant and the patrol boat departed, MacLean ordered the *Acapulco*'s butcher boats be dropped for a land raid. When the seal hunters reached shore, they warned the Pribilof guards not to get in the way, and the guards did not argue. The raid was successful, but after learning from a newspaper article that the US revenue cutter *Bear* was headed their way, the crew was spooked. Four men escaped in a butcher boat, rowing to freedom along Alaska's Inside Passage. MacLean sailed on without them, deciding it was time to head for port. On the voyage back to Victoria, "Captain" Bill Thomas keeled over and died of unknown causes. His fellow sailors shrouded his corpse for burial at sea.

To cash in on his illegal cargo of sealskins, MacLean stopped at

Clayoquot, on Vancouver Island's western coast, where there were no pesky customs agents demanding to know how he had come by so many seal pelts. He sent six men ahead of him to Victoria, where they made a point of telling everyone they met how the *Acapulco*'s elderly captain had died at sea. MacLean had been aboard, the men admitted, but the rumors of him advancing land raids of the Pribilofs were untrue. In fact, they said MacLean lacked a mouse's courage, and Jack London had been sorely mistaken to fashion the Sea-Wolf after him.

The Victoria customs officer was not so easily fooled. He sent word to Clayoquot that MacLean had best report there straightaway and turn over his ill-gotten sealskins. Feigning ignorance of customs laws, MacLean sent back word that he would certainly comply now that he understood what he was supposed to do. Then he took his time getting from Clayoquot to Victoria, stretching what should have been a one-day trip into nine days. When MacLean finally reached his destination, he looked dapper as usual in his Prince Albert coat and black plug hat. He signed himself in the customs house books as a Mexican citizen, then went home to his wife and daughter in Victoria. Writing to the US State Department, the American consulate called MacLean's Mexican registry a fraud. After paying a $1,600 fine for this fraud and other infractions, MacLean delivered his seal pelts to Victoria's R. P. Rithet and Company—an association for which he would soon be called into question—amid suspicions that he'd offloaded most of the pelts before reaching Victoria.

The *Acapulco* was stripped of its flag, and the nineteen men still on MacLean's crew filed suit in court for wages they claimed he owed them. When queried about the length of his journey and the relative paucity of skins (only 379) aboard the *Acapulco* after his slow trip around the tip of Vancouver Island, MacLean blamed the press. He said the newspapers had made such a fuss over him since *The Sea-Wolf* had come out, comparing him so closely with the book's brutal title character that he had not been able to get a lick of work from his crew. The attention he drew was in part a sign of the times. Victorian ideas about manhood had spilled over into the new century, cross-pollinating with worries about the effects of urbanization and industrialization on "real men." No wonder the press fell all over itself, reinforcing the idea that MacLean was every bit as ruthless as his fictional counterpart. Even accounts that decried MacLean's callous deeds left no doubt he was a man's man—adept, fearless, and resourceful. Like Wolf Larsen, MacLean was a man to be abhorred and yet also admired, a man who was, as one reporter wrote, "half monster, half philosopher and all demon, who fought his way through life with scorn for the hearts that were broken or stilled that he might triumph in even the pettiest design." At the same time, MacLean was depicted as a social bandit, a Robin Hood–like man whose misdeeds could be overlooked because of how boldly he challenged authority.

MacLean's 1905 misdeeds succeeded in part because only a duly commissioned British naval officer could arrest a Canadian captain or seize a vessel docked in Victoria, so the American consulate's hands were tied. But in Washington, the US Department of Justice was preparing papers to request the pirate's extradition to San Francisco to face trial. Weeks later, a court order would force the sale of the *Acapulco* to settle the crew's demand they be paid. All in all, it was bad season for MacLean.

TWELVE

ROUGH RIDE

*A*MERICA'S TWENTY-SIXTH PRESIDENT, TEDDY ROOSEVELT, inherited the seal crisis from the three presidents who had dealt with it before him—William McKinley, Benjamin Harrison, and Grover Cleveland in both his terms. Of these, Henry Elliott had found a ray of hope in McKinley, who took office in 1897. Like Elliott, McKinley hailed from Ohio, and the two had mutual friends. But McKinley had also had his share of distractions, including the Spanish-American War and a revolving door of cabinet officials.

When an anarchist shot and killed McKinley in 1901, Vice President Theodore Roosevelt assumed the nation's highest office. At age forty-two, he became the youngest president in American history, embodying the bold mix of intellect and adventure to which men of the era—especially men of means—aspired. Having been urged outdoors as an antidote to his childhood illnesses, he valued wilderness as equal parts restorative and invigorating. He was also a man of letters—even after losing vision in one eye during a White House boxing match, Roosevelt read, on average, a book a day.

Teddy Roosevelt's dream of leading a contingent of "harum-scarum roughriders" into battle had materialized in 1898, when he recruited and equipped the Rough Rider regiment during the Spanish-American War, from which he emerged a hero following the Battle of San Juan Hill. The gore and victory of war thrilled Roosevelt as much as big-game hunting expeditions. Both activities encouraged robust manliness, a quality he deemed essential above all others, in an individual and in a nation. While wars were occasional, hunting seasons came around throughout every year, presenting endless opportunities for men like him to get out in nature and demonstrate their bravado. In one storied hunting incident when Roosevelt came face-to-face with a cougar, he jumped off his horse, shoved aside his hounds, and thrust a knife into the big cat.

Roosevelt and his trophy-hunting counterparts took a sort of wistful pride in killing big-game animals that were threatened with extinction in the American West. After all, Charles Darwin himself had declared extinction as natural a process as speciation. But happening naturally, both speciation and extinction occur so slowly as to be nearly imperceptible to the human observer. By the early twentieth century, it was becoming clear that humans were accelerating extinction rates at an alarming pace. Due to wanton killing, previously abundant species including the passenger pigeon were dangerously close to dying out. Like the seals, these birds had relied on safety in numbers for survival. But their numbers also made them easy targets, and the expansion of railroads across America after the Civil War gave easy access to those looking to profit from pigeon meat. When there was money to be made, no method was beyond the pale. In addition to shooting passenger pigeons, hunters attacked them with pitchforks, burned sulfur to asphyxiate them, and poisoned them with corn soaked in whiskey.

Coming from a wealthy New York family, Roosevelt eschewed such crude methods, not so much for the birds' sake, but because he believed that hunters should be noble in their pursuit. As he saw his beloved Western landscape changing, he began to worry over the future of big-game hunting. After the bitter "blue snow" winter of 1886 decimated the cattle Roosevelt kept as a gentleman's hobby, he spent three weeks in the autumn of 1887 hunting alone in the Dakota Badlands. To his dismay, he found the territory greatly changed. Beavers had been trapped into near extinction, causing ponds and creeks to disappear. Free-range cattle had trampled freshwater springs and deposited dung that soured the soils. Where he had formerly heard the honking of geese and the bugling of elks, there was now only silence.

Roosevelt believed the blame for this desolation lay squarely on swinish game butchers—that is, men who hunted not for sport but as a way of feeding their families and earning a living. After observing the changes in the Badlands, he resolved to take action. Returning to New York, he summoned twelve wealthy friends to a dinner party. United by their mutual love of sport hunting, they formed a social club devoted to preserving large game. Named for two of Roosevelt's favorite frontiersmen, the Boone and Crockett Club propelled concerns about nature and wildlife into the national conversation. Its membership soon expanded to ninety well-to-do hunters, all of whom wielded significant influence in Congress. Most of the club's activities centered on preserving habitat to ensure a continuing supply of big game to kill. But the group was also instrumental in establishing the New York Zoological Park, which would later become the Bronx Zoo.

Here at last was a leader who valued wildlife. True, Roosevelt also had no qualms about killing wild creatures, but he still professed to love what he killed. On a 1902 bear-hunting expedition in Mississippi, he made headlines by showing compassion for a bear. As was the norm with the wealthy, Roosevelt hunted with dogs and with a guide. On his second day out, he retreated for lunch while the dogs and the guide tracked a bear into a swamp. There, the cornered bear killed one dog and injured another. The hunting guide countered by cracking the bear over the head with his rifle. Then he tied it to a tree so the president could shoot it when he returned from his meal.

Eyeing the wounded bear malnourished from drought, Roosevelt declared there was no honor in shooting such a creature. Instead, he demanded the guide put it out of its misery. Learning of the incident, a political cartoonist sketched Roosevelt holding out his hand to a plump, cuddly bear. Seeing the cartoon, a Brooklyn candy-store owner made a stuffed animal as a tribute to the president, calling it Teddy's Bear. The world of plush toys has never been the same.

Like Elliott, Roosevelt wrote with passion and clarity about nature and wildlife, publishing such work even while serving in the White House. He was also a reformer, lauded for his moral energy, an attribute Elliott cultivated even as his own enemies sought to undermine him. The president may have known privilege all his life, which could scarcely be said of Elliott, but Roosevelt was nevertheless unafraid to confront wealthy men like Stephen Elkins if he thought their underhanded dealings were harming the nation. In addition to his NACC involvement, Elkins had made big money in the railroad business. Initially, Roosevelt had embraced a laissez-faire policy toward railroads, but after men like Elkins had gotten past the point of risk and were enjoying their comfortable fortunes, the president advocated for regulation and anti-monopoly actions.

In keeping with Boone and Crockett Club efforts, Roosevelt became known as a conservationist, contending that humans needed to manage wildlife so it would be perpetually available for their enjoyment and profit. In the meantime, Elliott was becoming known as a preservationist, advocating not only for the wise use of wildlife but also for preserving species for their own sake. If pointing to the seals' value helped their cause, Elliott would do so, but he also argued that the seals should be saved on principle, whether or not anyone ever made another penny on their pelts. At a time when expansion and progress were the nation's bywords, preservation was an unpopular stance. Men like John Muir, who lauded the intrinsic value of wilderness, were politely viewed by men like Roosevelt as extremists.

Still, Elliott hoped the president would intervene on the seals' behalf as he had done with the buffalo, joining other wealthy sport hunters to form the American Bison Society in 1905. By then, only three hundred American bison remained in the wild, and they had only survived because a few concerned individuals, including displaced Native Americans, had moved them onto a private preserve. Before Europeans arrived in North America, buffalo had ranged throughout most of the continent. As with the fur seals, their sheer numbers, coupled with their constant roaming about the plains, complicated attempts to estimate the species' pre-contact population. Experts disagreed wildly over the numbers of American bison, with estimates ranging between thirty million and one hundred million existing in the year 1500 CE. In 1805, expedition leader Meriwether Lewis described herds of buffalo so vast they darkened the plains. But as settlers replaced buffalo habitats with farms, plantations, and cities, the species vanished east of the Mississippi by 1833.

Killing buffalo was considered essential to westward expansion primarily because getting rid of them meant also getting rid of the Indigenous Peoples whose cultures centered on the buffalo, which was also their primary food. From two-bit saloon owners to high-rolling railroad barons, white men seeking to profit from settlement of the West needed the Native Americans out of the way. General William Sherman, fresh off his scorched-earth Civil War notoriety, was among those who advocated eliminating the buffalo as a means of eliminating the Plains Indians. A market for buffalo robes brought civilians into the fray. When a recession hit, as it often did during the last decades of the nineteenth century, any American man with a gun and a train ticket could go to the Great Plains and pick off buffalo by the hundreds, generating profits to keep his family afloat. These market hunters were followed by sport hunters, some of whom shot their quarry in decidedly unsportsmanlike fashion, including from the windows of trains that would slow down to allow them to shoot. The captions on one set of contemporary engravings depicting the remains of buffalo killed for sport read "300 a day for pleasure" and "100,000 for tongues."

In nineteenth-century America, the prevailing notion was that extinction was the price the nation must pay for progress. Manifest Destiny was at odds with any animal species that roamed the country's vast open spaces and sustained Indigenous populations, who the government was systematically working to exclude from their traditional lands. But the men who formed the American Bison Society, including Roosevelt, wanted to save enough buffalo to hunt. The group rounded up the few specimens they could find, then shipped them to New York aboard the same railroads that had accelerated the species' decline. There, the zoological society set up a breeding program, with the goal of eventually reintroducing buffalo to hunting reserves in the West. Naturalists who were aligned with David Starr Jordan suggested that a similar effort might be tried with the Pribilof seals—capture a few, ship them off to a zoo, and hope they would breed. Elliott scoffed at the plan, contending that the seals would fare poorly in captivity. As it turned out, he was right—the fur seals transplanted to zoos failed to thrive. This outcome mattered little to the wealthy men of the American Bison Society though. Fur seals were not the sort of creature men hunted for sport.

No matter what affinities Elliott and Roosevelt might have shared, Elliott could not use sport hunting as a means of engaging with the president on the seals' behalf. He could, however, play the diplomatic angle, and he had just the man to help him do it.

Secretary of State John Hay came from William McKinley's administration, and Roosevelt was not entirely happy about it. In some ways, Hay was a holdover from an even earlier era. His first stint in lawyering had been at a Springfield, Illinois, office located next door to the office of Abraham Lincoln. Hay so impressed Lincoln that when he became president the following year, Lincoln brought the twenty-two-year-old Hay to Washington to serve as one of his personal secretaries. After Lincoln's assassination, Hay devoted a number of years to co-authoring a ten-volume biography on the president whose life had ended so tragically. Reentering the executive branch as McKinley's secretary of state, Hay had endured the assassination of yet another leader.

Diminutive and elegantly dressed, John Hay wrote poetry and suffered bouts of melancholy, making him not the sort of man toward whom Roosevelt was constitutionally inclined. But in the abrupt transition following McKinley's death, the new president understood the need for continuity, and so he asked Hay to stay on as secretary of state. Before long, Roosevelt was complaining about Hay's careful, measured approach to foreign relations. Likewise, Roosevelt's shifting energies wearied Hay, who bemoaned the fact that an hour's wait yielded only a minute of conversation with the president. He also found Roosevelt too confrontational, whether dealing with the Moroccan crisis, the Turkish crisis, the Venezuelan crisis, the Panama Canal, or the Alaska boundary dispute. Eventually Hay decided he had had enough and readied his resignation. But then an unusually pleasant interaction with the president reminded Hay that, whatever Roosevelt's flaws, the president was bright, compassionate, and gentlemanly. Setting aside his qualms, Hay continued in his office.

Elliott had first reached out to Hay for help with the seals in 1900, while McKinley was still alive. Elliott pointed out the inadequacies of the 1893 Paris Tribunal, which had been extended, and offered to help draft a better solution. Careful not to overstep, he asked his Ohio congressman to deliver this message to the secretary of state. Hay's reply was characteristically measured: if Elliott could get authorization from Congress to reassess the seal problem and devise a solution, Hay would do what he could to see it through.

This was all the encouragement Elliott needed. He packed his bags and was in Hay's Washington office two days later. Their meeting heartened and inspired Elliott. While the Joint High Commission—meaning his nemesis David Starr Jordan and his associates—continued to advise lawmakers on the seals, Hay acknowledged that the scientific commission was in a holding pattern, doing nothing to address the problem.

At last, Elliott saw a clear path to victory. Dusting off his charts and surveys and watercolors, he again made the rounds in Washington. It was a long slog, amounting to four years of unpaid lobbying for creatures oblivious to his efforts, pushing for an agreement of mutual concession and joint control of the Pribilofs. The essence of such an agreement lay in acknowledging that no nation could claim ownership of a migratory species and, therefore, all nations with a potential interest in the species—as well as the creatures themselves—were best served by a cooperative agreement in which any value derived from the wildlife was shared by all. Given that extinction benefited no one, least of all the seals, the concept should have gotten traction. But Elliott knew that any proposal with genuine potential to stop the pirates would be a nonstarter with the British and Canadians until the United States stopped the land lease.

Not surprisingly, four senators who had provided legal services to the NACC were doing all they could to disincline their colleagues in the Senate to Elliott's efforts. But when the United States and Canada finally settled the Alaska boundary dispute in 1903, Elliott saw a window of opportunity. For years Great Britain and Canada had pointed to the sticky boundary matter as yet one more reason not to bargain over the seals, and now that was out of the way. The United States was generally perceived as having gotten the better end of the settlement, which in turn amplified the need for it to make concessions in any negotiations over the seals.

In 1904, nearly four years after Hay first charged Elliott with drumming up support for an agreement of mutual concession and joint control, Congress finally passed legislation that essentially overrode Jordan's seal commission and opened the door to a fresh round of negotiations with the British and Canadians. Thus authorized, one of the first actions Hay took was to purchase Elliott's field surveys and charts. For a family scraping by, this $5,000 transaction would be a godsend. But the arrangement was about more than money. It proved to the nation—and to Elliott himself— that his reputation as a seal expert had been restored.

During the remaining months of 1904, Elliott worked closely with Hay on his proposal, but Hay's health, never robust, began to falter. In addition to his usual bouts of depression, he was suffering from heart pain, nightmares, and coughing spells. He asked more and more of Elliott, who happily obliged. When Elliott suggested that the United States would need to make more concessions in order to get Canada to the table, Hay asked him to put the details in writing. After Elliott drew up a sample treaty, Hay asked him to confer with the British ambassador on the proposed terms, then seek approval from the chairs of the Senate's Judiciary Committee and subcommittee on Alaskan affairs.

Shortly before Roosevelt's 1905 inauguration, Elliott accomplished all that Hay had asked. Having passed muster with the British ambassador and the requisite committee chairs, the proposal of mutual concession and joint control was ready for government action. Hay asked Elliott to see the plan through the committees and then deliver it to the secretary of commerce, who would bring it to Roosevelt's attention. Assuming the plan met with Roosevelt's approval, the president would convey it to the British ambassador, with whom Elliott had already consulted. The odds for meaningful action had never been better.

Only days after laying out these plans, Hay was wheeled aboard a cruise ship headed for Europe, where he hoped the German baths would cure his ills. His condition had deteriorated and he could no longer walk without assistance. While Hay was abroad, Elliott proceeded to get approval from the Senate committees as the secretary of state had requested. Per his instructions, Elliott then marched the proposed treaty over to Secretary of Commerce Victor Metcalf for delivery to Roosevelt.

But Metcalf did not convey the draft to the president. Instead, he sat on it. As time passed, Elliott grew increasingly frustrated. Spring had arrived, and in only a few weeks the seals would begin hauling out on the Pribilofs. Unwilling to risk their future on further delays, he approached Roosevelt directly. The president assured him he would follow through with the British ambassador as soon as Metcalf delivered the necessary documents.

Armed with the president's assurances, Elliott again approached the secretary of commerce. Metcalf stalled, saying he would not do anything until Hay returned from Europe. That meant the loss of more precious time, the seal population dwindling by the day. Finally, in June, Hay returned from his voyage. The baths had failed to restore his health. Traveling back across the Atlantic, he had dreamed that Lincoln had returned from the dead—a bad omen, it seemed. Following his arrival, the ailing secretary of state met with Roosevelt on a White House porch. A screeching owl interrupted their conversation, then perched on a nearby window ledge, its large eyes trained on Hay. It was another bad omen, portending death. Not two weeks later, Hay's time on earth ended.

THIRTEEN

STALLED

*T*HOUGH NOT UNEXPECTED, JOHN HAY's death hit Elliott hard. For four years, Elliott had enjoyed having an ally in his cause, an official who trusted him even as David Starr Jordan and his associates worked to undermine his efforts. That Secretary Metcalf had blocked their project when it was so close to completion while knowing full well the frail state of Hay's health was to Elliott yet more evidence of the NACC's corrupt influence.

By 1906, Elliott had spent sixteen years warning of the fur seals' looming extinction and proposing ways to stop it. During that time, his enemies had never relented in their attacks. To feed his children, the youngest of whom was only seven years old in 1905, Elliott was now relying on credit extended to the family by his neighborhood grocer. There must have been times when he regretted ever taking up the cause, times when he was tempted to give up. These were only seals, after all, on a pair of tiny islands in a remote northern sea. If they went extinct, who would care?

Yet Elliott never wavered in his conviction that the seals were remarkable and worthy of his efforts. He had always been easygoing, especially in his youth, readily admitting his errors and poking fun at himself, but he had also never shied from expressing a contrary opinion when his convictions demanded it. Above all, he clung to his principles—corruption must be exposed, the truth must prevail, and those incapable of defending themselves must be defended. It was more than just standing up for the seals. Elliott was standing up for himself—his honesty, his reputation, his integrity. He was not about to concede to a collusion of moneyed interests.

And so, in his writing, his art, and his winter campaigns in Congress, Elliott kept hammering away at the proposition, much revised from his early thinking, that the Pribilof seals should be saved simply for their own sake. Since the fallout over his 1890 report, he had been unable to convince Congress to send him back to the Pribilofs. But in 1903, at his suggestion, the Senate finally sent four of their own to the islands. What they saw must have been shocking. The slaughter the senators witnessed there, coupled with Elliott's charts and graphs, made believers of them. Returning from their journey, they agreed with Elliott that the killing of northern fur seals under the NACC lease must stop.

This was a huge step in the right direction. The more abuses Elliott found, the more convinced he became that no private entity should control the seals. Corporations had had their chance to do right by them, and they had failed miserably. With this in mind, Elliott began working with Ohio Senator Joseph Foraker on legislation to end the Pribilof lease entirely. The senator minced no words in characterizing the land harvest as an operation marred by shame, guilt, and blunder. Yet despite Foraker's bulldog reputation, the bill failed in the face of opposition from Senators Stephen Elkins and Charles Fairbanks, both of whom were affiliated with the NACC.

Having reached a dead end in the Senate, Elliott hoped Roosevelt's new secretary of state, Elihu Root, would pick up where Hay had left off. A longtime figure in Republican circles, Root got along with Roosevelt much better than Hay had. From Roosevelt's earliest days in politics, Root had served as an advisor, assisting with messaging and speeches. In turn, Roosevelt described Root as the "brutal friend to whom I pay the most attention."

From the start, Elliott was uncertain about Root, who had built a legal career representing corporate interests. But there was no need to win Root over to the cause. The groundwork had been laid. The new secretary of state simply needed to pick up where Hay had left off by prompting Metcalf to move Elliott's proposal off his own desk and onto Roosevelt's.

Root took his time getting to Washington, arriving three months after the president appointed him. When Elliott got word that the new secretary of state was finally installed in his office, he hastened from Ohio to meet with Root. Arriving at the State, War, and Navy Building, a five-story structure on acreage west of the White House, Elliott mounted the granite stairs to the suite of offices occupied by the secretary of state. Arriving ahead of his 9 a.m. appointment, he delivered his calling card to the department's messenger, a man named Eddie who Elliott knew from many previous visits to the State Department while Hay was alive.

Eddie ushered him into the office of Root's assistant secretary, Robert Bacon. Elliott briefly reiterated the reason he had come, and Bacon led him into the elegant second-floor room where Root conducted state business. Morning light streamed in through huge windows, illuminating a group of men and women seated on chairs and sofas throughout the room. A stout bald man was expounding on some injustice he wanted Root to address.

Bacon approached the secretary of state, and the two of them quietly exchanged words. Root then told the people assembled there that they would need to leave. When the room had emptied, he said, "Ah! Elliott. Ah, yes. The keeper of the great seal."

Elliott laid out the papers he had brought with him: letters and memos Hay had sent him, along with supplemental documents related to the treaty he had drafted at Hay's request. As he made his explanations, Root interjected from time to time, saying things like "most interesting" and "I never heard these things before."

The meeting lasted two and a half hours. At its conclusion, Root told Bacon to gather up the official forms for moving the seal treaty forward. Then he grasped Elliott by the hand, saying, "Mr. Elliott, you call up here tomorrow about noon and look over the draft. You can come, can't you?"

"That's what I came down here for, and nothing else," Elliott said.

Departing, his heart felt light. After all the trials, all the attacks, and all the delays, success actually looked within reach. Smiling, he said on the way out of the State Department, "I've got the seal business going again, Eddie."

"I hope so, sir," Eddie said. "I hope so. Indeed, I do."

As Root had requested, Elliott returned the next day before noon. Bacon warned him that the secretary was busy, but he would make time to see Elliott. Sure enough, Bacon beckoned him into Root's office only a few minutes past twelve.

The reception was unmistakably cooler than it had been the day before. Root remained seated, squinting coldly at his visitor. Elliott waited for him to speak, but the secretary of state said nothing. Finally, Elliott broke the silence. "Well, Mr. Secretary, here I am. Where are those papers you asked me to look over?"

"Oh, yes," said Root. "I remember. There's nothing to be done yet. I must see the secretary of commerce first, and then the president."

Then Root dropped his gaze, swiveled in his chair, and began shuffling papers on his desk. Looking uncomfortable, Bacon set a hand on Elliott's shoulder. "That's all there is today for us, Mr. Elliott."

Elliott was stunned. Retreating to Bacon's office, he said, "Why, I don't understand this, Mr. Bacon. You know I have put the papers in his hands, which the president and the secretary of commerce had given me, and which declare that they approve of the treaty terms, and I have had the entire question under consideration in connection with those senators who are to pass on it finally. You saw and heard me recite those matters over to Mr. Root yesterday, and you saw me leave the papers with him."

"I'm as much surprised as you are," said Bacon. "But Mr. Root has his own way of doing things."

"Am I to wait here an indefinite period of time, at my own cost, away from my personal affairs at home, which need my attention? How long is Mr. Root going to be about this job?"

"Come up every day to my office," said Bacon. "I'll let you know how the thing goes."

So it went. Day after day, Elliott mounted the granite steps. Day after day, Eddie ushered him in to see Bacon. Day after day, the news was the same—no progress.

Finally, Elliott went home to Ohio. Three years later, he finally learned exactly what had gone wrong. After Elliott's first meeting with Root, Bacon had delivered the treaty documents, at Root's request, to a clerk for transcription onto the proper forms. Another clerk had noticed what was being transcribed and had alerted his father-in-law, who was a NACC attorney. The attorney then phoned NACC principal Darius Ogden Mills, who instructed him to see Root immediately to assert the company's objection to any treaty provisions that would halt the Pribilof land harvest. Mills was a wealthy railroad and banking client of Root's, and his direct objection was sufficient to convince Root to shelve the project. He stalled, then stalled some more.

The seals would not survive much more stalling. By all accounts, fewer than two hundred thousand remained. If the rate of decline continued, they would have only a few years left. Root's solution was to drop press releases chastising the seal pirates, which, in Elliott's assessment, served only to annoy the British and Canadians and undo the relations he and Hay had forged to smooth the way for the treaty of mutual concession and joint control. Meanwhile, despite the fact that regulations prohibited the killing of seals that were younger than two years old—identifiable only after the fact by a pelt that weighed less than five and a half pounds—the NACC was killing more and more yearlings. How could a species be preserved if its young were never allowed to reach breeding age?

As he pored over reports by Pribilof Treasury Agent Walter Lembkey, Elliott discovered alarming discrepancies. Among the various Treasury agents assigned to the Pribilofs, Lembkey was an aberration. He had a law degree, but rather than enter the legal profession, he had worked a series of unrelated jobs—newspaper editor, director of a YMCA, a recorder of deeds. In 1899, he had somehow secured an appointment as an assistant US Treasury agent overseeing the seal harvest on St. George Island. In 1901, he was promoted and charged with supervising the entire Pribilof seal operation, a post he would hold for a remarkable twelve years.

As pirates became ever bolder in their land raids, Lembkey was in the thick of it. In 1906, he had supervised the guards who captured the Japanese pirates, and he had overseen the burial of the pirates Kozloff had killed. At the same time, as Elliott noted, Lembkey was overseeing harvests that included five-pound pelts, indicating that the seals being killed were yearlings. Lembkey was also allowing the Unangax̂ to harvest seals from a reserve of two thousand young breeding males. Ostensibly, this was so the Unangax̂ would have seal meat to last the winter. However, Elliott discovered that the NACC was selling the pelts of these reserve seals, evidence of their commercial rather than subsistence use.

Between the stalled treaty and concerns that Lembkey was not properly managing the land harvest, Elliott was becoming discouraged. In July 1906, he read news of the Japanese raids, a situation even more desperate than he had imagined. Three weeks after the raids, Elliott received a letter sent from the Pribilofs. While US Treasury regulations forbade the Unangax̂—or anyone, for that matter—from discussing the seals without the express permission of Commerce Secretary Metcalf, the sender, whose identity Elliott protected, believed conditions were urgent enough to override this prohibition. The letter outlined what had happened during the raids and stated that such raids had not stopped—pirate ships were still circling the islands just beyond the three-mile territorial limit. Whenever the fog descended, the pirates would rush in and kill as many seals as they could. The letter writer pointed out that to defend themselves and the seals, the Unangax̂ were risking everything while barely subsisting. This was because their earnings were based on the number of pelts the NACC sold each year. For every pelt delivered to the company, a few cents went into a communal fund which was then divided among the Unangax̂. This system had provided enough to sustain the workers when the lessees were making a quota of one hundred thousand pelts per year, but with the sharp decline in the seal population, the communal fund was running dry.

Elliott recognized that the circumstances were dire. President Roosevelt was the person best positioned to intervene, but he was walking a diplomatic tightrope and didn't want to further enflame tensions with the Japanese. The plight of the Unangax̂ people was not likely to move him—Roosevelt had spoken of Native Americans being "savage tribes" that were scarcely more than wild beasts. Likewise, the seals, being wildlife with no hunting potential, were not a cause that inherently moved him.

By the end of 1906, Elliott was ill with anxiety and nearly devoid of hope. Roosevelt's State of the Union address, delivered late in the year, only made him feel worse. In it, the president admonished

Americans to tamp down their hostility toward the Japanese, warning of grave consequences if tensions ratcheted up. Toward this end, Roosevelt proposed that Congress ease the naturalization process for Japanese immigrants. Addressing the Pribilof seal problem, Roosevelt acknowledged Elliott's initial count of 4.7 million seals, even though Jordan and his associates disputed this figure. He also recounted the Japanese raids, saying the seal pirates had been "beaten off by the very meager and insufficient armed guards." Roosevelt made clear the horror of the incident, noting that the pirates had skinned many of the seals alive.

Going forward, the president vowed there would be more patrol vessels, more guns, and more ammunition to defend the islands. The pirates might have surprised us once, he suggested, but they would not surprise us again. He also called for stronger laws to expedite the conviction of any would-be raiders and pirates, adding that Japanese officials had assured him they would do what they could to prevent future incidents. At the same time, Roosevelt also aligned himself in no uncertain terms with the wealthy NACC shareholders. There had been, he declared, "no damage whatever done by the carefully regulated killing on land." Only the pirates were to blame for the precarious status of the fur seals, he implied, exactly as Jordan and the NACC maintained.

Even more troubling was what Roosevelt suggested about the future. If at any point, as the United States attempted to negotiate an end to seal piracy, it was "compelled to abandon hope," the president advised Congress to enact a law that would authorize the killing of every last Pribilof fur seal—a drastic measure designed to end the trouble in the Bering Sea once and for all.

FOURTEEN

STUBBORN TRUTH

*T*HE PIRATES KEPT COMING AND coming to the Pribilofs. In 1907, only a few months after President Roosevelt assured Americans of Japan's promise to prevent further raids on American soil, an Unangax̂ watchman on St. Paul Island alerted Agent Walter Lembkey that three schooners were headed directly for Northeast Point, the same landing spot where Kozloff had shot the Japanese pirates the previous summer. By chance, a revenue cutter arrived the following day, and the pirate ships retreated into the fog before another international incident developed.

But Lembkey was taking no chances. He directed as many guards as he could muster to stand watch at Northeast Point, provisioning them with food and coal in case they were needed for the long haul. Soon, the guards began hearing rounds of gunfire coming from the waters near the Zapadnie rookery. Leaving the others at Northeast Point, four of the guards rowed through the mist to station themselves closer to the gunfire. The shooting continued all afternoon, followed in the evening by cannon fire, which was how pirate ship captains guided butcher boats back to their vessels.

In the days and weeks that followed, the Unangax̂ guards spotted so many schooners that they eventually quit reporting them. Even the *Kensai Maru*, the ship that had carried five Japanese pirates to their deaths in 1906, returned to the Pribilofs in 1907. Reports continued to connect Alex MacLean with the *Kensai Maru*, which the Unangax̂ called "the Terror" because of the raids conducted from its butcher boats and the liquor allegedly smuggled by its crew. Whoever masterminded the exploits of the ship's crew was indeed a master of deception, painting its hull white and installing a fake smokestack so that, through the fog, the schooner was readily mistaken for a steam-powered revenue cutter. Crewed by "desperate men" of various nationalities, the *Kensai Maru* remained the most aggressive of the vessels targeting the Pribilofs that summer.

In mid-July, an Unangax̂ worker on St. Paul Island was hauling a load of sealskins when he encountered three Japanese pirates trudging toward St. Paul village. The worker ordered the men into his wagon and delivered them to Lembkey, who enlisted the help of a Chinese laundry worker as a translator, despite the fact that this worker spoke no Japanese. Mostly by pantomime, the pirates conveyed that their schooner had struck a rock and sank, leaving them stranded on the island. The contents of their backpacks—guns, compasses, and several changes of clothing—suggested they had lost their way while attempting to raid a rookery.

Lembkey dispatched several Unangax̂ guards to investigate the truth of the story. They returned after midnight, reporting they had found an abandoned butcher boat with the usual greased oars, salt, and skinning knives. Nowhere had they seen any evidence of a pirate ship having run aground. From the island's West Point, they had counted sixteen schooners, six of them within four hundred yards of shore, plus thirty butcher boats. From Northeast Point, another guard counted seven more schooners for an all-time record of twenty-three pirate ships circling St. Paul Island.

As promised, Roosevelt had ordered more revenue cutters to patrol the Bering Sea that summer, but as usual, the pirates were so adept at handing off skins and concealing evidence that they were rarely apprehended. The president had also made good on his promise of delivering a stronger arsenal for protecting the islands, but the extra munitions did not arrive until August, when the pirates were preparing to sail back to port. From then on, the guards would have at their disposal three Hotchkiss Mountain guns, twenty-five rifles, five revolvers, and two .30-caliber Gatling guns. No one on the islands, including Lembkey, had ever seen a Gatling gun before and apparently the guns did not come with instructions. Lembkey and eight of the guards spent the better part of a day cleaning and mounting them. In the end, Lembkey concluded that while the Gatlings were superb machines, they would require considerable upkeep.

Confidential sources told Lembkey that the principal owner of the Japanese vessels encircling the island was Rithets LLC, a San Francisco firm owned by R. P. Rithet. Rithet was also a principal in the Victoria Sealing Company, a collective representing the pelagic sealing fleet. Ties between Rithet and Alex MacLean went back to 1894, when US authorities had seized the *Favorite*, a schooner fitted out by Rithet and owned by MacLean. Rithet had many shady associations and was also involved in a sugar industry scandal along with Louis Sloss, yet another person made wealthy from profits on the Pribilof seals.

Elliott mistrusted Rithet, though by 1907 Elliott's trust admittedly was in short supply all around. His friend William Dall had betrayed him, as had his friends at the ACC by failing to do right by the seals. So had Secretary of State James Blaine, who had authorized a secret quota while suppressing Elliott's report; David Starr Jordan, who had urged the Smithsonian to cut ties with Elliott; and Secretary of State Elihu Root, who had reversed course on the proposed treaty of mutual concession and joint control.

Small wonder Elliott began seeing enemies around every corner. For years, his opponents had accused him of being vain, self-serving, and downright crazy. They rejected his every effort, dismissing him as a crank and a tiresome fellow, as Elliott put it. Still, he persisted, doggedly doing research and presenting facts and advocating for solutions to the seal problem. In many circles, his persistence was taken for sheer stubbornness, and to some extent, it was. Yet it was also typical of a whistleblower. As Tom Mueller points out in his 2019 book *Crisis of Conscience: Whistleblowing in an Age of Fraud*, whistleblowers often devote themselves to proving the wrongdoing they have brought to light. Sidelined from their usual work, often to the point of financial ruin, they throw themselves into investigations. As their life's focus narrows, they become increasingly isolated. Digging deep into evidence of wrongdoing, they may spiral into paranoia as their opponents attack them at every turn.

The sensible course of action was for Elliott to give up on the seals. So what if the species went extinct? The world would go on and Elliott would no longer be the target of attacks. He could paint other subjects, pursue other work. But he had already come so far and given so much. He held fast to his ideals, his sense of duty unwavering. It was up to him to make sure the "sin and shame" of extinction did not befall his beloved seals. Furthermore, he was fed up with "that venal backroom of officialism," which he was certain would do in the seals. A writer at the *Toronto Globe* made a similar observation: "If this fur seal business has ever been equaled for organized deception and hidden political influence, the world has never been enlightened by the disclosure."

Unable to count on officialdom, Elliott needed public support. Muir had his Sierra Club while Roosevelt had his Boone and Crockett fellows, but Elliott was essentially a one-man team, and a nearly penniless one at that. Secretary of State Hay had died before making good on his promise to pay Elliott $5,000 for his work, and Hay's successor, Root, had refused to honor the commitment. Elliott had been forced to secure a bank loan to pay his bills and offered the local grocer fifty of his watercolors to pay down his bills.

Anxious and increasingly desperate, Elliott reached out to William Templeton Hornaday, director of the New York Zoological Park. The two men had become acquainted in the early 1880s, when Elliott was still in the good graces of the Smithsonian and Hornaday was employed as the museum's chief taxidermist. As president of the American Bison Society, Hornaday had helped establish the zoo's buffalo breeding program and lobbied for preserves where buffalo that had been bred in captivity could be returned to the wild. Hornaday was also a big-game hunter and had hobnobbed with influential men, including Teddy Roosevelt.

As Elliott's daughter Edith later put it, the zoo director gave her father the "finest and rarest thing in this world, the heart and heartening of a friend." Of similar background and temperament, Hornaday was a light in Elliott's darkest hours. Orphaned at age fifteen, Hornaday had picked up taxidermy while on scholarship at a small Iowa college. Chance encounters with Andrew Carnegie and Teddy Roosevelt taught him the value of networking. Yet like Elliott, Hornaday never shied from a cause he believed in, even if it made him an outlier among his influential friends. He was a warrior, fierce and determined to win whatever battles he took on.

When Hornaday read news accounts of how the buffalo were being slaughtered on the Great Plains, he went first to the Smithsonian. There, he discovered not a single worthy specimen of the species. Embarking on what was billed as the last scientific buffalo hunt, he went west. He asked ranchers and cowboys to show him where he might find a buffalo to take for science. They laughed at him, calling such an act a waste of time and money. The buffalo were history.

It took him another two trips, but Hornaday finally got his specimens. He was also well on his way toward deciding that wild game was best shot with a camera, not a gun. Like Elliott, he eventually had a falling out with the Smithsonian, but in Hornaday's case, the separation led to opportunity when two wealthy New Yorkers tapped him to manage their zoological park. At first, the vision of these benefactors was akin to a living museum where the public could view specimens from threatened species. Eventually, Hornaday convinced them of a broader mission, working to save those species from extinction.

President Roosevelt's 1906 remark about killing off every last fur seal was what had convinced Elliott he needed Hornaday's help. The zoo director was sympathetic to the cause, but he did not think it prudent to get between Roosevelt and his secretary of state, not with the president remaining on edge over tensions with Japan. Better to let the politics sort themselves out, Hornaday reasoned. Elliott had little choice but to hope that he was right. Still, his frustrations mounted. Testifying before a Senate committee in 1908, Elliott let loose a string of accusations against his opponents that did no favors for either the seals or himself.

Hornaday's decision to wait for the political winds to shift proved to be the right one, as Roosevelt opted not to run for a third term. In his place, the party nominated William Taft. Roosevelt liked Taft but feared that his lackluster style would doom his candidacy. Taft managed to prevail, and while he vowed to continue Roosevelt's policies, he would choose a new secretary of state. From Elliott's perspective, Root's departure was one huge obstacle out of the way.

After Taft took office, Elliott approached his secretary of commerce, Charles Nagel, about ending the Pribilof land kill. A

Texan by birth, Nagel was no stranger to big business, having worked as a corporate attorney for beermaker Anheuser-Busch. While employed by the brewery in St. Louis, Nagel had led a posse of upper-class vigilantes who guarded streetcars during a strike against the transit company. But armed thuggery was an aberration for Nagel, who generally preferred a pen to a shotgun as a means of promoting his no-nonsense, pro-business agenda. He was a pragmatic man with little sentiment to spare for the seals. In fact, he made no attempt to hide his purchase of a seal fur coat for his wife.

Still, Elliott pleaded with Nagel to conduct an audit of the Pribilof agents' logbooks, confident the figures would reveal how government agents were mismanaging the land harvest. When that appeal fell on deaf ears, Elliott tried another angle, arguing that the land lease should be canceled because the NACC had acted in bad faith from the start. Alex MacLean was the lynchpin of this argument. Elliott explained how, in procuring the NACC lease, Herman Liebes had sworn that neither he nor any of his associates had any sort of investment in pelagic sealing. But after the Russians captured MacLean during his 1891 raids on the Commander Islands and seized the *J. Hamilton Lewis*, Liebes had filed for damages. In 1903, a tribunal at the Hague awarded Liebes—and by extension, his captain, Alex MacLean—$50,000 in damages to compensate for the seized vessel and lost revenues.

Elliott testified before a congressional committee that Liebes's perjury was grounds for revoking the NACC lease. But the NACC still had friends in high places, and a State Department official had Elliott's testimony struck from the record. So, Elliott took his complaint directly to President Taft, who delegated it back to Nagel, who delegated it to Fisheries Commissioner George Bowers. Nothing good for the seals had ever happened under Bowers's watch, which began in 1898 and would last until 1913 when some of his less-than-scrupulous dealings came to light. A West Virginia banker with no scientific background, Bowers responded to Elliott's concerns by circulating a document within the Fisheries Department titled "Elliotanna." In it, Bowers portrayed Elliott as a washed-up former expert, now somewhat confused.

More than ever, Elliott needed assistance. In the fall of 1909,

Hornaday finally sprang into action, working through the Camp Fire Club of America, which he had co-founded in 1897. Hornaday's Camp Fire Club, a different organization from the later-formed Camp Fire Girls, was conceived as a social outlet for outdoorsmen who lacked the high status required for membership in Roosevelt's Boone and Crockett Club. While Boone and Crockett members had to prove they had personally bagged several big-game animals, men were eligible for the Camp Fire Club if they had "camped on the ground in the howling wilderness" and either killed or made artistic portrayals of big game.

With its roster of influential men, the Camp Fire Club provided gravitas for Hornaday's efforts on behalf of the fur seals. Toward the end of 1909, he reached out to Montana Senator Joseph Dixon, who had helped set up the American Bison Society's buffalo preserves. Hornaday acknowledged missteps in prior efforts to save the seals—a not-so-subtle reference to Elliott's increasingly strident and defensive interactions with those who disdained him—and affirmed that now was the time to wipe the slate clean and start fresh with new champions in Congress.

Hornaday told Dixon that he had acquired a great deal of information on the seals in recent years and knew exactly what action was needed. To end the piracy, the United States required the full cooperation of other nations who also had a vested interest in the seals, especially Canada. To secure that cooperation, a ten-year moratorium on the land harvest would be necessary. After the seal population recovered and the land harvest was resumed, the US must participate in a profit-sharing arrangement that would give its international partners incentive to enforce a total ban on seal piracy. This was, of course, virtually the same solution Elliott had been advocating for nearly twenty years, but true to his vow to start anew, Hornaday did not mention that.

From Senator Dixon, Hornaday got results where Elliott had not. In part, this was because Hornaday had the Camp Fire Club behind him. He also had not been under attack for almost two decades as Elliott had. In his determination to protect the seals at all costs, Elliott had alienated potential allies with his zeal. As Senator Dixon admitted, Elliott's appeals to him had become so "voluminous and frequent" that Dixon had chosen to ignore them altogether. Now that Hornaday had lain the matter before him, though, Dixon said he was quite interested in helping to preserve the fur seals. In fact, he promised to take up a bill on their behalf when he returned to Washington in the spring. Conveying this news to Elliott, Hornaday warned that Dixon's pledge must be kept under wraps. They must be as "wise as serpents," Hornaday said, stifling all controversy and all history of controversy. He and Elliott were walking a field littered with land mines, and they would need to tread carefully, he warned, presenting the facts in a formal, passionless way and allowing logic to do its work.

Their efforts would begin with determining which department should have oversight over the Dixon bill and whether the profit-sharing component should be exclusive to Canada or should also include Japan. After the details were decided and the legislation drafted, Hornaday would publicize the cause, compelling the American people to choose sides: were they for the fur seals, or were they for the wealthy interests that exploited them? Though Hornaday and Elliott agreed that the seals should be preserved for their own sake, they also planned to play the money card. In the sixteen years since the 1893 Paris Tribunal, the US Treasury had lost out on millions of dollars in fur tariffs because the seal population had declined so sharply. And with the surge in piracy, the Japanese were now clamoring for the United States to settle damage claims from their seized vessels, including the *Kensai Maru*, which US authorities had finally apprehended in 1908.

Grateful for Hornaday's guidance, Elliott agreed to stay in the background, providing facts that would strengthen their case as needed. Hornaday made sure Dixon knew this, acknowledging that Elliott's indignant accusations of mistakes and wrongdoing had not landed well with certain government officials. Hornaday also made sure Dixon knew that in Hornaday's assessment, Elliott remained the world's foremost authority on the seals.

There was not a moment to lose. During the 1909 season, pirates had killed at least fourteen thousand seals, with the NACC slaughtering a similar number. Treasury Agent Lembkey claimed that 138,000 seals remained in the Pribilof herd. By Elliott's estimate, derived from poring over sales records from the London fur market, the number of surviving seals was only thirty-eight thousand, a far cry from the nearly five million seals he estimated in 1872. Individual rookeries also bore evidence of the decline. In 1872, Elliott had painted a vibrant scene at English Bay on St. Paul Island, estimating half a million seals in residence there. By 1890, that number had dropped by 99 percent to five thousand seals, and in 1909, according to Agent Lembkey's report, not a single seal remained at English Bay.

Even Taft's Secretary of Commerce Charles Nagel was now admitting that within a few years, the seals would be extinct. Meanwhile, David Starr Jordan and his cadre of scientists were recommending that the Pribilof reserves, protecting two thousand young seals from slaughter, were no longer necessary. One scientist from the Jordan contingent proposed instead that twenty orphaned pups be moved from the Pribilofs to an island in the Atlantic so that Canada could have its own fur seal population to kill. Elliott chafed at the idea. Even if the twenty pups survived transport to the Eastern Seaboard, he doubted they would adapt to an unfamiliar island halfway around the world, where their food sources and migration routes would be totally disrupted.

In February 1910, Senator Dixon made good on his promise to Hornaday, holding committee hearings on legislation that included a ten-year moratorium on the Pribilof seal harvest and a profit-sharing arrangement with Canada. The sole witness to testify was Hornaday, who came equipped with Elliott's prodigious charts, maps, chronologies, and paintings. The other prong of Hornaday and Elliott's strategy, the public relations effort, also got underway. With constituents beginning to take notice of the seals' plight, the Senate committee members unanimously called for an end to Pribilof lease, which was set for renewal later that spring.

Despite this victory, Hornaday worried that the committee would rescind its decision, bowing to NACC pressure tactics. The company seemed determined to harvest pelts until the last seal was gone, and Secretary of Commerce Nagel fully supported their position. As Hornaday pointed out, it had always been within Nagel's power to roll back the land-harvest quota, but even as extinction threatened,

Dixon bill with Nagel's revisions.

Nine days later, Fisheries Commissioner Bowers, Nagel's subordinate, authorized a 1910 Pribilof land harvest, with the government managing the slaughter instead of a leaseholder. The reason Bowers gave was simple and blunt—for their own good, the seals must be killed. It was the same twisted logic Jordan and his Fur Seal Advisory Board championed, that despite much evidence to the contrary, man knew better than nature.

Once again, the seals had been betrayed.

FIFTEEN

BUTCHERS OF LAND AND SEA

*N*o matter the seals' desperate plight, the United States intended to keep on killing them. Relying on Jordan's theory that slaughter was somehow necessary for the species' survival, Nagel and Bowers clearly intended to authorize as much killing as they wanted. And with the continuing land harvest, there was little reason for any country—not Canada, Great Britain, Russia, nor Japan—to join in any sort of meaningful negotiations to stop the pirates, who seemed intent on hunting seals to the bitter end.

The reign of terror that had begun in 1906 was still raging in 1910. In each of those five summers, at least twenty pirate ships had anchored around the Pribilofs, right outside the three-mile territorial limit. Under cover of fog, the land raids had continued. When butcher boats drifted off, US authorities sometimes caught up with them and arrested the seal hunters, who were mostly Japanese. They were tried in Alaskan courts, served light jail sentences, and then were sent home. If the killing of matkas had ever been a matter of shame, it was no more. Fur catalogs now advertised the skins of "black pups," meaning the tiny pelts of unborn seals. And prices for seal furs in general were higher than ever, bringing an average of $22 per pelt at auctions in London.

Despite the strong market, Alex MacLean had been conspicuously absent from the Pribilofs, at least as noted in official reports. Since US officials had indicted him for taking seals in the Bering Sea in the falsely registered *Carmencita/Acapulco*, MacLean seemed to have steered clear of San Francisco. With Herman Liebes dead and his other American financiers in legal trouble, there had been little reason for MacLean to risk capture and trial, even if the end result was only a fine.

Elliott was among those who believed that MacLean remained a threat. The pirate could continue his involvement in pelagic sealing without necessarily commanding his own ship, instead operating under wraps out of Hokkaido or Victoria. Elliott shared his concerns about MacLean with Nagel's Department of Commerce, but when pressed for proof that the real-life Sea-Wolf was working behind the scenes, Elliott hedged, wary of trusting Nagel. If Elliott's evidence got into the wrong hands, MacLean would dodge the authorities as he had in the past. Instead, Elliott offered to travel to San Francisco and Victoria to procure written statements that he claimed would make an iron-clad case against the pirate. Of course, he was in no financial position to make such a trip, and his offer was seen in some circles as an attempt at a government-funded fishing expedition. A Department of Commerce solicitor admitted to hearing rumors about MacLean working behind the scenes, but he found them too vague to pursue. In some ways, these rumors made sense, since high fur prices had previously drawn MacLean back to piracy. In addition, his experience and connections would have made him a valuable partner to Japanese pirates, and given his notoriety, it would have made sense for him to manage or advise other pirates rather than risk sailing himself.

There is also evidence that MacLean simply gave up seal pirating after the 1905 season. Short on funds, he spent at least some time in command of a twenty-ton fishing boat, the *Ella G.* Early in 1906, he told reporters he was taking the *Ella G* on an exploratory voyage, refusing to say where he intended to go. Setting out from Victoria, he sailed straight into a storm—no surprise, since it was the winter storm season. MacLean may have timed the expedition to discourage pursuit by American authorities who still had an open indictment against him.

A week later, when the *Ella G* failed to return to port, headlines in newspapers around the world declared that the infamous Sea-Wolf, Alex MacLean, had gone down with his ship. MacLean's wife, Lucy, held out hope, declaring to a reporter that her husband was not the sort of sailor who let a storm get the best of him. Sure enough, two days later, Alex MacLean sailed the *Ella G* into a port on Vancouver Island's west coast, the boat only a little worse for the wear. From there, he resumed the unspecified purpose of his expedition. By March, his crew had had enough of whatever it was that MacLean was fishing for—a smuggler's profits, perhaps—and all of them quit.

For the next several months—sealing season—MacLean's whereabouts were a mystery, but by August 1906, he was reportedly piloting a small Vancouver tugboat for an old friend. For an adventurous man like MacLean, this might have been a dull venture, but it no doubt paid the bills. Perhaps he had wearied of a pirate's life or was fed up with people expecting him to embody Wolf Larsen. Perhaps he was wary of the increasing attention Elliott and Hornaday were drawing to the butchers of land and sea, as Elliott liked to call those profiting from the seals. Perhaps he had decided that, with the seals' looming extinction, there was no sense carrying on until the bitter end.

In April 1908, MacLean hired out to run gunpowder by boat to construction camps on British Columbia's Skeena River. In October, he actually did go fishing. Once again, he was reported missing in a gale. Eight days later, he turned up in Metlakatla, a Native village in Southeast Alaska. This time, he had all his crew plus six tons of fish. None of these reports about MacLean preclude his ongoing involvement in seal pirating. But given the amount of interest in his exploits, both in popular culture and on the part of US authorities, it would have been difficult for him to escape detection, even in the murky world of pelagic sealing. Then again, MacLean had a knack for evading detection. Somehow, after years of prodigious spending, he was earning enough money after 1905 to maintain a comfortable home near downtown Victoria with his wife and daughter.

EVEN WITHOUT MACLEAN, THERE WAS PLENTY OF pirate activity. Based on reports of seventy-five to one hundred Japanese schooners headed to the Pribilofs, two US cutters were deployed in the summer of 1910 to circle the islands in what those in the service facetiously called a "Waltz Me Around Again, Willie" assignment.

The increased pirate activity made Elliott and Hornaday all the more determined to stop the land slaughter so that negotiations to end pelagic sealing could resume. Furious with Nagel for going back on his word and allowing his fisheries commissioner to authorize a seal harvest quota, Hornaday now understood why Elliott was so mistrustful of government officials. He and Elliott resolved that their common enemies—the enemies, ultimately, of the seals—must be resoundingly defeated, even if it required confrontations that Hornaday had been trying to avoid. Indeed, Hornaday was no longer inclined to rein in Elliott. From now on, they would both be in full-battle mode.

Hornaday began by confronting Nagel in a series of angry letters. What was the intent behind Taft's special message to Congress, he asked Nagel rhetorically. "TO STOP THE KILLING OF FUR-SEALS ON THE PRIBILOF ISLANDS," he wrote, emphasizing his point in all capital letters. "DID THE PRESIDENT, OR DID SENATOR DIXON'S COMMITTEE, OR THE UNITED STATES SENATE, INTEND FOR ONE MINUTE THAT YOU SHOULD GO ON IN THE BLOODY KILLING BUSINESS, WITHOUT A HALT? NO! A THOUSAND TIMES NO! AND YOU KNOW IT." Hornaday also bluntly reminded Nagel that the past fifteen years of fur seal history were "black with official blunders and some other things even more serious."

In response, Nagel offered the rather illogical claim that an end to the land slaughter would somehow play into the pirates' hands. He also reiterated Jordan's belief that killing most of the male seals was essential to preserving the species. These unproven theories further incensed Hornaday and Elliott. Based on Elliott's research, they were certain that Treasury Agent Lembkey, who now had full control of the land harvest, had been inflating the total seal count while simultaneously allowing the slaughter of yearlings. Hornaday told Nagel that he was getting bad advice from so-called experts who disliked Elliott for exposing their flawed science and misguided motives. In this correspondence, Hornaday had the backing of the Camp Fire Club—men whose "fighting blood was right up," as Hornaday told Elliott. Several of these men were attorneys who stood ready to lead the charge in Congress if Nagel refused to rescind the quota Fisheries Commissioner Bowers had authorized.

As Hornaday went after Nagel, Elliott went after Bowers, the erstwhile banker who Elliott claimed could not tell a fish from a whale when he first assumed his government post. Elliott considered Bowers a dangerous lackey acting on Jordan's behalf. Elliott also wanted to expose Treasury Agent Lembkey for defrauding the government with lax supervision and false reports on the land harvest. In turning attention to Bowers and Lembkey, Elliott hoped to expose connections to NACC shareholders, including Darius Ogden Mills and Stephen Elkins. Behind the scenes, he pressed sympathetic legislators to open an investigation.

Meanwhile, Hornaday continued to rally public support for the seals, primarily through the press. Elliott was positively gleeful about how such efforts could eventually expose backroom deals among those who had harmed the seals. "Publicity will shrivel them quick, and quick now for that publicity!" he wrote Hornaday. Toward that end, Elliott had letters ready to submit to Canada's leading newspaper, the *Globe and Mail*, which had previously commented on the corruption surrounding the US land lease. But the publicity efforts hit a rocky patch when the Associated Press misrepresented Elliott on two counts: a reporter claimed Elliott said President Taft had overruled Nagel's decision, when in fact the president had taken no such action, and also tagged Elliott as a member of the Camp Fire Club, which he was not.

Writing on official Camp Fire Club letterhead, Hornaday conveyed to Elliott the club's concerns over the interview, saying these errors annoyed some members of the club's wildlife committee. He also reminded Elliott, as Elliott surely knew, that scientific experts were working to discredit him. In further response to the misinformation, the New York Zoological Society instructed Hornaday to refrain from writing to congressmen and publishing newspaper editorials on the Pribilof seals.

Meanwhile, the land slaughter went on as Bowers had authorized, with Lembkey overseeing the kill. At the end of the 1910 season, Bowers garnered some publicity of his own by claiming that the government, under Lembkey's supervision, had made a net profit of

$500,000 by killing nearly thirteen thousand seals, compared to previous net profits of $150,000 when the lease was in effect. A deal for the US Treasury, Elliott noted privately, but at what price to the seals? By poring over records from the London fur market, he would soon learn that nearly eight thousand of the thirteen thousand slaughtered seals that year were pups, yearlings, and matkas who had been swept up in close drives. If such killing continued much longer, there would be no seals left to fight for.

The Victoria sealing fleet also had a strong 1910 season, the average catch higher than it had been in a decade. Sealskins attained at sea also accounted for an increasingly large percentage of the total number brought to market. Only a few ships had sailed under the Canadian flag in 1910, but R. P. Rithet's collective, the Victoria Sealing Company, was still paying dividends to its shareholders. Elliott took this as evidence that Rithet and his collaborators, perhaps including Alex MacLean, were profiting from Japanese sealing ventures.

Fortunately, public sentiment was finally turning in the seals' favor. Those who had once thrilled to tales of the real-life Sea-Wolf were now studying the Camp Fire Club's widely circulated press releases and its pamphlet "A Square Deal for the Fur Seal." With the public increasingly rooting for the seals, Hornaday decided it was time to confront the scientists (or "scientists," as Elliott always referred to them) who opposed their efforts, chiefly David Starr Jordan. In November 1910, Hornaday traveled across New York City to meet with Jordan at the Holland House, an upscale Fifth Avenue hotel. At the time, Jordan was embroiled in fish conservation efforts along the US-Canadian border. Unlike the seals, which the United States still claimed as their own, fish quite clearly belonged to neither nation. Jordan was pushing to solve this dispute by instituting federal licensing requirements for fishermen, but US State Department attorneys said Jordan's proposed licensing mandate was likely unconstitutional.

On every side, the fishing industry was attacking Jordan for his efforts, a problem Elliott understood all too well. Jordan's overtures with Canada had fallen flat in part because he had previously antagonized the Canadians by insisting that only pelagic sealing was a threat to the Pribilof seals. Jordan also lacked congressional support. While Elliott had been able to recruit congressional leaders to his cause by exhibiting paintings of dewy-eyed matkas and their adorable pups, it seemed that only an ardent ichthyologist like Jordan became passionate about saving fish. Had Elihu Root more vigorously pursued the seal treaty that Elliott had crafted, Jordan would have at least had a precedent for an international fisheries agreement.

In light of these challenges, Jordan was more conciliatory on the seals during their meeting than Hornaday had expected. Predictably, Hornaday disagreed with Jordan on several points: Jordan's claim that the seals were holding their own, his stubborn assertion that killing was necessary to preserve the species, and his trust in Nagel. But in a huge turnaround, Jordan agreed to support a five-year moratorium on the land slaughter as long as the preamble to any such measure asserted that the slaughter had no deleterious effects whatsoever on the seals. In other words, Jordan wanted language that would preserve his pride and reputation.

Elliott and Hornaday had major hurdles yet to tackle, but they felt they were now well positioned for success if they continued to work strategically. Despite what they viewed as Nagel's treachery— the man was a crook, Hornaday said privately, and eventually Elliott came around to agreeing—the Senate had done away with the Pribilof land lease. Elliott and Hornaday still wanted a moratorium on the land kills, and Elliott also wanted investigations into the corruption that had brought the seals to the brink of extinction, but at least the shadowy interests of wealthy shareholders were no longer in play now that the government had taken over management of the seals. And without the land lease, the United States was much better positioned to negotiate the agreement of mutual concession and joint control that Elliott had long sought. Now they needed the Taft administration to see it through.

SIXTEEN

SEAL DEAL

*A*s ELLIOTT HAD BITTERLY AND sometimes publicly complained, Elihu Root had done little during his five years as secretary of state to advance an agreement to stop pelagic sealing. But with a new administration and the end of the Pribilof lease, that agreement now seemed within reach. Hoping to ensure that neither apathy nor corruption sidelined current efforts, Elliott and Hornaday leveraged their relationship with Senator Dixon and his Natural Resources Committee, demanding Taft's secretary of state, Philander Knox, produce State Department documents that would reveal whether his predecessor had made a good faith effort to negotiate on the seals' behalf.

A portly man with an aloof, butleresque gaze that had grown sterner with age, Philander Knox was a privileged sportsman like Teddy Roosevelt. A native of Pennsylvania, Knox was a charter member of the exclusive South Fork Fishing and Hunting Club, the group responsible for the infamous Johnstown Flood. To create a picturesque hillside lake for its wealthy members to enjoy, the club patched up an earthen dam on the Little Conemaugh River that had fallen into disrepair. In 1889, a large rain event caused the poorly engineered and poorly maintained dam to fail. Twenty billion tons of water flooded the working-class towns below the dam, killing over two thousand people. Amply stocked with attorneys, including Knox himself, the club fended off attempts to hold its members liable. To his credit, Knox volunteered funds from his personal assets to help rebuild the stricken communities.

The flood did little lasting damage to Knox's reputation. He went on to work for some of the nation's largest industrialists, notably as legal counsel for the Carnegie Steel Company. Shortly before William McKinley's assassination, the president had tapped Knox to serve as his attorney general. In that role, which continued through the early years of Roosevelt's presidency, Knox showed himself not entirely beholden to industrialists by initiating anti-trust actions against railroad barons. As a sportsman, his interest in wildlife aligned with Roosevelt's. Ruling that game reserves within national forests needed to be established by Congress and not by the secretary of the interior, Knox lamented that the process could not be more expedient. As Taft's secretary of state, Knox engaged in dollar diplomacy, which had the goal of advancing American commercial interests abroad. But after the Senate ended the land lease, commercial interests were no longer at play in the Pribilofs. Instead, the government managed the seals, an arrangement with more socialist overtones than a man like Knox was inclined to admit.

While Knox's predecessor, Elihu Root, had done little to further an international agreement to stop seal piracy, he had not been entirely negligent. In 1906, he floated an offer to the British ambassador: if Britain and Canada would stop sanctioning pelagic sealing, the United States would share 20 percent of its land-harvest profits with Canada. This was a step toward the mutual concessions Elliott had envisioned, but as Canadian officials pointed out, Root's proposal did not allow for joint control. American leaseholders could kill all remaining seals, as Roosevelt had threatened, and Canada would have little to show for the arrangement.

When Knox became secretary of state in 1909, he faced an additional hurdle. In May of that year, Britain had established the Canadian Department of External Affairs. Though Britain's Parliament had made Canada a dominion in 1867, America's northern neighbor would not achieve full independence until 1931. Establishment of Canada's Department of External Affairs, later called the Department of Foreign Affairs, in 1909 was one in a series of steps that was moving Canada closer to full independence.

For Knox, the move meant that he now had to deal with both the British ambassador and Joseph Pope, who was appointed head of Canada's Department of External Affairs. Like Alex MacLean,

Pope was originally from Canada's eastern maritime region. Immigrants on Prince of Wales Island, where Pope grew up, reveled in their British heritage. But when Pope took over as the first "under-secretary" of the Department of External Affairs, he felt considerable pressure to agitate on behalf of Canada. Now that London was no longer entirely in charge of Canada's foreign policy, Pope had a duty to look out for his country's interests above those of all others. Whatever concessions Canada might make in a seal agreement, Pope wanted something equitable in return.

One sticking point for Pope was the huge discrepancy between Elliott's estimated seal counts, which he based on figures from the London market, and the official figures from the United States, which were based on Agent Lembkey's rosy estimates. If there were 50,000 seals left in 1908, as Elliott had claimed, and 150,000 left in 1909, as Lembkey maintained, then pelagic sealing could scarcely be blamed for harming the seal population. Why should Canada make any concessions at all? Further, Pope believed that Canada had more at stake than the United States in any seal-related negotiations. As he saw it, the US was concerned solely with profits. For Canada, the issue was freedom of the seas.

Besides addressing multiple and sometimes conflicting representations of Canadian interests, Knox had to deal with Jordan and his scientists, who, under the auspices of the 1909 Fur Seal Advisory Board, had been making foreign policy recommendations. The board wanted a conference of diplomats and scientists from the United States, Russia, Japan, Canada, and Great Britain to negotiate an agreement to end pelagic sealing. Knox wanted the scientists to stay out of foreign policy.

As Elliott continually pointed out, Canada was the lynchpin to a broader international agreement to end seal piracy. With heightened public interest in the seals and legislation that ended the land lease, plus some prodding from Great Britain, Knox was able to hammer out a tentative arrangement with Pope. Under its terms, Canada would enforce a fifteen-year ban on pelagic sealing in the eastern Bering Sea. In exchange, the United States would share 20 percent of the profits from any land harvest with Canada. However, this agreement would not take effect until a broader North Pacific treaty was negotiated to extend the pelagic sealing ban to Russia and Japan.

In May 1911, scientists and diplomats from the United States, Canada, Great Britain, Russia, and Japan gathered in Washington, DC, to discuss possible terms for a first-ever international wildlife treaty. As Knox feared, each delegation's scientists skewed the facts to suit their own national interests. Given all that had transpired, it was no surprise that Elliott had not been chosen to represent the United States. He was, however, called to testify before the delegates, and at least one foreign diplomat noted that he seemed to know more about the seals than any of the other scientists.

Though not part of the deliberations, Elliott believed he could help the process along by prodding Congress to open investigations into years of fraud and deception in the US seal industry. In effect, he was blowing the whistle all over again, offering evidence he had been accumulating for over twenty years, going all the way back to the secret 1890 quota, granted during the first season of the NACC lease. In short order, a congressional committee on expenditures chaired by Congressman John Rothermel of Pennsylvania opened the inquiry Elliott sought. This was an important development, one that Elliott had hoped for. At the seal negotiations, foreign delegates took note. Perhaps the United States was concerned with more than lining wealthy pockets after all.

After the United States revealed the details of the tentative agreement with Canada, much posturing, along with a few blunders, peppered discussions at the seal conference. The Japanese wanted terms similar to the Canadians but argued that they deserved a larger share of the Pribilof land-kill profits because their pelagic sealing industry was now more robust than Canada's, and so they stood to lose more by ending it. This demand inflamed the US delegation, which proceeded to revive Teddy Roosevelt's threat to exterminate all the seals. So much for the moral argument against killing seals, which delegates liked to bring up as an added bargaining chip whenever it suited.

Pope called this bluff, claiming that Canada was not especially invested in the Pribilof seals. If the United States killed them all, only a few hundred pelagic sealers in British Columbia would be out of work, and a good number of those were Indigenous Peoples, so overall, Canada would get by. This cavalier claim angered Nagel, who was part of the American team. If sealing truly had so little impact on the Canadian economy, Nagel suggested that Canada should relinquish a portion of its 20-percent share of US profits to Japan. But Japan wanted more than a percentage of a percentage—their team demanded a 35-percent share in profits from both the Russian and American land harvests. Even Pope, who was hoping to align Canada's interests with Japan, thought that seemed like extortion. With negotiations at a standstill, the Japanese began to talk of withdrawing from the conference and going home. This alarmed Pope, who recognized that Canada's interests were much like Japan's. Both nations shared the view that efforts to curtail pelagic sealing threatened their maritime rights, and while Japan once had had its own Kuril seals to protect, the population had declined to the point that they might as well have had none, like Canada.

Eager to keep the Japanese at the table, Pope circled back to the moral argument for saving the seals. He reminded his fellow diplomats that pelagic sealing was wasteful, and if it continued it would surely lead to the fur seals' extinction. Public sentiment was with the seals, he asserted, and nations that failed to act on their behalf risked the world's moral judgment. With these considerations in mind, Pope offered a compromise: Canada would split 30 percent of the American and Russian land-kill profits with Japan to compensate for a full ban on pelagic sealing.

For Elliott, Pope's offer signaled that a deal was within reach—and not just any deal, but one that aligned with what he had been suggesting all along. Even Nagel would be under pressure to agree. On May 26, 1911, Elliott sent a telegram from Washington, relaying the hopeful news to his son Frank, now grown and living in Seattle:

> *Japs were coaxed by Canada and Russia yesterday, to agree on the "Elliott plan"; they would not treat with Nagel and [US negotiator] Anderson; my settlement will come at once, after signatures are appended. Hurrah! Am in fine health, and flush with satisfaction.*

> *Henry W. Elliott*
> *c/o Smithsonian*

But the settlement and signatures did not come quite as soon as Elliott had predicted. The Japanese balked at Pope's proposal, threatening again to pull out of the discussions entirely. At this point, the United States had too much at stake to let the conference fall apart without an agreement. Increasingly invested in the "square deal for the fur seals" that Camp Fire Club pamphlets championed, the public might be outraged if the United States did not do everything possible to get a treaty banning seal piracy. Nagel reached out to President Taft, who then sent a carefully worded telegram to be conveyed to the Japanese emperor. In it, he warned that without an agreement, the fur seals would surely become extinct, and if the Japanese pulled out of negotiations, they would shoulder the blame.

After the message was delivered, the Japanese delegation began negotiating in earnest. For a nation still finding its place among world powers, reputation mattered a great deal. In addition, Japan was trying to hammer out a trade agreement with the United States and could not afford additional anti-Japanese sentiment. With prodding from Tokyo, the Japanese delegation agreed in principle to the terms Pope had proposed. In exchange for enforcing a complete ban on seal piracy, Japan and Canada would each get a 15-percent stake in profits from the Russian and American herds. They would also each get a $200,000 advance on those profits from both Russia and the United States. In exchange, the US and Russia reserved the right to manage, as they saw fit, the seals that bred on their soil.

This was the treaty of mutual concession and joint control that Henry Elliott had championed for so many years, the treaty he believed would have been signed in 1905 had John Hay not died. Most significantly, from Elliott's perspective, it included a clause that bound all parties to the agreement even if Russia or the United States were to declare a moratorium on the land kill to allow their seal populations to recover. As he had long recognized, the arrangement was by necessity pragmatic, hinging on the economic value of the seals instead of their inherent value as wildlife—and of course, without economic value, the seals would never have been threatened in the first place. Although Elliott had long ago come to believe the species must be saved for its own sake, he and Hornaday recognized the need to come at the problem from both angles, economic and moral, in order to avert extinction.

Representatives from the United States, Great Britain, Canada, Japan, and Russia signed the North Pacific Fur Seal Treaty on July 11, 1911. It was a precedent-setting agreement, the first that acknowledged that the world's wildlife could and should be protected by nations working together. The principles of international cooperation embodied in the 1911 Fur Seal Treaty would facilitate the negotiation of the 1916 Migratory Bird Treaty, which Hornaday would champion using many of the public relations tactics that had proved successful with the seals. Later would come far-reaching international agreements like the Convention on International Trade in Endangered Species, the Convention on Migratory Species, and the Convention on Biodiversity, with specialists in international law to aid in the enforcement of each.

Even if Elliott had been able to foresee the far-reaching impact of the agreement he had fostered, he had more immediate concerns. The 1911 treaty promised to put the seal pirates out of business for good, but only if legislative bodies in the signatory nations ratified it. In the United States, congressional support was far from certain. Elliott also understood how much the species still needed a land-kill moratorium. Otherwise, with the powers Nagel had retained for his department, Lembkey and Bowers could easily mismanage the Pribilof seals into extinction, even with the pirates sidelined.

Elliott also wanted to make sure that Congressman Rothermel's fraud and corruption investigations were thorough and complete. Privately, Elliott shared with Hornaday a "Codex Criminus" in which he detailed the people and offenses he wanted Rothermel to investigate. Toward this end, he shared with Rothermel's congressional committee volumes of data and documents he had amassed alleging mismanagement of the Pribilof seals. In session after session, the committee studied this and other evidence. They also heard witness testimony, much of it focused on Elliott's assertion—backed up with data from agent logs and sales figures from the London market—that Treasury Agent Walter Lembkey had allowed hard, close drives to the killing fields that had drawn pups and matkas into the slaughter.

In a break from the tedium of facts and figures, Hornaday livened up the Rothermel proceedings by arranging for a trained seal to perform. Since fur seals fared poorly in captivity, the entertainment was provided by a hair seal. In demonstrating its innate capacity to learn, the seal also showed committee members it knew who its friends were. When the trainer mentioned Fisheries Commissioner Bowers, the seal hid under a chair. When the trainer mentioned Professor Elliott, the seal barked and waved its flippers.

The seal's opinions aside, Elliott's opponents also had their day before the committee. During his appearance, David Starr Jordan reneged on what he had told Hornaday at the Holland House meeting: he would not support a moratorium after all. Jordan also renewed his accusations about Elliott's lack of scientific training, calling him a discredited adventurer. And in a bizarre move, Jordan accused Elliott of having worked for twenty years on the side of the pirates, though Jordan could produce no evidence of this.

Jordan remained as committed to opposing the land-kill moratorium as Elliott was to getting it enacted. Unsurprisingly, Secretary of Commerce Charles Nagel sided with Jordan, claiming that such a moratorium would cause signatory nations to withdraw from the 1911 Fur Seal Treaty. But the treaty also included language that nullified this threat: should Russia or the United States suspend their seal harvests, the treaty stipulated they compensate Japan and Canada. In fact, this provision had already been put into effect when Russia instituted a harvest moratorium on the Commander Islands shortly after the treaty was signed. As Congress deliberated over a pause in the land kill, the worst the Canadians could muster by way of objection was that the press might have a heyday with it. The Japanese politely asked that Taft consider vetoing a moratorium if Congress passed one, but they showed little sign they cared much one way or the other.

At the crux of the matter was science—specifically, the recommendation by Jordan and his associates that, for the good of the seals, the government should kill up to 95 percent of the bachelors each year. Jordan's secretary, George Clark, who had no scientific training, proposed that this slaughter would not harm the species because, in his assessment, the seals had reached a state of equilibrium back in 1906, never mind the alarms he had raised in 1909. Clark vowed to perpetually fight any attempt to enact even a temporary moratorium in order to keep the beachmasters from trampling pups. With a convert's zeal, he also disparaged Hornaday for letting Elliott do his thinking. After all, Clark noted smugly, Hornaday had never even been to the Pribilofs.

In a scathing response, Hornaday pointed out that if Clark was going to accuse Elliott of doing all the thinking, Clark had best be prepared to also give Elliott 100 percent of the credit for saving the Pribilof seals. As for the accusation that Hornaday had never taken a government-funded pleasure cruise to the Pribilofs, as Hornaday put it, he pointed out that Clark, Jordan, and their cohorts had not traveled to the islands until twenty years after Elliott made his first seal studies there. Hornaday also chided Clark for his continued insistence that the seals be treated like livestock, an error in thinking that Elliott had long ago acknowledged. "That pernicious idea shows how easy it is for experts to start with a wrong premise and reach wrong conclusions," Hornaday wrote. "Even on 'secondhand information,' I can safely assure you that the fur seal is yet a wild animal, with some of the wildest habits imaginable, and that it is not to be handled as domestic cattle are handled. In the breeding of fur seals, Nature is yet superior to Man; and the way to bring up any decimated species is to protect it with a long-closed season and then let it severely alone."

With this, Hornaday resurrected the larger question of whether humans should perpetually dominate nature, controlling and bending it for what they perceived as gain. Though man's domination of nature had long been assumed, the excesses of the Industrial Revolution and the Gilded Age contributed to a growing sense that nature was better off left alone. Declaring that an army of experts could not convince him that Mother Nature could be improved upon, Nebraska Senator Gilbert Hitchcock attached an amendment to the Fur Seal Treaty ratification bill. To Elliott's delight, it called for a ten-year moratorium on the Pribilof land harvest.

Nagel tried to block Hitchcock's amendment, arguing that it would make the United States look bad. He succeeded in getting the moratorium cut to five years, but it remained attached to the bill. In

August 1912, thirteen months after US delegates signed the North Pacific Fur Seal Treaty, Congress ratified it in legislation that included this five-year land harvest moratorium. After decades of abuse, some of it self-inflicted, Henry Wood Elliott had finally emerged the victor. Though others had abandoned the fight to save seals, he had never given up. Despite attacks on all fronts, especially from fellow naturalists, Elliott had succeeded in his goal of stopping seal piracy through a treaty of mutual concession and joint control. He had also achieved the land-kill moratorium he believed essential to the seals' survival.

Elliott's victory lap including a lengthy *New York Times* article celebrating his accomplishments. "No More Slaughtering of the Seals for Five Years" read the headline. The piece featured a full-length photo of Elliott and side-by-side reproductions of two of the paintings he had used in his relentless advocacy. "You can't kill any seals for five years to come, no matter how bloodthirsty you may be or however much you want to sell the skins of mother seals and their infants," the article began. The reporter went on to denigrate David Starr Jordan as the leader of the "so-called experts" who armed the seal "murderers" with a "semblance of argument for their bad cause." Also named as enemies of the seals were Commissioner Nagel and Treasury Agent Lembkey. In their enthusiasm to turn a profit for the government, the article said, they had neglected to look beyond the present administration to a potentially seal-less future. In contrast, Elliott had for years fought single-handedly for the seals' survival. Joining forces with Hornaday and the Camp Fire Club, their collective efforts were "honest and unmercenary." Now "almost an old man," Elliott "never had an axe to grind," the reporter wrote.

After all he had suffered, after all he had put himself through, Elliott was finally getting the recognition he deserved. Sadly, it would not last.

SEVENTEEN

NEVER SAY DIE

A STEAMSHIP SLUICES THROUGH CHOPPY WAVES, sea and sky twinned in gray, the air damp and thick and smelling faintly of salt. Beneath the waves, spot-bellied pollock swarm, feeding on plankton stirred by summer storms. Beyond the ship's wake swims a matka intent on reaching her pup, her belly plump with fish and her teats full of warm milk. Watching from the deck, Henry Wood Elliott feels a familiar sense of wonder and excitement. Ahead, shrouded in fog, are the islands that gave his life shape and purpose. For twenty-three years he has been away, his longest stretch ever. And yet he still feels the magic, the sense that he is going home to a place that has never stopped calling to him. At sixty-seven, he has long ago lost the innocence he had at age twenty-six, when he first journeyed to the Pribilofs with the enthusiastic notion that he would enjoy easy success at the intersection of art and science. Back in 1872, he could never have imagined himself in the throes of politics and international diplomacy, nor could he have imagined how much he would lose along the way.

It is 1913, and pirate ships no longer bob in a daisy chain around the Pribilof Islands. The revenue cutter transporting Elliott has made a peaceful journey—no chasing of vessels through the fog, no volleys of gunfire sounding all around. The treaty of mutual concession and joint control is working exactly as Elliott knew it would, with the United States, Japan, Great Britain, Canada, and Russia committed to the protection of the migrating fur seals. Overhead, gulls careen, raucously screeching, the engine noise seeming to attract them. Steam now rules the sea, the clippers favored by men like Alex MacLean having faded into history. Sailors have had to either leave the sea for steam, as they put it, or give up a mariner's life altogether. When war comes, as it soon will, it will be the death knell for sail-powered ships.

Beyond the pounding of the waves, Elliott hears a faint rumble that grows to a steady roar. Ahead, a dark shape emerges from the fog, revealing the curve of a hill. Vaguely at first and then with precision, he spots a rookery filled with clamoring seals. This is the homecoming he has long dreamed of, one that few humans will ever be privileged to enjoy. Nothing has changed, and yet everything has. Coming ashore from the steel-hulled *Tahoma*, which recently rescued a commercial steamship in the eastern Aleutians, Elliott walks among family and friends from long ago. Many are old now, as is he. The young ones, born since his last visit, know him only by reputation, as Alexandra Milovidov's husband, the man who saved their seals.

But Alexandra is not at his side. Months ago, as the leaves on Lakewood's big oaks and maples turned orange and red, he and Alexandra were forced to sell their Ohio home. For a time, Alexandra will live with their son Frank and his wife and daughters. Later, she will move to California, to live with their oldest daughter, Grace, near her brother's poultry farm. Henry and Alexandra will remain legally married the rest of their lives, but they will never again live together. Publicly, Alexandra will say nothing of why she left her husband, though many assume she simply tired of his seal obsession, which cost them nearly every comfort they had known. Now grown, the ten Elliott children have scattered across the country, the youngest ones moving in with their older siblings. Henry Elliott has put most of his papers and paintings in storage. He now lives in a rented room in a Washington, DC, boardinghouse.

Much has also changed on the islands. The drafty two-hundred-square-foot wooden houses built by the ACC forty years earlier are aging poorly, with only one outhouse for every seven households. With the lessees out of the picture, the Unangax̂ are now considered wards of the United States government, which controls their lives down to the smallest details, including whether or not they may move from the islands. Funds designated by Congress to sustain the Unangax̂ through the five-year moratorium have been woefully inadequate, a pittance of what they might have earned had they been able to live where they chose.

The Pribilof Islanders are increasingly distraught. They want the government to recognize that they have been loyal, industrious workers at a distasteful enterprise that contributed millions of dollars to the US Treasury. They want the freedom to hunt and fish when and where they choose. If they must abide by rules that prohibit them drinking alcohol, they want the US government agents who keep tabs on them to abide by the same rules. They want the freedom to speak their own language without retribution, and they want to be able to reopen the church school so their children can learn Russian again. But it is 1913, and remedies will be a long time coming. At least the seals are doing well. With piracy ended and the land-kill moratorium in place until 1917, the population is beginning to rebound as Elliott predicted it would. In addition, none of the threats David Starr Jordan warned of have come to pass. Beachmasters are not trampling pups nor tearing matkas to shreds, and no pups are dying of hookworm.

Dispatched to the Pribilofs by Rothermel's committee, Elliott rises early each morning. He treks over wild grasses, gentian, and creeping pea-vines to visit rookeries on the island's farthest reaches. As always, he makes careful notes and sketches. He estimates the seal count, believing his data will discredit Jordan's 1897 seal census, which Jordan in turn had used to dispute Elliott's original 1872 count.

Though the seals are faring well, full recovery is still in the distant future. From Old John Rock, Elliott surveys a scene even more desolate than the one he witnessed in 1890. From Grand Parade Pinnacle in 1874, he had observed not a single patch of vegetation because a seemingly endless parade of 150,000 bachelor seals marching to and from the sea had kept the ground bare. Now a luxurious mat of mosses, grasses, and flowers covers the area, with only tufts of matted fur and hair to suggest the bachelors had ever been there at all. At other rookeries, Elliott takes comfort in familiar scenes. With tender, intelligent eyes, matkas gaze at him as they fan themselves with one flipper, heads tossed back as if they have not a care in the world. Pups huddle against the rocks, mewling for food, their distress only temporary. Now, no pup will starve because pirates have shot its mother. With no drives to the killing grounds for Jordan's proposed 95-percent slaughter, a good many of the bachelors that frolic in the waves will now live to become beachmasters, restoring the breeding capacity of their species.

Elliott has brought a camera with him, but he still favors sketches and watercolors. His renderings from this 1913 visit depict tranquil scenes—the seas calm, the skies placid, the landscape large and luminous. With pen and brush, he captures a sense of nostalgia, portraying the affection for the seals and their islands that changed his life's course. He does not paint himself, nor any person, into these scenes. The only evidence of human influence is when he depicts a distant steamship on the sea, chugging black smoke into the sky.

BUT ALL WAS NOT TRANQUILITY DURING ELLIOTT's 1913 Pribilof visit. Over his objections, Walter Lembkey was still the government's agent on the islands, charged with overseeing both the moratorium and the Unangax̂ people, who from the government's perspective could not be trusted to look after themselves. Lembkey knew that because of Elliott, Rothermel's committee would now pore over his reports for evidence of fraud. With a history of harsh accusations between them, Elliott and Lembkey did their best to avoid one another during Elliott's visit—no easy task on an island as tiny as St. Paul.

One July day, Lembkey trekked out to Lagoon Rookery to inform Elliott that George Clark, the clerk who had made a bitter vow to forever fight the land-kill moratorium, would be arriving the next day, dispatched by Fisheries Commissioner Bowers to corroborate Elliott's work. By Bowers's orders, Clark and Elliott were to work as a team, preparing a joint report that both men would sign.

Elliott felt ambushed. Months earlier, Commissioner Bowers had publicly disparaged the moratorium, issuing a press release that said it was a grave mistake. He claimed that like teenage hoodlums, bachelor seals would soon be tearing matkas to pieces. The surviving matkas would mostly bear stillborn pups, with beachmasters trampling the few that were born alive. Inciting this mayhem would exhaust the beachmasters' vitality and virility, Bowers said, rendering them impotent. As if these outrages were not enough, he hastened to add, the government was missing out on handsome profits by not killing the bachelors and selling their skins.

This was the "science" Bowers had sent Clark to prove. Elliott would have none of it. He had traveled to the Pribilofs on assignment from a committee that was making an independent investigation into both Clark and Bowers. He was not about to take orders from Bowers or collaborate with Clark on a joint report. Fuming, he told Lembkey that Clark could tag along with him if he wanted or he could go to hell, whichever he pleased. Either way, Elliott was not going to vouch for Clark's so-called science, especially not after Clark said he would never stop opposing a moratorium.

Lembkey snapped back that he was only following orders. He said someone had to keep an eye on Elliott, and if Elliott was not going to allow Clark to do it, then Lembkey would do it himself— and he had no intention whatsoever of going to hell. As Elliott would soon discover, Lembkey had much less authority than his posturing suggested. Well before Elliott's arrival, he had received a telegram informing him that his position had been abolished. He was only in charge until a new naturalist arrived, replacing the naturalist who had died the previous winter. In fact, the new naturalist arrived the next day, on the same steamer as George Clark, but this new man was also in ill health, his lungs racked with what the village doctor would soon diagnose as tuberculosis. Within two days of his arrival, he was confined to bed, creating doubt over who was actually in charge of the Pribilofs.

Upon arriving, Clark marched out to Northeast Point to confront his opponent with a fervor that matched Elliott's. Elliott reiterated his resolve. His was an independent investigation and he would work with no one but himself. The two men spent an uncomfortable night camped within view of one another. The next morning, Clark retreated to the village. Two days later, Elliott proceeded to St. George Island, putting a swath of the Bering Sea between himself and Clark. On St. George, he found more evidence of Clark's meddling. The previous summer, Clark had traveled to St. George to revive Jordan's failed attempt at branding matkas. To facilitate this task, he had driven them from the beaches to high ground. Now the matkas bunched unusually close to the water instead of in their usual pods at the rookeries. Elliott believed this new behavior was because they had been traumatized the previous summer.

From the rookeries at Keetavie, Lukannon, Zapadnie, and Polavina, Elliott recorded his observations, including the green and gray lichens that covered rocks once polished by seals and the clusters of matkas huddled uncharacteristically at the water's edge. The beachmasters were older than they should have been, he noted, and their numbers were low, further evidence of damage incurred by Jordan's insistence that bachelor seals be killed. Still, Elliott remained hopeful that the moratorium would correct this imbalance. Already, the ban on pelagic sealing was yielding results. At the base of Hutchison Hill, in a rookery that had been nearly empty in 1890, some six thousand matkas now chuckled and piped—welcome sounds to Elliott's ears.

On July 24, Elliott met with nine Unangax̂ sealers at the Unangax̂ Town Hall. Among them was twenty-five-year-old Nicholai Kozloff, brother of Mikhail Kozloff, who had shot and killed the Japanese pirates seven years earlier. Elliott asked whether the men had been pressed into killing yearlings. Yes, they said, beginning in 1896. To affirm this, Elliott studied the logbooks, where he discovered notable discrepancies with Lembkey's official reports. At the end of July, the deposed agent left the Pribilofs on the same revenue cutter as Elliott. It was undoubtedly a long trip for both of them.

For another crusader, this might have been the end of the story. Elliott had amassed volumes of evidence. He had pressed his case. With Hornaday's help, Elliott had seen through the measures required to save the seals from extinction. Now he had seen for himself the promising signs of their recovery. It might be time for him to rest on his laurels. But whatever pleasure Elliott took in returning to the islands, whatever satisfaction he enjoyed from observing his beloved seals free from the threat of butchers at land and sea, he still believed he had wrongs to right.

Back in Washington, he set to work with his usual diligence, compiling a report filled with facts and figures and maps and conclusions that Clark was sure to counter. In December 1913, he turned his report over to Rothermel's committee. In it, he defended his past work, which Jordan had attacked, though Elliott said Jordan could be forgiven for not being able to imagine the seals as Elliott had first observed them back in 1872. But bad theories were another matter. He pointed out that despite Jordan's dire warnings, Elliott had observed not one matka torn to pieces, not a single trampled pup. He also took Jordan to task for claiming that harsh winters killed off the weaker seals, when in fact the seals spent the winter in southern waters. In addition, he critiqued Jordan's 1897 seal census and his cruel branding of matkas, which Clark had tried to reinstate in 1912.

By 1913, there had been decades of attacks on Elliott. First had been Herman Liebes and the Anti-Monopoly Association, upset over the ACC's 1870–1890 monopoly and Elliott's contract work with the company. Then came the NACC in 1890, including wealthy shareholders Darius Ogden Mills and Stephen Elkins, alarmed that Elliott would cut into their profits with his proposed moratorium. In 1896, Jordan had entered the fray as a competing seal expert, despite the rather obvious conflict of interest with Mills on his university's Board of Trustees. For the most part, Elliott had borne these attacks stoically, even when they turned unfairly personal, questioning his sanity and his marriage to an Indigenous woman. That changed in 1908, when he had been forced to hawk his paintings to pay the bills. The hard realities of challenging corporate greed and complicit officials were taking a collective toll and had made him bitter. He began pointing fingers and calling names, vowing that the seals' enemies would one day get their just rewards. Though not above throwing an occasional punch himself, Hornaday sought to separate himself from Elliott's methods. "I do not believe in pinpricking my enemies, nor in cherishing a vindictive spirt," he wrote to George Clark in 1913. "Mr. Elliott believes in both of these things; and therein we differ."

Believing Rothermel's investigations would bring his enemies to justice, Elliott threw himself into the hearings, winning over members of Congress with his documentation and his examinations of witnesses who came before the committee. He knew the seals' natural history, and he had also made it his business to understand the complex political, diplomatic, and capitalistic forces at play in the seal controversy. He was delighted when one senator, reportedly "a warm personal friend of Jordan," made a fiery speech deriding the ignorance and deceit of certain men of science who opposed the land-kill moratorium.

But Elliott also knew that most congressmen had neither the time nor the inclination to sift through the voluminous evidence he had accumulated. Complied over decades, the information gathered into official documents on the seal crisis was nothing short of overwhelming. Elliott's solution was to prepare annotated versions for decision makers. From the Government Printing Office, he purchased multiple copies of bound volumes containing various lengthy US government reports on the seals, work that stretched back over three decades. With pen and ink, he set to work, underlining key passages in red and making sometimes acerbic notes in the margins. For instance, he annotated a page of testimony on the killing of yearlings with a T. H. Huxley quote: "There are three kinds of liars—liars, damned liars, and scientific experts." On the first page of another volume, he copied a quote from Gerald Stanley Lee: "For a man to have an ideal in this world, for a man to know what an ideal is, this is also to have lived." Where Elliott's commentary was lengthy or he wanted to include news items pertaining to a certain topic, he bound in blank pages, then attached the supplemental material, creating a scrapbook of sorts.

He also inserted cartoons. Some were his original work, including one in which a portly, double-chinned Fisheries Commissioner Bowers says, "Say Jordan, what is a Venus Mercenaria—is it a fish, or?" Dapper in ascot and tails, Jordan replies, "It's a clam, Bowers. Not a lobster like you, see?" Beneath this cartoon, Elliott penned the caption "Official 'Science'" and "Par nobile fratum," meaning a pair of noble brothers. But mostly, Elliott illustrated these volumes with cartoons he clipped from newspapers and then annotated. Carefully, he would excise the original speech bubbles and captions. Then, with pen and ink, he would insert his own commentary on his foes. Nagel, Bowers, Lembkey, Jordan, and Clark were all targets. Some cartoons Elliott also embellished using ink washes and watercolors. In one rendition, a child lies back on a sickbed, a doctor hovering nearby. Elliott's revised caption reads, "No use, my dear child—it is uncinaria [hookworm], Dr. Jordan says." In another, Elliott identifies a cartoon figure as Jordan, who tells a stout man labeled Bowers, "Liebes must have those yearlings, see." In yet another, inserted into a scrapbook below an excerpt from Elliott's testimony connecting Liebes with the pirates, a man clutches a woman to his chest, both of them gazing toward some unseen threat. In Elliott's caption, the woman exclaims, "Oh, John, don't buy that seal coat—don't you go near that fellow's store—the brute!"

As the Rothermel hearings dragged on, Elliott sent copies of these annotated books, as well as the individual cartoons, to congressmen and newspaper editors. The subject of some of his most caustic work, David Starr Jordan, accused Elliott of mailing these items using congressional franks, a privilege afforded members of the US Congress via a mail allowance. Jordan suggested there was something nefarious in Elliott asking congressmen to distribute his work. Clearly the congressmen themselves, or at least their staffers, had no problem disseminating material that was related to a congressional investigation.

Finally, after three years and thirty-one sessions of investigations that included Elliott and Clark's separate 1913 reports, Rothermel's committee delivered its findings in a 1,031-page document. Their conclusions went entirely in Elliott's favor. The committee began by documenting the numbers of fur seals over the forty years of Pribilof leases. In 1870, at the beginning of the ACC lease, there had been 4.7 million Pribilof fur seals. Over the next twenty years, the ACC had killed 1.8 million of them, raking in a cool $18.7 million in profits. Even after subtracting expenses that included beefed-up revenue cutter patrols during the final years of the ACC lease, the US government had still done quite nicely, clearing $5.2 million in fur seal revenues from 1870 to 1890.

When the NACC procured the Pribilof lease in 1890, the seal count was at 959,000. The herd had been substantially diminished by pelagic sealing and land-kill quotas of one hundred thousand per year, which the ACC had fulfilled in the latter years of its lease with hard drives to the killing grounds that indiscriminately swept in matkas and yearlings. The committee also noted that when Treasury Agent Charles Goff reported declining seal numbers in 1889 and again in 1891, the Treasury Secretary had removed him from his post. The hard drives had continued on the NACC's watch until the Pribilof fur seal population reached a low of 133,000 seals, and possibly fewer. The committee determined that seal piracy accounted for a substantial share of the decline, but they also blamed the NACC for depleting the population.

In addition, the Rothermel report chided government officials for failing to adequately supervise the leaseholders, beginning at the end of the ACC lease and continuing through the NACC's tenure. This lack of oversight was so blatant that some agents, including Walter Lembkey, admitted to having allowed corporate managers to call the shots on the Pribilofs. The committee also cited Jordan for overlooking violations of the "Carlisle rule," which prohibited the killing of yearlings as evidenced by pelts weighing less than six pounds. Rothermel's committee also said that because NACC principal Darius Ogden Mills was a Stanford trustee, Jordan had a clear conflict of interest. In a related example of corporate influence, NACC principal Stephen Elkins had endorsed his friend George Bowers for the post of fisheries commissioner. Assuming the position in 1898, Bowers had broad discretion over the seals' fate. On his watch, the London markets showed increasing numbers of yearling pelts. Onsite counts of live seals might be complicated or purposely inflated, but dead seals did not lie. By 1909, the final year of the Pribilof land lease, the lessees were entirely in charge of the land kill with virtually no government oversight, the committee noted. They were killing as many bachelors as they could, along with matkas and yearlings pulled in due to hard driving. Yet that same year, the Fur Seal Advisory Board had somehow seen fit to endorse renewal of the lease.

Owing to bad-faith management by the NACC, Rothermel's committee recommended that the US government demand the company surrender the $500,000 bond it had put up to secure the lease. In particular, they noted that NACC principal Herman Liebes had vowed that neither he nor any of his NACC associates had ever engaged in pelagic sealing, when in fact there was ample evidence that he had financed seal pirate Alex MacLean, including the ill-fated voyage of the *J. Hamilton Lewis*, for which MacLean and Liebes had both filed for and received a settlement from the Russian government.

The Rothermel report infuriated Jordan and Clark, who responded by lashing out at Elliott. In an article published in the *New York Times*, Clark claimed that Elliott had addressed letters disparaging him to Stanford University's trustees. The letters had also gone to Mrs. Leland Stanford, whose relationship with Jordan was strained at best. According to Clark, these letters were written on Cleveland hotel stationery in Elliott's handwriting but were signed "Junius," a well-known pseudonym used by an eighteenth-century Englishman to expose corruption. Jordan and Clark wanted a congressional investigation into these letters, which they also claimed were sent using congressional franks. The minority members of Rothermel's committee wrote up an alternate set of findings to the majority report, which *Science* magazine published. Authored by an associate of George Clark, this minority report accused Elliott of being a disgruntled former federal employee. It called his 1913 Pribilof visit a farce and recommended a Department of Justice investigation of him on charges of perjury and misuse of congressional franks. No one in Congress took up either Jordan's or the minority's request.

By any measure, the battle over the Pribilof seals had been ugly. There had been the bloody land slaughter, the greed of those who violated the breeding grounds for their own gain, and the wanton killing of matkas and starving of their pups by pirates. There had been oversea chases, seized vessels, and the shooting of marauders. There had been low blows shot across the bows of science and the duplicity of government officials to the benefit of industry barons.

Alex MacLean's death in 1914 added another ugly element to the mix. In Jack London's novel, the Sea-Wolf goes down fighting. The well-to-do man and woman who the pirate rescues eventually get the upper hand, chaining him belowdecks to protect themselves from his increasingly erratic and violent behavior. Time and again, the Sea-Wolf breaks free and threatens their lives, but a cancer is eating away at his brain. Eventually, it paralyzes his body's right side even as he insists he is wholly functional. Finally, in the middle of a dark storm, the Sea-Wolf's life flickers out. His great strength no longer shackles him, the narrator observes. His spirit is free. Far less protracted, MacLean's death lacked the metaphorical meaning a novelist can bestow. On the afternoon of August 26, 1914, MacLean was drinking with the proprietor of the Clarence Hotel, a drab, three-story brick building a few blocks from Victoria's waterfront. Shortly afterward, a friend happened upon MacLean on the street, but he did not seem especially drunk. After that, no one reported seeing him that evening.

The next day, MacLean failed to show up for a contract project with his tugboat. Thinking he might have fallen asleep belowdecks, the man who had hired him went to check the tug. Named the *Favorite* after the first sealing ship MacLean owned, the boat was moored at False Creek, an inlet that separates downtown Victoria from the rest of the city. Aboard the tug, the man found no sign of MacLean except for his big black Stetson hat, the one he wore everywhere. Alerted that the famous seafarer was missing, police combed the waterfront but found nothing to suggest what had become of him. They dragged the harbor for his body, then dragged it again, but they turned up nothing. A week later, an engineer starting his morning shift at the power plant noticed something unusual along the shoreline. Investigating, authorities discovered the body of Alex MacLean, age fifty-six.

Some of MacLean's friends attended the next day's inquest. According to the coroner, MacLean's lungs and stomach were filled with seawater, and there were no signs of violence. One theory was that the infamous seal pirate, perhaps under the influence of alcohol, had slipped on one of the small decks that led to where his tugboat was moored. Hitting his head, he had then drowned in three feet of water. Not everyone agreed with the findings, as it seemed impossible to some that an experienced mariner like MacLean, who had survived shipwrecks and storms, could die in such a hapless way. Elliott was among those who questioned the cause of death. He had never met Alex MacLean in person, but for decades the two men's fates had intertwined. Elliott had despised MacLean's ruthless disregard for the seals and his underhanded dealings with Liebes. But in zeal, resilience, and sheer determination, the artist and the pirate were more alike than either would have wanted to admit.

Elliott had his own ideas about how and why MacLean died. In the recently released Rothermel report, the NACC had come under fire. There was big money at stake if the government followed the report's recommendations and sought damages from the NACC's $500,000 bond. The rationale for the government's claim to the bond would have been Alex MacLean's dealings with the Liebes Fur Company. As a star witness against his former associates, MacLean could have done grave financial damage. With seal pirating outlawed, he no longer had reason to protect men like Isaac Liebes, Stephen Elkins, and Darius Ogden Mills. Asked for comment on the Rothermel findings, MacLean had hinted as much. Smiling, he told a reporter, "It will be a fight of the heavyweights that will put Jack Johnson and his heavyweights in the shade, you may reckon on that." Elliott surmised that to avoid the fight, Alex MacLean's former associates had forever silenced the Sea-Wolf.

EIGHTEEN

THOSE HARROWING DAYS

*A*T THE SEATTLE AQUARIUM, a few blocks south of the city's iconic Pike's Place Market, a northern fur seal named Flaherty swim laps in a glass enclosure. Compared to the crowded rookeries where millions of fur seals once piped and roared, the aquarium tank is quiet. As of 2021, Flaherty is one of only nine fur seals in captivity in the United States, all notable exceptions to Henry Wood Elliott's point made more than a century ago that unlike hair seals, fur seals typically fare poorly when removed from the wild. The few fur seals in American zoos and aquariums now act as ambassadors for ocean conservation.

The man who saved their species spent his final years not far from where the Seattle Aquarium sits today, a few miles west in what is now the suburban enclave of Renton, Washington. After the Elliotts sold their Ohio home, several of their adult children ended up in Seattle. Consumed as he was with the seal investigations, Elliott still found time to send affectionate letters and "little checks" from Washington, DC, asking his children to keep their eyes open for a property in the Seattle area that they could turn into another grand, open home like their Rockport cottage with its ponds and expansive green lawns. In his letters, he asked after the family dog and said he looked forward to a good rest when his business was done, not to mention the payment he hoped to receive for supplying evidence to Rothermel's committee.

Even after the committee's report delivered the hoped-for vindication, Elliott was unable to rest. Still focused on the seals, he kept up his winter campaigns in Washington, DC. Insistent that the

NACC must be held to account for killing yearlings, he lobbied for the government to pursue the civil case over the NACC's $500,000 bond. In the end, the solicitor general declined to pursue the case, claiming that the accused had not intentionally defrauded the government. In addition, the government had larger concerns, as shortly after the Rothermel committee released its findings, war broke out in Europe following the assassination of Archduke Franz Ferdinand. The world's attention shifted quickly to what would become the bloodiest conflict to ever engage humanity.

William Hornaday told Elliott that the time had come to stand down, but as much as he trusted his good friend and ally, Elliott would not—and perhaps could not—abide this advice. He shifted his attentions to the Fouke Fur Company, a US venture that had taken over processing sealskins from the government's land harvest. In 1921, the US government had awarded Fouke a ten-year monopoly on processing the pelts. This alarmed Elliott, who feared a monopoly on fur processing could too easily become another monopoly on the entire Pribilof venture and once again relegate the seals' fate to profiteers.

Elliott convinced Robert La Follette, an influential Progressive Party senator, to open investigations into what he called the Fur Trust. La Follette drew up legislation that would prohibit the monopoly, which Elliott estimated had deprived the US Treasury of $5 million in revenue. Each year from 1921 to 1926, Elliott pushed for this trust-busting legislation to advance, and each year it went nowhere. After a final round of congressional testimony in 1926, at age eighty, Henry Wood Elliott finally gave up. Retreating from Washington, DC, he first stayed with his son Frank and his family in Lakewood, Ohio, then went west to the property his children had finally purchased outside Seattle—a family compound of cottages, gardens, orchards, and greenhouses tended by his son Lionel. A fire in the Cleveland warehouse where Elliott had stored many of his belongings had destroyed over one hundred of his paintings, along with much of the documentation of his fight for the seals. But he seemed not to dwell on the loss, enjoying instead a respite from what he called the harrowing days of the past. In the lily gardens outside his cottage, he turned his brush to producing dozens of paintings of

Mount Rainer. Like the Pribilofs, the mountain often hides among clouds, which in some of Elliott's watercolors resemble the sea. Rising majestically from the foothills, the mountain exudes a degree of calm. Small wonder that after his trials, Elliott found himself drawn to it.

Not long after Elliott arrived in Seattle, a reporter came calling at his "little rose-bound cottage." It was the height of summer, the dry season in Seattle, and Elliott's skin was tanned and leathered from hours outside at his easel, capturing the mountain's many moods. None of Elliott's paintings were for sale, nor did he plan to exhibit them. "They are too sacred for that," the reporter wrote. In the interview, Elliott spoke fondly of his early days in Washington, DC. He recalled President Lincoln coming to the Smithsonian's Castle tower to watch new, rebel-defying signal codes being tested by the Union Army and noted that the president's infectious laugh made him seem every bit as homely and affable as history had made him out to be. He noted what a tiny burg Seattle had been in 1865, when he passed through on his way to British Columbia with the Western Union Telegraph Expedition. He spoke of studying the Pribilof seals and working on what he always referred to as "the Hay-Elliott treaty." He downplayed the battles he had fought over the seals, saying only that although he had emerged the victor, the conflicts had made him weary of public life. Now living with four of his children in the shadow of Mount Rainier, Elliott said he was supremely happy. Seated among the lilies, painting the great mountain the Puyallup people called Tahoma, he found his life was a peaceful respite from those harrowing days.

A few years later, in early 1930, Hornaday interrupted Elliott's idyllic existence. He was writing a memoir, *Thirty Years War for Wildlife,* and he hoped that Elliott could tell him more about his first meeting with Secretary of State Elihu Root. Writing in response to this query, Elliott showed that his mind was as sharp as ever, offering details long buried in his memory. Yet despite still being able to recount the specifics of the battles and the cause to which he devoted his life, Elliott did not write memoir. Instead, he painted Mount Rainier in various times and seasons—a lavender sunrise, at sunset, rising from fog.

On May 25, 1930, as the roses surrounding the little cottage were coming into bloom, Elliott's heart gave out. He died peacefully, surrounded by four of his children. He likely would have been pleased with the article about him that ran in the *Seattle Daily News*. It called him "an internationally acclaimed scientist" and "an associate of the Smithsonian Institution" who "collaborated with many of its famous members." The article also credits Elliott as author of the 1911 Fur Seal Treaty, noting that his investigations laid the foundation for the agreement.

Unlike many of his fellow naturalists, Elliott made no broad Arctic explorations, only intimate studies of a tiny group of islands and the fur seals that bred there. Not a single river or mountain or glacier would be named for him, nor would any newly identified species bear his name. Beyond his ties to the Smithsonian, he never sought to rise within scientific circles. He was content with his seals and his art. His detractors, men of power and influence, attacked his character, portraying him as vain, mendacious, spiteful, bitter, and even treasonous and insane. That he had readily admitted his mistakes, that he doggedly pursued truth, that he worked tirelessly without reward—these facts would be overlooked in favor of the notion that Elliott was, as he himself put it, simply a "crank." Yet he persisted against all odds in a quest to save a single species of marine mammals on a pair of small, remote islands.

Like any of us, Elliott was far from perfect. He was bold and opinionated and impulsive. He was also amiable, enthusiastic, hard-working, and a keen observer of the natural world. His sketches and paintings evoke feelings of solitude and splendor, a sense that in the earth's vast expanses, one human is small indeed. And yet as one human, Elliott made an enormous difference.

Epilogue

*I*N THE *SEATTLE DAILY TIMES*, Elliott's death announcement ran beneath an article with the headline "Astronomers pick 'Pluto' as Name for New Planet." By the twenty-first century, scientists would acknowledge their error—Pluto was not a planet after all. Such is the way of science. By design, it evolves. New experiments and more extensive observations result in fresh sets of data, prompting scientists to cast aside old theories in favor of previously unknown truths.

The first naturalist to make detailed studies of the Pribilof fur seals, Henry Wood Elliott made errors that subsequent scientists would correct, most notably his inflated estimates of the Pribilof seal population in 1872. William Dall made errors too, such as claiming fur seals mated in the water. So did Dall's mentor, Louis Agassiz, who rejected evolution and monogenism, asserting that humans of differing races belonged to different species.

The scientist who did the most to discredit Elliott, David Starr Jordan, accused him of hubris, but Jordan showed a good deal of hubris himself, especially when he recast his failures as successes. For instance, Jordan wrote in his memoir that he had missed out on a college botany prize because he thought more expansively than tests could measure. He also claimed to have let an etymology prize go to another student who needed the money. When Jane Stanford accused him of only hiring his friends to teach at the university, he said it was because he knew all the best people.

There is also the not-so-small matter of Jordan's role in Jane Stanford's death. After Leland Stanford died in 1893, his wife became increasingly dissatisfied with how Jordan was running Stanford University. Following Jane Stanford's death in 1905, the coroner's jury ruled the cause to be poisoning. Jordan intervened, and with the help of a doctor he hired, made the case for overeating as the cause of death. Given his distrust of Jordan, Elliott would likely be pleased to know that recent investigations suggest that if Jordan was not complicit in the poisoning, he certainly went to great lengths to cover it up.

In another case of mysterious death, Elliott's own theories about the cause have recently been proved wrong. When Robert Kennicott, darling of the Megatheria, was found on the banks of the Yukon River in 1866, Elliott thought the lingering effects of yellow fever coupled with Kennicott's self-medicating with alcohol caused his untimely death. But in 2001, a team from the Smithsonian exhumed the naturalist's body and determined he had died from heart failure likely caused by long QT syndrome, a congenital disorder that can lead to life-threatening arrhythmias.

In a sense, the field of natural history as Elliott knew it also died, at least for a time. By the mid-twentieth century, studies of life forms had largely moved from the field into laboratories. Gone were partnerships like the ones the Smithsonian's Spencer Baird forged with railroads, telegraph companies, and the US government. Museums disposed of specimens collected in bygone days, not foreseeing their potential for helping modern-day scientists better understand the effects of the climate crisis on the world's animals.

In the Pribilofs, the seal population recovered, as Elliott predicted it would, following the five-year moratorium on the land harvest, but for the Unangax̂, conditions worsened. In 1916, an agent of the Fisheries Bureau—no longer led by Bowers, who had resigned in the wake of the Rothermel report—visited the islands and discovered that conditions were as bad as Elliott had indicated in his 1913 report. Food was scarce. Families were hauling their drinking water from ponds. Unangax̂ children were undernourished and lacked sufficient clothing. And yet government agents still would not allow the Unangax̂ to leave the islands unless they had an amount of money that was nearly impossible for them to acquire. If the American public were to learn of these conditions, the investigating fisheries agent wrote, there would be nationwide outrage.

Congress did finally authorize funds to replace the rundown Pribilof houses that had been built in the 1870s. In 1924, Congress also finally recognized Alaska Natives as naturalized citizens. Then the Depression struck, followed by another world war. Withdrawing from the Fur Seal Treaty, Japan deployed fishing boats to gather military intelligence from the Aleutian and Pribilof islands. Six months after the Japanese attack on Pearl Harbor, Japanese aircraft carriers approached the Aleutian Islands under cover of fog. Launched from the decks of the aircraft carriers *Jun'yō* and *Ryūjō*, airplanes bombed the town of Dutch Harbor on Unalaska Island, about three hundred miles southeast of the Pribilofs.

On the Pribilofs, the first clue that something was amiss came when the fisheries office in Seattle radioed the Unangax̂ instructing them to make sure the barges they used for offloading supplies from cargo ships were in working order. Days later, several Unangax̂ men who had gathered to play baseball spotted a military transport ship approaching from the south. When the officers came ashore on St. Paul Island, they told the Unangax̂ that the Pribilofs were now in a war zone and they had to evacuate. They did not say where the Unangax̂ would be taken. Families hurried to pack what little they were allowed to bring. The next morning, everyone in the village was loaded onto the transport ship. Nine American soldiers stayed behind to guard St. Paul Island. The ship then swung toward St. George Island, where the commanding officer gave residents there only one hour to pack their belongings. Zigzagging through the northern Pacific to avoid attack by enemy submarines, the transport ship eventually offloaded the Pribilof Islands Unangax̂ at an abandoned salmon cannery on Admiralty Island, along Alaska's Inside Passage. The towering trees and dark forests could scarcely have been more different from the landscape they'd come from.

Among the displaced was David Fratis, whose father, John Fratis Jr., had defended the Pribilof seals from Japanese pirates. In filthy, long-abandoned dormitories, David and the other Unangax̂ men used scrap lumber and chicken wire to put up privacy walls. Now that they were citizens, some of the men would be drafted into military service, but Fratis was compelled to a different sort of government work. Even in wartime there was a market for furs, and the government needed money to fund the war effort. So in 1943, David Fratis boarded another government transport ship. This time, it would take him and other Unangax̂ men back to the Pribilofs to serve their country by killing seals.

One hundred American soldiers now occupied tiny St. Paul Island. When the tired, hungry Unangax̂ men arrived after the long voyage from Admiralty Island, they were herded into a bunkhouse without bedding, food, or water. Fratis took charge, refitting a stovepipe so he could cook dinner for himself and his friends using some old tins of salmon. During their stay on the island, Fratis and his companions were allowed to go only between the bunkhouse, the killing fields, and the salting garage. They were not allowed to spend time in their own homes, which the soldiers had ransacked, placing a full drum of kerosene in each dwelling so they could blow them up in the event of an enemy attack.

When the seal harvest ended, the government shuttled Fratis and the other sealers back to the Admiralty Island cannery, where the Unangax̂ were suffering from a measles outbreak. A woman named Alexandra Milovidov, who was married to Alexander Milovidov, Elliott's nephew, was tending to the sick, hauling soup from the communal kitchen and emptying chamber pots. Those who died from measles and other diseases that swept through the internment camp were buried in shallow graves near Funter Bay.

By the time World War II ended and the Unangax̂ were allowed to return to the Pribilofs, 118 villagers—about a quarter of the total population—had died, most of pneumonia and tuberculosis. Those who lived to return found their circumstances much the same as they had been. The US Fisheries Bureau still governed their lives, they still earned only rations instead of cash, and they had no control of their destiny. A reporter for the *Tundra Times*, a newspaper focused on issues affecting Alaska Natives, wrote that anyone who believed that slavery had been abolished in the United States needed to take a good look at the Pribilofs.

In 1951, Alexander Milovidov, the son of Alexandra Milovidov, joined three other St. Paul leaders in launching a claim against the US government on behalf of the Pribilof Unangax̂. In it, the leaders alleged maltreatment of their people and demanded legal recognition, the return of lands wrongfully taken, and monetary compensation. In 1980, the claim was settled out of court, and in 1983, after centuries of servitude, the Pribilof Islands Unangax̂ finally achieved control of their land and their lives. However, the circumstances were not entirely of their own choosing. Once again, the issue involved seals.

In 1976, Greenpeace Canada began a campaign to end the killing of harp seal pups in the Gulf of St. Lawrence and Newfoundland. The pups were being killed for profit by Canadian commercial fishermen who clubbed two-week-old harp seal pups before they began shedding their soft white fur coats. Photographs of tiny, wide-eyed harp seal pups who might have been among the brutally slaughtered evoked outrage around the world. In 1983, the European Economic Community banned seal pup furs, and the bottom dropped out of the market. Simultaneously, Americans discovered that their own government was profiting from killing Pribilof fur seals. The public outcry was intense. Pups or bachelor seals—it made no difference to Americans angered by the practice of clubbing seals for coats.

Yielding to pressure, the US government finally withdrew from controlling the Pribilofs in 1983, effectively buying out the Unangax̂ with a $20 million trust fund to help them transition into self-reliance. The collapse of the fur market left the Unangax̂, who for generations had known no other livelihood than sealing, without a means of supporting themselves. Eventually, the Alaska legislature, flush with Prudhoe Bay oil money, appropriated funds for dredging two deep-sea harbors at the Pribilofs. Once again, the Unangax̂ adapted, turning to commercial fishing as well as servicing the Bering Sea fishing vessels Americans would later come to recognize from the popular reality TV show *The Deadliest Catch*.

Around the world, environmentalism and wildlife protection efforts have evolved greatly since the seal-war era, as have perspectives on animal consciousness, measures to curb animal cruelty, and respect for the subsistence practices of Indigenous Peoples. Where Henry Wood Elliott pioneered the relentless, groundbreaking work of saving wildlife in a faraway place, interest in wildlife preservation now abounds. Hornaday's New York

Zoological Society, now called the Wildlife Conservation Society, works on behalf of wildlife in sixty nations and in every ocean of the world. It is just one of hundreds of organizations dedicated to saving species from human-caused extinction.

Likewise, the seminal 1911 Fur Seal Treaty, achieved in no small part through Elliott's relentless and unconventional methods, still stands as a model for wildlife protection the world over. Through similar agreements of mutual concession and joint control, the international community works to secure the future of the world's wildlife—and the future of the planet itself. The Migratory Bird Treaty Act, the Endangered Species Act, the Marine Mammal Protection Act, and the Paris Climate Accord advanced the core concepts of the Fur Seal Treaty, as did the Convention on International Trade in Endangered Species (CITES), an agreement between 177 member nations to protect nearly thirty-five thousand species of endangered plants and animals. Without such measures, humankind would have lost countless species that are essential to a healthy ecosystem.

Although a 2018 survey showed that 80 percent of Americans support the Endangered Species Act, shifting political winds still threaten wildlife. In 2017, President Donald Trump's secretary of the interior issued a memo reinterpreting the 1918 Migratory Bird Treaty Act, effectively releasing oil companies from liability for any damage their spills did to migratory waterfowl. By executive fiat, Trump also substantially weakened the Endangered Species Act, credited with saving notable species such as the bald eagle, the northern gray wolf, and the California condor, along with many lesser-known species. The Trump administration also poked holes in the Marine Mammal Protection Act, allowing "incidental" harassment of protected marine mammals, including seismic blasting. Likewise, Trump's withdrawal of the United States from the 2015 Paris Agreement on November 4, 2020, would have threatened any number of species, including humans, had President Joseph Biden not signed an executive order to rejoin the agreement on January 20, 2021, his first day in office.

Yet in our current epoch, dubbed "Anthropocene" to reflect the effects of human domination, the threat of human-caused extinctions looms large. According to the World Wildlife Federation's *Living Planet Report 2018*, human-caused extinctions have wiped out an astounding 60 percent of the earth's wildlife since 1970. But as Henry Elliott learned firsthand, getting accurate census numbers on wildlife can be tricky. Some species are more studied than others, and a good number of species—especially insects—have yet to be discovered. Still, the essential fact remains that in prior epochs, species on earth rarely went extinct—on average, one species of mammals disappeared every seven hundred years, and when they did, it was the result of cataclysmic events. Now, according to an extended global assessment by the United Nations released in 2019, one million species are threatened with extinction worldwide. Among the most vulnerable are the world's marine mammals, with a full third of existing species at risk.

Across far-flung reaches of the planet, human migration is spreading diseases that harm animals. As humans encroach into wildlands and climate change upends whole ecosystems, habitats are disappearing at alarming rate. Though the 1911 Fur Seal Treaty ended the poaching of northern fur seals, poachers today shoot endangered Asian elephants for their tusks, kill rhinos for their horns, illegally harvest sea turtle eggs, and strip scales from pangolins. The value of the global wildlife trafficking industry is estimated at between $7 and $23 billion.

When a species goes extinct, it chips away at the biodiversity upon which our planet depends, a fact that is far better understood today than it was in Elliott's day. Even so, human-centric views of our world prevail in many circles, and efforts to save wildlife come under attack. One of many examples is the spotted owl. In the 1990s, efforts to protect these endangered owls were blamed for a decline in timber jobs in the Pacific Northwest, despite the fact that mechanization was having a greater effect on jobs in the logging industry.

In the Pribilof Islands seal controversy, the human threat was simple and obvious: men were killing seals on land and at sea. Today, the cascading effects of different types of human activity compound the troubles that species face, in some cases pitting the survival of one animal against that of another, such as the rats that literally jumped ship long ago on an uninhabited Aleutian Island and have recently been exterminated in hopes native wildlife will return. Scientific advances help decision makers navigate these complexities. Using sophisticated tools and techniques, biologists today understand how various species contribute to an ecosystem, the threats each face, and which interventions stand the best chance of ensuring a species' survival far better than did any of the dueling naturalists of Elliott's era. Armed with data, advocacy groups employ a variety of tactics— some controversial, some commonplace—to promote wildlife preservation. Sometimes they get it wrong, as Greenpeace Canada admitted in a 2014 apology to Canada's Indigenous Peoples for the unforeseen consequences of their campaign to end commercial seal hunting. As part of its conciliatory effort, Greenpeace drafted a policy in conjunction with First Nations leaders to support the right of Indigenous Peoples to pursue a subsistence lifestyle.

Regarding northern fur seals, modern-day scientists have conducted an astounding amount of research on the species, documenting site fidelity, territorial behaviors, female foraging behaviors, mating systems, and population changes. Though far more empirical and nuanced, much of the data coming forth corroborates Elliott's observations, including the fact that beachmasters go out of their way to avoid trampling pups. In addition, biologists have determined that Jordan's proposed killing of 95 percent of bachelor seals—now called "peripheral males"— would have gravely damaged the population. As Elliott had pointed out, peripheral males are important in replacing breeding males. They also impregnate matkas unclaimed by the beachmasters and reduce disturbances among the seals by discouraging the youngest males from making forays into breeding grounds.

When the United States government relinquished control of the Pribilofs in 1983, it had no further revenues from the seals to divide among the signatory nations of the 1911 Fur Seal Treaty. Ongoing advocacy by the Humane Society and other likeminded groups has convinced thirty-seven countries, including the United States, to ban the commercial seal trade. But Canada, Japan, Greenland, and Namibia still allow commercial harvests of various types of seals. In 2016, Canada's harp seal quota was four hundred thousand, though because there is little market for seal fur these days, only sixty-six thousand were killed. Harp seals are not a threatened species, but the Humane Society continues to advocate for an end to the commercial harvest, citing cruel methods and the fact that 97 percent of the seals killed are under three months old.

On the Pribilofs, the seals that Elliott devoted himself to saving are once again in decline. Beginning with the five-year moratorium in 1912 and continuing until 1924, the population grew at a rate of 8 percent per year. Then, climbing at slower rates for three decades, the population reached 2.1 million in the 1950s. In a move Henry Elliott would surely have opposed, US government wildlife managers began purposely killing female seals to curb the herd's growth. By that point, seal census methods had advanced significantly from Elliott's first estimates in 1872. Instead of mapping beachmaster territories, biologists began estimating the number of pups with a mark-and-recapture method—not branding the seals as Jordan did, but shearing a portion of fur so the pups could be re-identified. Multiplying by pre-determined expansion factors based on age and sex distribution, biologists then extrapolated the number of yearlings and older seals.

By 1974, wildlife managers had overseen the culling of 315,000 female seals from Pribilof rookeries, with another sixteen thousand killed at sea. In 1983, the US government quit killing seals altogether. The Pribilof seal population rebounded slightly, then began dropping again. By 1988, their numbers had declined by more than 50 percent from the 1950s peak of 2.1 million. Under the provisions of the Marine Mammal Protection Act, the herd was designated "depleted." The birth rate of seal pups on St. Paul Island began declining at a rate of 4 percent per year, though on St. George Island, the birth rate remained stable. At this steady rate, the fur seal population on St. Paul Island dropped by almost 60 percent between 1999 and 2019.

Without pirates or commercial harvests to blame, scientists are looking for other factors to account for this alarming change. Entanglements in marine debris such as fishing nets are one significant cause of fur seal deaths. Commercial fishing appears to be another culprit. In 2016, fishermen caught and sold a whopping 1.5 million metric tons of Bering Sea pollock, a staple for both fur seals and humans—pollock is used in McDonald's fish sandwiches. At the same time, the size of the pollock being caught has been decreasing. As a result, matkas may not be finding enough food, causing some younger females not to go into estrus and be able to mate while older ones may produce too little milk to sustain healthy pups.

Scientists also speculate that killer whales may have turned to eating more seals because the human overharvesting of great whales has depleted this source of prey. The climate crisis is yet another factor in the fur seals' decline. Warmer oceans mean less phytoplankton, which means less food all the way up the food chain. In all, biologists worry that fur seals, especially those that breed on St. Paul Island, are going the way of the Bering Sea's Steller sea lions, which are now endangered.

Had Henry Wood Elliott not devoted his life to the Pribilof fur seals, it is hard to say when the public would have finally recognized the intrinsic value in preserving wildlife for its own sake. As a self-trained artist and naturalist, he was uniquely positioned to rally support. His fervent commitment to his ideals and his persistence made all the difference. Yet for his efforts, he received far more attacks than recognition. As William Hornaday sardonically remarked, "By the year 2000, Mr. Elliott's great-grandchildren may receive for him 'the thanks of Congress.' But I doubt it!" Indeed, Congress has yet to thank Elliott. However, the National Oceanic and Atmospheric Association (NOAA) has made some amends. In addition to cleaning up debris and contamination from 116 years of government control of the Pribilofs, NOAA has also drawn attention to Elliott's legacy with a short documentary film, *Henry Wood Elliott: Defender of the Fur Seal.*

Now more than ever, we need advocates who fervently and relentlessly confront human-caused threats to the world's wildlife, activists who are determined to stand against those who would pirate the earth's wild creatures for their own gain. We need people like Henry Wood Elliott, who was willing to confront corruption while holding fast to his ideals no matter the cost.

AUTHOR'S NOTE

I AM GRATEFUL TO A NUMBER of authors who delved into the Pribilof seal controversy before me, especially Briton Cooper Busch (*The War Against the Seals*, 1985) and Kurkpatrick Dorsey (*The Dawn of Conservation Diplomacy*, 1998). In many cases, they have characterized Elliott as stubborn, quarrelsome, and inept. I do not fault them for this. Elliott triumphed in saving the seals, but his enemies won the war on his reputation.

In writing this book, I did not set out to vindicate Elliott. I began by taking him at his word while at the same time looking for evidence of mendaciousness, an accusation that seems to have originated with William Dall. I found little, though Elliott did fail to openly state that he had independently contracted with the ACC. I also weighed his unquestionably healthy ego against the egos of men like Dall and Jordan, and I found none of them lacking. In addition, I considered the ways Elliott's foes provoked him, especially after he turned whistleblower. I acknowledge that some readers will find my assessment of Elliott too generous for their liking.

I am also deeply indebted to Don MacGillivray for his meticulously researched biography, *Captain Alex MacLean: Jack London's Sea Wolf* (2008). In it, MacGillivray masterfully unravels the facts of MacLean's life from the fictions that arose around him. I have chosen to present MacLean mostly as Elliott—and much of the American public—perceived him during his lifetime, knowing that there is always more to the man than the myth. MacLean did not like being called a pirate, but I have used the term liberally because, like many of his contemporaries, Elliott did.

An abundance of primary source material is available to any who want to make a deep dive into the Pribilof seal controversy. Smithsonian archivist Tad Bennicoff and the staff at the Cleveland Museum of Natural History Archives were especially helpful in responding to my repeated requests for "just one more document," as was Clatsop Community College librarian Rhonda Alderman, who graciously processed my many interlibrary loan requests. In addition to all the other good work done by the Wildlife Conservation Society, its archivists have masterfully digitized and indexed all of William Hornaday's Wildlife Conservation Scrapbooks, which contain a great deal of relevant material not accessible elsewhere. Among other notable resources is a massive volume commissioned by the US Department of Commerce/NOAA, *Pribilof Islands, Alaska: The People* (2010). I wish a similar collection of illustrated biographies would be compiled for every Alaska Native community so that valuable personal histories would be preserved.

A special thanks to the fabulous team at West Margin Press/ Alaska Northwest Books, to Louis Lehmann for his help with research, and to the Pribilof School District students and staff who welcomed me to their remarkable islands and pointed me toward this incredible piece of history.

Deb Vanasse
April 2021

ENDNOTES

PROLOGUE

7   **Of a swath of land:** Krista Langlois and Heather Pringle, "A Sunken Bridge the Size of Australia," *Hakai Magazine* (Sept. 20, 2016), https://www. hakaimagazine.com/features/sunken-bridge-size-continent/

8   **these are the official charges:** Don MacGillivray, *Captain Alex MacLean* (Vancouver: UBC Press, 2008), 173.

8   **The world is watching:** Noel Robinson, "The Real Sea-Wolf," *Maclean's* (Jan. 1, 1922), 12–13, 22.

8   **"Captain Alexander Woodside":** MacGillivray, 185.

8   **As London says:** Jack London, "Small Boat Sailing," *Delphi Complete Works of Jack London* (East Sussex, UK: Delphi, 2012).

8   **Stopping at Clayoquot Sound:** MacGillivray, 172–3.

9   **One account:** MacGillivray, 177.

9   **Another posed a series:** MacGillivray, 177.

10 **three hundred thousand hairs per square inch:** Briton Cooper Busch, *The War Against the Seals: A History of the North American Seal Fishery* (Toronto: McGill-Queen's University Press, 1985), 99.

10 **As it stands in 1905:** Busch, 103.

12 **In no other species:** Nicholas Mathevon, Isabelle Charrier, and Thierry Aubin, "A memory like a female Fur Seal: long-lasting recognition of pup's voice by mothers," *Anais da Academia Brasileira de Ciências*, 76 (June 2004): 2, https://doi.org/10.1590/S0001-37652004000200007.

12 **her flippers working almost like legs:** "Northern Fur Seal," National Oceanic and Atmospheric Administration, https://www.fisheries.noaa.gov/ species/northern-fur-seal, accessed June 22, 2021.

ONE

17 **"He was a pal of mine":** "He Was a Pal of Mine," http://www.traditionalmusic. co.uk/songster/29-he-was-a-pal-of-mine, accessed June 22, 2021.

18 **Originally of Cape Breton Island:** MacGillivray, *Captain Alex MacLean*, 7–8.

18 **renowned for fighting and seafaring:** MacGillivray, 7.

19 **As cosmopolitan as New York City:** M. Louisa Locke, "Victorian San Francisco in 1880: Social Structure and Character Development," August 20, 2012, https://mlouisalocke.com/2012/08/20/victorian-san-francisco-in-1880-social-structure-and-character-development/.

21 **he said he came up with the idea:** MacGillivray, 17.

23 **$200,000 in profits:** MacGillivray, 25.

23-24 **Extinction was inevitable:** MacGillivray, 95.

24 **Alex refused the label of pirate:** MacGillivray, 183.

24 **The Greek biographer Plutarch:** "The Time Julius Caesar Was Captured by Pirates," https://www.britannica.com/story/the-time-julius-caesar-was-captured-by-pirates, accessed June 22, 2021.

24 **When confronted with the label:** MacGillivray, 183.

24 **Renegade warriors:** "A Brief History of Piracy," https://www.royalnavalmuseum.org/info_sheets_piracy.html, accessed June 22, 2021.

24 **the swashbuckling collection:** Charles Johnson, *A General History of the Robberies & Murders of the Most Notorious Pyrates* (Guilford, CT: Lyons Press, 1998).

24 **a companion volume:** Charles Johnson, *A Complete History of the Lives & Robberies of the Most Notorious Highwaymen* (Farmington Hills, MI: Gale ECCO, 2010).

25 **a thoughtful and well-spoken man:** MacGillivray, 121.

25 **Once, when his crew was readying:** Andrew Walter Roy, "The Life and Death of the Sea Wolf," *Atlantic Advocate* 98 (1958), 84.

TWO

25 **To punish transgressions:** MacGillivray, *Captain Alex MacLean*, 244-6.

28 **From the Galápagos:** Briton Cooper Busch, *The War Against the Seals* (Montreal: McGill-Queen's University Press, 1985), 36.

29 **Arriving by boat:** William R. Hunt, *Arctic Passage: The Turbulent History of the Land and People of the Bering Sea, 1697–1975* (New York: Charles Scribner's Sons, 1975), 37.

29 **That changed in 1745:** James R. Gibson, "Russian Dependence on the Natives of Alaska" in *An Alaska Anthology: Interpreting the Past*, ed. Stephen W. Haycox and Mary Childers Mangusso (Seattle: University of Washington Press, 1996), 25.

32 **"Walrussia":** "Formal Transfer of Walrussia," *The San Francisco Examiner* (Nov. 14, 1867), 2.

34 **The son of an enslaved African woman:** James M. O'Toole, "Racial Identity and the Case of Captain Michael Healy, USRCS," *Prologue Magazine* 29, no. 3 (Fall 1997), https://www.archives.gov/publications/prologue/1997/fall/michael-a-healy-1.

THREE

39 **Born on November 13, 1846:** Margaret Manor Butler, *The Lakewood Story* (New York: Stratford House, 1949), 96.

39 **But when Emerson wrote:** Dorceta E. Taylor, *The Rise of the American Conservation Movement: Power, Privilege, and Environmental Protection* (Durham, NC: Duke University Press, 2016), 35.

40 **a stop on the Underground Railroad:** Mazie Adams, "Lakewood in the Civil War: Anti-Slavery Activities," *The Lakewood Observer*, September 21, 2011, http://lakewoodobserver.com/read/2011/09/21/lakewood-in-the-civil-war-antislavery-activities.

40 **In addition to the Elliotts:** Margaret Manor Butler, *The Lakewood Story* (Lakewood, OH: Stratford House, 1949), 78.

40 **Going forward:** Butler, 96.

40 **In 1856, when Henry was ten:** Butler, 96.

42   **when five o'clock came:** "The Megatherium Club," Smithsonian Institution Archives, https://siarchives.si.edu/featured-topics/megatherium/introduction, accessed June 22, 2021.

44   **"warm friend":** Henry Wood Elliott, "Robert Kennicott: An account of the causes which led to his unexpected and sudden death on the Yukon River, May 13, 1866, Told by Mr. Henry W. Elliott; in Washington, D.C. on June 11, 1914," Robert Kennicott Biographical Notes and Athapascan Manuscripts, Alaska State Library Archives, 17. https://library.alaska.gov/hist/hist_docs/docs/asl_PM641_K46_OVERSIZE.pdf.

44   **"was the very ideal man":** Elliott, "Robert Kennicott," 31.

44   **"day in and day out":** Elliott, "Robert Kennicott," 21.

45   **After a period of remission:** Pan American Health Organization, "Yellow Fever," https://www.paho.org/en/topics/yellow-fever, accessed June 22, 2021.

45   **"fairly self-possessed":** Elliott, "Robert Kennicott," 21.

45   **hard country full of swamps:** Henry Wood Elliott to Joseph Henry, March 20, 1866. William Healey Dall Papers, circa 1839–1858, 1862–1927, Smithsonian Institution Archives, RU 7073, Box 10, Folder 10.

46   **He confessed to Baird:** Henry Wood Elliott to Spencer Baird, April 30, 1869. William Healey Dall Papers, circa 1839–1858, 1862–1927, Smithsonian Institution Archives, RU 7073, Box 10, Folder 10.

47   **"elegant":** Henry Wood Elliott to Spencer Baird, October 28, 1870, Henry Wood Elliott correspondence, 1863–1873, Smithsonian Institution Archives, RU 7002, Box 19, Folder 29.

48   **"gaily-colored lichens and crinkled mosses":** Henry Wood Elliott, *A Monograph of the Seal-Islands of Alaska* (Washington: U.S. Government Printing Office, 1882), 11.

49   **"Their fat bodies writhe":** Elliott, *Monograph*, 32.

49   **"The head and eye of the female":** Elliott, *Monograph*, 35.

FOUR

51   **"free Creoles":** "Alaska Natives at Fort Ross," Fort Ross Conservancy, https://www.fortross.org/alaska-natives.htm, accessed July 9, 2021.

52   **Alexandra was counted:** Betty A. Lindsay and John A. Lindsay, *Pribilof Islands, Alaska: The People: A Historical Account Told Through Illustrated Biographies* (Seattle, WA: U.S. Department of Commerce, National Oceanic and Atmospheric Administration, National Ocean Service, Office of Response and Restoration, 2010), 12.

53   **"It is the wind":** Elliott, *Monograph*, 14.

53   **At the end of December:** Lisa Demer, "Orthodox Christmas melds Yup'ik and religious traditions," *Anchorage Daily News*, September 28, 2016, https://www.adn.com/rural-alaska/article/orthodox-melds-yupik-and-religious-traditions/2015/01/09/.

54   **he attempted the seemingly impossible feat:** Henry Wood Elliott, *Monograph*, 63.

54   **For ten cents:** "Lantern Slides," Magic Lantern Society, http://www.magiclanternsociety.org/about-magic-lanterns/lantern-slides/, accessed June 22, 2021.

55 **she could play the piano:** Henry Wood Elliott to William Dall, July 22, 1873, Smithsonian Archives, Henry W Elliott 1865-1874 Correspondence Complete, RU 7073, Box 10, Folder 10.

56 **While Elliott was adamant:** Henry W. Elliott, *A Report upon the Condition of Affairs in the Territory of Alaska*, (Washington: Government Printing Office, 1875), 20-28.

56 **On one occasion:** Elliott, Henry Wood, The Lakewood Historical Society, from Early Days of Lakewood – D.A.R. 39-40, https://www.lakewoodhistory.org/research/library-local-history-files/biography-a-f#h.p_-ANh-_ffMKYc, accessed June 22, 2021.

FIVE

58 **known as Rotten Row:** MacGillivray, *Captain Alex MacLean*, 35.

58 **The Army pulled out in 1877:** National Park Service, Sitka: Administrative History, Chapter 2: Sitka—Historical Overview, http://npshistory.com/publications/sitk/adhi/chap2.htm, accessed June 23, 2021.

58 **"drunken judge":** "Lafayette Dawson," *Daily Alta California*, Vol. 42 (April 12, 1888), 2.

59 **The pirates, including MacLean:** MacGillivray, 37, 125.

60 **According to some reports:** MacGillivray, 41.

60 **In 1887, the MacLeans and their fellow pirates:** Busch, *The War Against the Seals*, 148.

60 **As one pirate put it:** McGillivray, 37.

60 **The revenue cutters captured:** Peter Murray, *The Vagabond Fleet* (Victoria, BC: Sono Nis Press, 1988), 64.

60 **Henry Elliott addressed a separate appeal:** Henry Wood Elliott to T. F. Bayard, December 3, 1887, Cleveland Museum of Natural History Archives, Henry Wood Elliott Fur Seal Controversy, HWE_B11F74_UncheckedHunting.

61 **240 shirts:** David Crane, *Scott of the Arctic: A Biography* (New York: Knopf, 2008), 27.

61 **a letter from a British ambassador:** Robert Mitchell, "The fake letter historians believe tipped a presidential election," *Washington Post*, June 21, 2018, https://www.washingtonpost.com/news/retropolis/wp/2018/06/20/the-fake-letter-that-historians-believe-tipped-a-presidential-election/.

62 **In a separate incident:** Fredericka Martin, *Sea Bears* (New York: Chilton Company, 1960), 114.

62 **The pelagic catch that year:** Busch, *The War Against the Seals*, 146.

SIX

64 **Fur seals are descended:** National Park Service, Channel Islands, The Northern Fur Seal, https://www.nps.gov/chis/learn/nature/northern-fur-seal.htm, accessed June 23, 2021.

64 **Elliott described the beachmaster's large, expressive eyes:** Henry Wood Elliott, *Monograph*, 29–30.

65 **Up to seven feet long:** "Northern Fur Seal," National Oceanic and Atmospheric Administration, https://www.fisheries.noaa.gov/species/northern-fur-seal, accessed January 4, 2021.

66   **Then there were the nonbreeding females:** Elliott, *Monograph*, 50.

66   **From the ACC's annual quota:** *Hearings Before the Committee on Expenditures in the Department of Commerce and Labor, House of Representatives on House Resolution No. 73 to Investigate the Fur-seal Industry of Alaska*, Committee on Expenditures in the Department of Commerce and Labor, No. 1 (May 31 and June 2, 1911), 963.

67   **From one Government House window:** Henry Wood Elliott, *Monograph*, 71–72.

67   **a method, he wrote:** Henry W. Elliott, *Our Arctic Province: Alaska and the Seal Islands* (New York: Charles Scribner and Sons, 1886), 333.

69   **Noting a precipitous drop:** Henry W. Elliott, *Report on the Condition of the Fur-Seal Fisheries of the Pribylov Islands in 1890* (Paris: Chamerot & Renaurd, 1893), ix.

69   **In 1883, the year the MacLeans:** Busch, *The War Against the Seals*, 136.

70   **Tingle denied these improprieties:** Lindsay and Lindsay, *Pribilof Islands, Alaska*, 263.

71   **"a conceited old goose":** Lindsay and Lindsay, 455.

72   **"wonderous strength and desperate courage":** Elliott, *Monograph*, 32.

72   **"sickening contrast":** Henry Wood Elliott, *Report on the Condition of the Fur-Seal Fisheries of the Pribilov Islands*, produced April 4, 1893 by the Agent of the United States to the Tribunal of Arbitration Convened at Paris (Paris: Chamerot and Renouard, 1893), 32, 34–35, 45.

72   **Recently, a revenue cutter captain:** Henry Wood Elliott, *Report on the Condition of the Fur-Seal Fisheries*, 85.

74   **Even preservationist John Muir:** Dorceta E. Taylor, *The Rise of the American Conservation Movement* (Durham, NC: Duke University Press, 2016) 183.

74   **"We are a selfish people":** Elliott, *Report on the Condition*, 5–6.

75   **In his manuscript:** Elizabeth Kolbert, *The Sixth Extinction* (New York: Picador, 2014), 44.

SEVEN

78   **eight seal-hunting vessels:** Richard Ravalli, "Herman Liebes and Sea Otters," *Alaska Historical Society Blog*, February 5, 2014, https:// alaskahistoricalsociety.org/herman-liebes-and-sea-otters/.

80   **MacLean dropped anchor:** MacGillivray, *Captain Alex MacLean*, 72.

81   **Despite his habit:** Roy, "Life and Death of the Sea-Wolf," 84.

81   **A prime example:** MacGillivray, 73.

83   **twenty-three armed naval cruisers:** Charles S. Campbell Jr., "The Anglo-American Crisis in the Bering Sea, 1890–1891," *Journal of American History* 48, no. 3 (1961): 403, doi:10.2307/1891985, 403.

83   **As a writer for the *New York Herald*:** Campbell, "Anglo-American Crisis," 403.

85   **He published a summary:** James T. Gay. "Harrison, Blaine, and Cronyism," *The Alaska Journal*, Vol. 3 (1973), 18.

85   **He also published a letter:** Gay, 18.

EIGHT

88   **At the helm:** MacGillivray, *Captain Alex MacLean*, 85.

88   **"I'll sing about a sailor man":** Foulke, "Life in the Dying Age," 115.

88-89   **As one Liebes employee admitted:** Busch, *The War Against the Seals*, 132.

90   **Bering died while awaiting rescue:** Henry Wood Elliott, *Monograph*, 5.

90   **"For life it is that":** Rudyard Kipling, "The Rhyme of the Three Sealers," The Kipling Society, http://www.kiplingsociety.co.uk/poems_threesealers.htm, accessed June 25, 2021.

90   **As their schooners approached:** MacGillivray, 86.

92   **Years later, MacLean would gloss over:** MacGillivray, 91.

92   **Maclean reportedly had a new swagger:** MacGillivray, 92.

92   **Exposed to smallpox:** MacGillivray, 93.

92   **For ten years:** MacGillivray, 87.

93   **"practically under my command":** MacGillivray, 98.

93   **It was the worst patch:** MacGillivray, 101.

93   **During one especially bad gale:** MacGillivray, 99–100.

94   **At a favorite Oakland watering hole:** MacGillivray, 87.

NINE

96   **"He went into the drive":** David Starr Jordan, *Matka and Kotik* (San Francisco: The Whitaker and Ray Company, 1897), 62.

97   **Raised in New York State:** Lulu Miller, *Why Fish Don't Exist* (New York: Simon & Schuster, 2020), 22.

99   **In what would become a duplicitous pattern:** Lindsay and Lindsay, *People of the Pribilofs*, Alaska, 236.

100   **In turn, Dall wrote to the Smithsonian's Spencer Baird:** William Dall to Sebastian Baird, November 14, 1973, Smithsonian Archives, RU 7002, Box 18, Folder 23.

101   **According to a report in the Portland newspaper:** MacGillivray, *Captain Alex MacLean*, 107.

103   **Jordan spoke admiringly:** David Starr Jordan, *The Days of a Man*, Vol. I (New York: World Book Company, 1922), 579.

104   **Jordan once ordered:** Lindsay and Lindsay, 585.

104   **Belonging to a phylum:** Perry Klass, "War of the Worms," *The New Yorker*, December 14, 2015, https://www.newyorker.com/tech/annals-of-technology/war-of-the-worms.

105   **Recent studies show:** Mauricio Seguel et al., "Immune-mediated hookworm clearance and survival of a marine mammal decrease with warmer ocean temperatures," Ecology, Microbiology, and Infectious Disease, November 6, 2018, DOI: 10.7554/eLife.38432, https://elifesciences.org/articles/38432.

105   **he also penned a letter:** David Starr Jordan to Samuel Langley, Smithsonian Institution Archives, RU 31, Box 37, Folder 22.

TEN

109   **A total of sixteen schooners… Five Japanese dead:** Martin, *Sea Bears*, 135–139 and Busch, *The War against the Seals*, 147. Lindsay and Lindsay, *People of the Pribilofs*, Alaska, 545–549.

117   **If you must strike a blow, don't hit soft:** Teddy Roosevelt, speech in New York City, February 17, 1899, https://www.theodoreroosevelt.org/content. aspx?page_id=22&club_id=991271&module_id=339333.

ELEVEN

118   **The *San Francisco Chronicle*:** "A Family Rupture: Mrs. Herman Liebes Leaves Her Husband," *San Francisco Chronicle*, October 30, 1891, 12.

118   **He joined a South Seas pearling venture:** Roy, "Life and Death of the Sea-Wolf," 77–79, 81.

118   **In one night:** Kenneth Brandt, "The Short, Frantic, Rags-to-Riches Life of Jack London," Smithsonianmag.com, December 14, 2016, https://www. smithsonianmag.com/smithsonian-institution/short-heroic-rags-riches-life-jack-london-180961200/.

119   **Prince of the Oyster Pirates:** Brandt, "Rags-to-Riches Life."

119   **Returning to San Francisco:** "Jack London's Writings," Sonoma State University, https://london.sonoma.edu/writings, accessed June 28, 2021.

119   **London signed with *Century Magazine*:** John Mancini, "Jack London: Russo-Japanese War Correspondent," https://www.historynet.com/ jack-london-russo-japanese-war-correspondent.htm, accessed June 28, 2021.

120   **One day the author delivered:** Roy, "Life and Death of the Sea-Wolf," 83.

120   **With typical aplomb:** MacGillivray, *Captain Alex MacLean*, 163.

121   **As MacLean's butcher boat crews rowed:** MacGillivray, 165.

121   **twenty-two-year-old Missouri boy:** MacGillivray, 165–166.

122   **The detective claimed:** MacGillivray, 167.

123   **When asked if he and his crew:** MacGillivray, 185.

123   **When the third patrol boat:** MacGillivray, 185–186.

124   **MacLean lacked a mouse's courage:** MacGillivray, 189.

124   **He signed himself in the customs house books:** American Consulate, Victoria, to Herbert H.D. Pierce, Assistant Secretary of State, September 16, 1905. Cleveland Museum of Natural History Archives, Henry Wood Elliott Fur Seal Controversy Papers, Box 8, Folder 42.

125   **"half monster":** MacGillivray, 181.

125   **But in Washington:** American Consulate, Victoria, to Herbert H.D. Pierce, Assistant Secretary of State, October 5, 1905. Cleveland Museum of Natural History Archives, Henry Wood Elliott Fur Seal Controversy Papers, Box 8, Folder 42.

125   **Weeks later, a court order:** Consul Smith, American Consulate, Victoria, to Herbert H.D. Pierce, Assistant Secretary of State, September 30, 1905. Cleveland Museum of Natural History Archives, Henry Wood Elliott Fur Seal Controversy Papers, Box 8, Folder 42.

TWELVE

126   **When an anarchist shot:** "Theodore Roosevelt's Libraries," Theodore Roosevelt Center at Dickinson State University, https://www. theodorerooseveltcenter.org/Learn-About-TR/TR-Encyclopedia/ Reading%20and%20Writing/Roosevelt%20Libraries, accessed June 29, 2021. "Happy Birthday, Mr. President," Theodore Roosevelt Center at

Dickinson State University, https://www.theodorerooseveltcenter.org/Blog/Item/Happy%20Birthday%20Mister%20President, accessed June 29, 2021. Ellis W. Bell, "How Roosevelt changed America," Theodore Roosevelt Island National Memorial, June 18, 1968, https://www.theodorerooseveltcenter.org/Research/Digital-Library/Record?libID=o274212.

126 **"harum-scarum roughriders":** Edmund Morris, *The Rise of Theodore Roosevelt* (New York: The Modern Library, 1979), 642–3.

127 **In one storied hunting incident:** Sarah Watts, *Rough Rider in the White House: Theodore Roosevelt and the Politics of Desire* (Chicago: University of Chicago Press, 2003), 182.

127 **In addition to shooting passenger pigeons:** Barry Yeoman, "Why the Passenger Pigeon Went Extinct," *Audubon Magazine*, May–June 2014, https://www.audubon.org/magazine/may-june-2014/why-passenger-pigeon-went-extinct, accessed March 23, 2021.

127 **As he saw his beloved Western landscape:** Morris, *The Rise of Theodore Roosevelt*, 388-389.

129 **thirty million and one hundred million:** Shepard Kretch III, "Buffalo Tales: The Near-Extermination of the American Bison," National Humanities Center, http://nationalhumanitiescenter.org/tserve/nattrans/ntecoindian/essays/buffalo.htm, accessed March 23, 2021.

129 **In 1805, expedition leader Meriwether Lewis:** "American buffalo (*bison, bison*)," U.S. Fish and Wildlife Service, January 1998, https://www.fws.gov/species/species_accounts/bio_buff.html.

130 **In nineteenth-century America:** David Starr Jordan, 1851-1931, "The Fur Seals and Fur-Seal Islands of the North Pacific Ocean, Part 2," BC Historical Books (Washington: Government Printing Office, 1899), 381, doi:http://dx.doi.org/10.14288/1.0343634.

131 **Diminutive and elegantly dressed:** Morris, *Theodore Rex*, 238–241, 368.

131 **Elliott had first reached out to Hay:** Hearings Before the Committee on Expenditures in the Department of Commerce, House of Representatives: Investigation of the Fur-seal Industry of Alaska. [Oct. 13, 1913-Apr. 2, 1914], Vol. 1, United States Congress, House Committee on Expenditures in the Department of Commerce, U.S. Government Printing Office, 1914, 824.

134 **Armed with the president's assurances:** Morris, *Theodore Rex*, 394–395.

THIRTEEN

136 **"brutal friend to whom I pay the most attention":** Edmund Morris, *Theodore Rex* (New York: Random House, 2001), 13.

137 **"Ah! Elliott."** Henry W. Elliott to William Hornaday, April 6, 1930. Wildlife Conservation Society Archives, William T. Hornaday Wildlife Conservation Scrapbooks, Vol. 6: "The Saving of the Fur Seal Industry, 1909–12," Part III, 1894–1930, 48.

137 **"most interesting" "I never heard these things before":** Elliott to Hornaday, April 6, 1930. Hornaday Wildlife Conservation Scrapbooks, Vol. 6, 48.

137 **The meeting lasted two and a half hours:** Elliott to Hornaday, April 6, 1930, 48-49.

138 **"As Root had requested":** Elliott to Hornaday, April 6, 1930, 49.

140   **Three weeks after the raids:** Lindsay and Lindsay, *People of the Pribilofs*, Alaska, 546.

140   **a quota of one hundred thousand pelts per year:** Dorothy Jones, "From Wage Earners to Wards" in Century of Servitude, http://arcticcircle.uconn. edu/HistoryCulture/Aleut/Jones/ch3.html, accessed October 15, 2019.

140   **"savage tribes":** Morris, *Rise of Theodore Roosevelt*, 476.

140   **By the end of 1906:** Lindsay and Lindsay, 311.

141   **"beaten off by the very meager and insufficient armed guards":** Theodore Roosevelt, State of the Union Address, December 3, 1906, https://www. infoplease.com/primary-sources/government/presidential-speeches/state-union-address-theodore-roosevelt-december-3-1906, accessed March 23, 2021.

141   **"no damage whatever done":** Roosevelt, State of the Union Address.

FOURTEEN

143   **Crewed by "desperate men":** MacGillivray, 211; Lindsay and Lindsay, 399.

143   **They returned after midnight:** Lindsay and Lindsay, 399.

143   **three Hotchkiss Mountain guns:** Lindsay and Lindsay, 402.

144   **For years, his opponents:** Alaskan Seal Fisheries: Hearings Before the Committee on Conservation of National Resources, United States Senate on the Bill S. 9959, to Amend an Act Entitled "An Act to Protect the Seal Fisheries of Alaska, and for Other Purposes," Approved April 21, 1910, United States Congress, Senate Committee on Conservation of National Resources Jan (U.S. Government Printing Office, 1911), 21.

144   **As Tom Mueller points out:** Tom Mueller, *Crisis of Conscience* (New York: Riverhead Books, 2019), 31, 40-41, 62.

145   **"sin and shame":** Henry W. Elliott, "The Depredation of the Seal Rookeries," *The Pacific Fisherman* VII, no. 8 (August 1909), Vol. 7, No. 8, 11.

145   **"If this fur seal business":** Fredericka Martin, *Sea Bears* (New York: Chilton Company Books, 1960), 144-5.

145   **As president of the American Bison Society:** Taylor, *American Conservation Movement*, 183-184. Gregory J. Dehler, *The Most Defiant Devil* (Charlottesville: University of Virginia Press, 2013), 91-94.

145   **"finest and rarest thing":** Edith Elliott to William Hornaday, March 1, 1931. Wildlife Conservation Society Archives, William T. Hornaday Wildlife Conservation Scrapbooks, Vol. 6: "The Saving of the Fur Seal Industry, 1909-12," Part III, 1894-1930, 265.

145   **Orphaned at age fifteen:** Gregory J. Dehler, *The Most Defiant Devil* (Charlottesville: University of Virginia Press, 2013), 48.

146   **the president remaining on edge over tensions with Japan:** Morris, *Theodore Rex*, 534.

147   **$50,000 in damages:** MacGillivray, *Captain Alex MacLean*, 158.

147   **In the fall of 1909:** "Hornaday and the Camp Fire Club of America," *Wild Things: The Blog of the Wildlife Conservation Society Archives*, March 27, 2014, http://www.wcsarchivesblog.org/hornaday-and-the-camp-fire-club-of-america/.

148   **"camped on the ground in the howling wilderness":** "Hornaday and the Camp Fire Club of America," *Wild Things*.

148-9   **"voluminous and frequent":** Joseph Dixon to William Hornaday, November 3, 1909. Wildlife Conservation Society Archives, William T. Hornaday Wildlife Conservation Scrapbooks, Vol. 4: "The Saving of the Fur Seal Industry, 1909–1912," Part I, 1890–1930, 80.

149   **Their efforts would begin:** William Hornaday to Henry Wood Elliott, November 8, 1909. Wildlife Conservation Society Archives, William T. Hornaday Wildlife Conservation Scrapbooks, Vol. 4: "The Saving of the Fur Seal Industry, 1909–1912," Part I, 1890–1930, 81.

150   **Even if the twenty pups survived:** Henry W. Elliott to William Hornaday, February 24, 1910. Wildlife Conservation Society Archives, William T. Hornaday Wildlife Conservation Scrapbooks, Vol. 4: "The Saving of the Fur Seal Industry, 1909–1912," Part I, 1890–1930, 94.

151   **the National Audubon Society:** The Audubon Society was founded in 1886 by George Grinnell, who also co-founded the Boone and Crockett Club with Teddy Roosevelt the following year. In establishing the Audubon Society, Grinnell had hoped to pressure the millinery industry to stop killing birds for their feathers. Unlike Boone and Crockett and the Camp Fire Club, women were welcome in the Audubon Society as long as they pledged not to buy or wear hats with feathers. Unprepared for the rush of interest from women eager to support a cause, Grinnell disbanded the society after two years. In 1896, two well-to-do women had restarted the effort, recruiting society ladies who blamed not only milliners but also cats, mischievous boys, African Americans, immigrants, and Native Americans for threatening songbirds. See Taylor, *Rise of the American Conservation Movement*, 192–211.

151   **In putting together a chronology:** William Hornaday to Elihu Root, March 3, 1920. Wildlife Conservation Society Archives, William T. Hornaday Wildlife Conservation Scrapbooks, Vol. 4: "The Saving of the Fur Seal Industry, 1909–1912, Part I," 1890–1930, 98.

151   **President Taft issued a special message:** US Senate, Official message from the President of the United States William H. Taft recommending that the North American Commercial Company be denied further lease to collect fur seals from the islands of St. Paul and St. George, Document No. 430, March 15, 1910. Wildlife Conservation Society Archives, William T. Hornaday Wildlife Conservation Scrapbooks, Vol. 4: "The Saving of the Fur Seal Industry, 1909–1912," Part I, 101a.

152   **The board proposed only one restriction:** Report of the Commissioner of Fisheries to the Secretary of Commerce and Labor, 1910. 1-4, 27-29. Wildlife Conservation Society Archives, William T. Hornaday Wildlife Conservation Scrapbooks, Vol. 4: "The Saving of the Fur Seal Industry, 1909 -1912," Part I, 95.

154   **"reeking with selfish interests":** William T. Hornaday, *Thirty Years War for Wildlife: Gains and Losses in the Thankless Task* (New York: Scrivner & Sons, 1931), 176.

155   **The reason Bowers gave:** Hornaday, *Thirty Years War*, 180.

FIFTEEN

156   **$22 per pelt at auctions in London:** MacGillivray, *Captain Alex MacLean*, 213.

157   **headlines in newspapers around the world:** MacGillivray, 200.

158   **six tons of fish:** MacGillivray, 213.

158   **Based on reports:** "Strict Watch on Japanese Sealers," *Seattle Post Intelligencer*, May 19, 1910.

159   **Hornaday began by confronting Nagel:** William Hornaday to Charles Nagel, May 18, 1910. Wildlife Conservation Society Archives, William T. Hornaday Wildlife Conservation Scrapbooks, Vol. 4: "The Saving of the Fur Seal Industry, 1909–1912," Part I, 1890–1930, 116.

159   **In response, Nagel offered the rather illogical claim:** Charles Nagel to William Hornaday, May 23, 1910. Wildlife Conservation Society Archives, William T. Hornaday Wildlife Conservation Scrapbooks, Vol. 4: "The Saving of the Fur Seal Industry, 1909–1912, Part I," 1890–1930, 120–3.

159   **"fighting blood was right up":** William Hornaday to Henry W. Elliott, November 15, 1910. Cleveland Museum of Natural History Archives, Henry Wood Elliott Fur Seal Controversy Papers, Box 6, Folder 46.

160   **As Hornaday went after Nagel:** Henry W. Elliott, Memorandum titled "Who is Fish Commissioner Bowers?" June 2, 1910, in William T. Hornaday Wildlife Conservation Scrapbooks, Vol. 4: "The Saving of the Fur Seal Industry, 1909–1912, Part I," 1890–1930, 133.

160   **"Publicity will shrivel them quick":** Henry W. Elliott to William Hornaday, undated. Wildlife Conservation Society Archives, William T. Hornaday Wildlife Conservation Scrapbooks, Vol. 4: "The Saving of the Fur Seal Industry, 1909–1912, Part I," 1890–1930, 124.

160   **the New York Zoological Society instructed Hornaday:** William Hornaday to George Clark, February 13, 1913. Wildlife Conservation Society Archives, William T. Hornaday Wildlife Conservation Scrapbooks, Vol. 5: "The Saving of the Fur Seal Industry, 1909–1912, Part II," 1910–1935, 245.

160   **At the end of the 1910 season:** "US Finds Profits in Seals," undated clipping. Wildlife Conservation Society Archives, William T. Hornaday Wildlife Conservation Scrapbooks, Vol. 5: "The Saving of the Fur Seal Industry, 1909–1912, Part II," 1910–1935, 164.

161   **"A deal for the US Treasury, Elliott noted privately":** "US Finds Profits in Seals," William T. Hornaday Wildlife Conservation Scrapbooks, Vol. 5, 164.

162   **the man was a crook:** Henry Wood Elliott to William Hornaday, July 17, 1910, in William T. Hornaday Wildlife Conservation Scrapbooks, Vol. 5, 24.

SIXTEEN

165   **If there were 50,000 seals left:** Kurkpatrick Dorsey, *The Dawn of Conservation Diplomacy: U.S.–Canadian Wildlife Protection Treaties in the Progressive Era* (Seattle: University of Washington Press, 1998): 147.

166   **at least one foreign diplomat noted:** Dorsey, *The Dawn of Conservation Diplomacy*, 160.

169   **Privately, Elliott shared with Hornaday:** Henry W Elliott, Codex criminis Americanus sum in re fur seals. Chronological list of names associated with the ruin of the Alaskan fur seal herd, 1910-06-18, Wildlife Conservation Society Archives, William T. Hornaday Wildlife Conservation Scrapbooks, Vol. 6: "The Saving of the Fur Seal Industry, 1909–1912," Part III, 1909-1912, 3-6b.

169   **They also heard witness testimony:** Andrew F. Gallagher and Henry Wood Elliott, *The Report of the Special Agents of the House Committee on Expenditures*

in the Department of Commerce Upon the Condition of the Fur-seal Herd of Alaska and the Conduct of the Public Business on the Pribilof Islands: As Ordered by the Committee, June 20, 1913, and Made by the Said Agents, August 31, 1913, to the Chairman, Hon. J.H. Rothermel. United States: U.S. Government Printing Office, 1913, 98.

170   **When the trainer mentioned:** Ken Ross, "Fur Seal's Friend: Henry W. Elliot," in *Pioneering Conservation in Alaska* (Boulder, Colorado: University Press of Colorado, 2006), http://www.jstor.org/stable/j.ctt1wn0r8r.12, 49, accessed July 1, 2021. Dorsey, *The Dawn of Conservation Diplomacy*, 160.

170   **discredited adventurer:** Dorsey, *The Dawn of Conservation Diplomacy*, 161.

170   **Jordan accused Elliott:** "Accuses Elliott in Seal Inquiry," *New York Times*, February 24, 1914, 2.

171   **"That pernicious idea":** William Hornaday to George Clark, September 9, 1911. Cleveland Museum of Natural History Archives, Henry Wood Elliott Fur Seal Controversy Papers, Box 10, Folder 72.

172   **a lengthy *New York Times* article:** "No More Slaughtering of Seals for Five Years," *New York Times*, September 1, 1912, 10.

SEVENTEEN

174   **Sailors have had to either leave:** Foulke, "Life in the Dying Age," 137.

174   **Later, she will move to California:** Their California residence was also near vineyards belonging to Gustave Niebaum, a Finnish sea captain who finagled his way into the ACC and used his seal profits to set himself up in the wine business. He proved as adept with wine as he was with the sail. As of this writing, his Inglenook label is still being sold.

174   **The drafty two-hundred-square-foot wooden houses:** Barbara Boyle Torrey, *Slaves of the Harvest: The Pribilof Islands* (Anchorage: Tanadgusix Corporation, 1983), 108.

176   **to corroborate Elliott's work:** Lindsay and Lindsay, *Pribilof Islands*, Alaska, 193.

176   **Months earlier, Commission Bowers:** Andrew F. Gallagher and Henry Wood Elliott, *The Report of the Special Agents of the House Committee on Expenditures in the Department of Commerce Upon the Condition of the Fur-seal Herd of Alaska and the Conduct of the Public Business on the Pribilof Islands*: As Ordered by the Committee, June 20, 1913, and Made by the Said Agents, August 31, 1913, to the Chairman, Hon. J.H. Rothermel. United States: U.S. Government Printing Office, 1913, 98.

177   **Fuming, he told Lembkey:** Lindsay and Lindsay, 193–194.

177   **He said someone had to keep an eye on Elliott:** Lindsay and Lindsay, 194.

177   **Within two days of his arrival:** Lindsay and Lindsay, 402–403.

177   **Upon arriving:** Lindsay and Lindsay, 194.

178   **Elliott believed this new behavior:** Andrew F. Gallagher and Henry Wood Elliott, *The Report of the Special Agents of the House Committee on Expenditures in the Department of Commerce Upon the Condition of the Fur-seal Herd of Alaska and the Conduct of the Public Business on the Pribilof Islands*: As Ordered by the Committee, June 20, 1913, and Made by the Said Agents, August 31, 1913, to the Chairman, Hon. J.H. Rothermel. United States: U.S. Government Printing Office, 1913, 23.

179 **"I do not believe":** William Hornaday to George Clark, March 14, 1913. Wildlife Conservation Society Archives, William T. Hornaday Wildlife Conservation Scrapbooks, Vol. 5: "The Saving of the Fur Seal Industry, 1909–1912," Part II, 1910–1935, 115.

180 **"a warm personal friend of Jordan":** Henry W. Elliott to William Hornaday, December 4, 1912. Wildlife Conservation Society Archives, William T. Hornaday Wildlife Conservation Scrapbooks, Vol. 5: "The Saving of the Fur Seal Industry, 1909–1912," Part II, 1910–1935, 233.

180 **"There are three kinds of liars":** "Lucas' Wake at Cosmos Hall," Cleveland Museum of Natural History Archives, Henry Wood Elliott Fur Seal Controversy Papers, Box 1, Folder 1.

180 **"For a man to have an ideal in this world":** Henry Wood Elliott, A monograph of the seal islands of Alaska (Washington, D.C., Government Printing Office, 1882), scrapbook version in Henry Wood Elliott Collection, Washington State Historical Society Archives, Box 2, IA37, scrapbook page (unnumbered).

180 **He also inserted cartoons:** Lisa M. Morris, "Keeper Of The Seal: The Art of Henry Wood Elliott and the Salvation of the Alaska Fur Seals" (Thesis [Ph.D.] University of Alaska Fairbanks, 2001), Scholar Works @UA, http://hdl.handle.net/11122/8624, 126–132.

183 **"Junius":** "Accuses Elliott in Seal Inquiry," *The New York Times*, February 24, 1914, 2.

183 **It called his 1913 Pribilof visit a farce:** Raymond C. Osburn, "The Fur Seal Inquiry, the Congressional Committee, and the Scientist," *Science*, Vol. XL, No. 1033 (October 16, 1914), 557–558.

184 **Thinking he might have fallen asleep belowdecks:** MacGillivray, *Captain Alex MacLean*, 228–230.

184 **According to the coroner:** MacGillivray, 230.

184 **One theory was that the infamous seal pirate:** Memorandum Concerning "The 'Sea-Wolf' Found Dead," Investigation of the fur seal industry of Alaska; hearings of House of Representatives, 1913—1914, Washington D.C., Government Printing Office, 1914, scrapbook version in Henry Wood Elliott Collection, Washington State Historical Society Archives, Box 2, IA37, scrapbook page (unnumbered).

185 **"It will be a fight":** *Vancouver, BC, Daily News and Advertiser*, February 6, 1913, 13. Transcribed by Henry W. Elliott, Washington State Historical Society Archives, Henry W. Elliott Collection, Folder 15.

185 **Elliott surmised that to avoid the fight:** Memorandum Concerning "The 'Sea-Wolf' Found Dead," Henry Wood Elliott Collection, Washington State Historical Society Archives.

EIGHTEEN

186 **In his letters, he asked after the family dog:** Henry Wood Elliott to Lionel Elliott, November 6, 1916, Baldwin Wallace: CMNH Henry Wood Elliott Collection - Ohio Private Academic Libraries - Digital Collections, https://digital.opal-libraries.org/digital/collection/p16708coll10/id/67/rec/122.

187 **the harrowing days of the past:** "Aged Artist Finds Repose, Paints Mount Rainier Every Day," *Seattle Daily Times*, July 24, 1927, 53.

188 **Not long after Elliott arrived in Seattle:** "Aged Artist Finds Repose."

188   **Hornaday interrupted Elliott's idyllic existence:** Henry W. Elliott to William Hornaday, April 6, 1930. Wildlife Conservation Society Archives, William T. Hornaday Wildlife Conservation Scrapbooks, Vol 6: "The Saving of the Fur Seal Industry, 1909–12," Part III, 1894–1930, 48-50.

189   **the article about him that ran in the *Seattle Daily News*:** "HW Elliott Dies; Drafted Fur Seal Pact," *Seattle Daily Times*, May 26, 1930, 2.

190   **He also claimed to have let an etymology prize:** Lulu Miller, *Why Fish Don't Exist*, 102.

190   **When Jane Stanford accused him:** Miller, 59.

190   **Following Jane Stanford's death:** Miller, 113.

191   **If the American public:** Torrey, *Slaves of the Harvest*, 115–6.

193   **When the seal harvest ended:** "Aleutian Islands World War II: Evacuation and Internment," National Park Service, https://www.nps.gov/aleu/learn/historyculture/unangax-internment.htm, accessed July 1, 2021. Torrey, *Slaves of the Harvest*, 127–135.

193   **By the time World War II ended:** John Smelcer, "The Other WWII American-Internment Atrocity," NPR, February 21, 2017, https://www.npr.org/sections/codeswitch/2017/02/21/516277507/the-other-wwii-american-internment-atrocity.

193   **A reporter for the *Tundra Times*:** Torrey, *Slaves of the Harvest*, 155.

193   **Alexander Milovidov, the son of Alexandra Milovidov:** An alternate spelling for the surname Milovidov is Melovidov, used more commonly in recent decades. Alternate spellings for Alexander and Alexandra are Aleksander and Aleksandra.

195-6   **World Wildlife Federation's *Living Planet Report 2018*:** *Living Planet Report - 2018: Aiming Higher*, World Wildlife Fund, https://www.worldwildlife.org/pages/living-planet-report-2018.

196   **species on earth rarely went extinct:** Elizabeth Kolbert, *The Sixth Extinction: An Unnatural History* (New York: Henry Holt and Company, 2014), 15.

196   **global assessment by the United Nations:** United Nations, "UN Report: Nature's Dangerous Decline 'Unprecedented'; Species Extinction Rates 'Accelerating,'" *Sustainable Development Goals* (blog), May 6, 2019, https://www.un.org/sustainabledevelopment/blog/2019/05/nature-decline-unprecedented-report/.

196   **between $7 and $23 billion:** Simon Worrall, "Inside the Disturbing World of Illegal Wildlife Trade," *National Geographic*, November 9, 2018, https://www.nationalgeographic.com/animals/2018/11/poaching-tigers-bears-bile-farming-book-talk/.

196   **rats that literally jumped ship:** "Hawadax Island (formerly Rat Island)," Fish and Wildlife Service, Alaska Maritime National Wildlife Refuge, July 2, 2020, https://www.fws.gov/refuge/alaska_maritime/what_we_do/partnership/rat_island.html.

197   **Greenpeace Canada admitted in a 2014 apology:** Joanna Kerr, "Greenpeace Apology to Inuit for Impacts of Seal Campaign," Greenpeace, June 24, 2014, https://www.greenpeace.org/canada/en/story/5473/greenpeace-apology-to-inuit-for-impacts-of-seal-campaign/.

197   **As Elliott had pointed out:** Roger L. Gentry, *Behavior and Ecology of the Northern Fur Seal* (Princeton, NJ: Princeton University Press, 1998), 62, 214.

197   **In 2016, Canada's harp seal quota:** Jani Hall, "Demand for Seal Products Has Fallen—So Why Do Canadians Keep Hunting?" *National Geographic*, April 5, 2017, https://www.nationalgeographic.com/news/2017/04/wildlife-watch-canada-harp-seal-hunt/.

198   **Beginning with the five-year moratorium:** "About the Canadian Seal Hunt," The Humane Society of the United States, https://www.humanesociety.org/resources/about-canadian-seal-hunt, accessed February 3, 2021.

198   **the population reached 2.1 million:** Gentry, *Behavior and Ecology*, 27.

198   **By that point, seal census methods:** M. M. Muto, V. T. Helker, B. J. Delean, R. P. Angliss, P. L. Boveng, J. M. Breiwick, B. M. Brost, M. F. Cameron, P. J. Clapham, S. P. Dahle, M. E. Dahlheim, B. S. Fadely, M. C. Ferguson, L. W. Fritz, R. C. Hobbs, Y. V. Ivashchenko, A. S. Kennedy, J. M. London, S. A. Mizroch, R. R. Ream, E. L. Richmond, K. E. W. Shelden, K. L. Sweeney, R. G. Towell, P. R. Wade, J. M. Waite, and A. N. Zerbini, *Alaska Marine Mammal Stock Assessments 2019, NOAA Technical Memorandum NMFS-ADSC-404*, July 2020, 30, https://media.fisheries.noaa.gov/dam-migration/2019_sars_alaska_508.pdf, accessed February 4, 2021.

198   **By 1974, wildlife managers:** Gentry, *Behavior and Ecology*, 28.

198   **By 1988, their numbers:** "Northern Fur Seal."

198   **At this steady rate:** Muto, et al., *Alaska Marine Mammal Stock Assessments*, 31.

198   **In 2016, fishermen caught:** Brian Hagenbuch, "Bering Sea pollock fishery wraps about 2020 with difficult B season," *Seafood Source*, November 9, 2020, https://www.seafoodsource.com/news/supply-trade/bering-sea-pollock-fishery-wraps-about-2020-with-difficult-b-season.

199   **Scientists also speculate:** Sarah Kershaw, "Decline of Hardy Alaskan Fur Seals Baffles Experts," *New York Times*, February 22, 2005, F00004.

199   **"By the year 2000":** William T. Hornaday, *Thirty Years War for Wildlife: Gains and Losses in the Thankless Task* (Stamford, CT: Permanent Wildlife Protection Fund, 1931), 181.

199   **a short documentary film:** "Henry Wood Elliott: Defender of the Fur Seal," NOAA Fisheries, https://videos.fisheries.noaa.gov/detail/videos/alaska/video/1437362002001/henry-wood-elliott:-defender-of-the-fur-seal, accessed July 2, 2021.

W

Y

DEB VANASSE is an author of novels, nonfiction books, and children's books. She is also a reporter, historian, and the co-founder of the Alaska statewide writing center 49 Writers. Deb's writing has been published in *Alaska Magazine*, and she has been interviewed by the *Globe and Mail* and CBC radio. She has given lectures for the National Park Service and several museums among other programs. For several years Deb lived in the Alaskan bush, and she has spent time on the Pribilof Islands. She currently lives in Oregon. Visit her at DebVanasse.com.

CPSIA information can be obtained
at www.ICGtesting.com
Printed in the USA
BVHW041528041221
622841BV00010B/18

9 781513 209579